JANIS BALODIS was born in Australia of Latvian parents who settled in North Queensland after the Second World War. He trained at Townsville Teachers' College, majoring in drama, and worked as a primary school teacher until 1972. He then had a varied acting and directing career based in Brisbane and later in London where he was a director and tutor at E15 Acting School.

His first play, *Backyard*, was workshopped at the Australian National Playwrights' Conference and produced at the Nimrod Theatre in 1980. Other plays include *Happily Never After, Beginning of the End* (1982), *Summerland* (1984), *Wet and Dry* (1987), *Heart for the Future* (1989) which premiered with Melbourne Theatre Company as its 500th production, and *Double Take* (1996). Much of the material for the trilogy of plays comprising *Too Young for Ghosts* (1985), *No Going Back* (1992) and *My Father's Father* (1996) is drawn from his Latvian heritage. All three plays premiered with Melbourne Theatre Company. He has also written for television and radio.

Janis Balodis was an Associate Director of Melbourne Theatre Company (1988–1993), Dramaturg-in-Residence and Artistic Associate at Queensland Theatre Company (1995–1996).

THE GHOSTS TRILOGY

JANIS BALODIS

Currency Press · Sydney

CURRENCY PLAYS
General Editor: Katharine Brisbane

Too Young For Ghosts first published in 1991 by Currency Press

This edition first published in 1997 by
Currency Press Ltd,
PO Box 452, Paddington,
NSW 2021, Australia

10 9 8 7 6 5 4 3 2 1 0

NATIONAL LIBRARY OF AUSTRALIA CIP DATA

Balodis, Janis.
   The ghosts trilogy: too young for ghosts, no going back, my father's father.

   ISBN 0 86819 504 9.

   I. Balodis, Janis. Too young for ghosts. II. Balodis, Janis. No going back.
   III. Balodis, Janis. My father's father. IV. Title. V. Title: Too young for ghosts. VI.
   Title: No going back. VII. Title: My father's father. (Series: Currency plays).

A822.3

Australia Council
for the Arts

Publication of this title was assisted by the
Commonwealth Government through the Australia
Council, its arts funding and advisory body.

Printed by Southwood Press, Marrickville, NSW.
Cover design by Anaconda Graphic Design/Trevor Hood.

Cover photograph: John Dicks as Leichhardt and Warren Oates as Brown in the
Melbourne Theatre Company's 1996 production of *My Father's Father*.
(Photo: Jeff Busby)

Contents

Left to right: Deidre Rubenstein (Marta), Peter Adams (Karl), Paul English (Armand) and Monica Maughan (Ilse) in the 1996 Melbourne Theatre Company production of My Father's Father. *(Photo: Jeff Busby)*

Ghosts and Doppelgänger

Terence Clarke

In 1980, as artistic director of the Australian National Playwrights Conference (now Centre), I read all the 150 or so plays submitted for consideration. The one that most attracted me, by a country mile, was a play called *Backyard*—funny, disturbing, instinct with life lived, the characters strong and original, the language often poetic in its understanding of the inarticulate. The playwright, Janis Balodis, was unknown to me. The two outside assessors, Robyn Nevin and Arthur Dignam, were similarly excited in their reports and the play was given an excellent workshop by Kerry Dwyer. Later that year I directed its premiere for Nimrod Theatre. The production starred Bryan Brown, who commissioned Balodis to develop it as a screenplay; the film, sadly, never eventuated. So began my association with the plays of Janis Balodis.

Nimrod had instituted from its early days a scheme of patronage called 'Dead Authors Subsidise the Living'. For the right to produce a play still subject to copyright, a theatrical producer pays the author an agreed percentage of gross box-office receipts. When presenting plays in the public domain, Nimrod set aside a notional 10% royalty for the commissioning of new plays. Richard Wherrett, ex Nimrod, took this idea to the Sydney Theatre Company when he became its director. So it was that in 1981 the STC advertised for ideas for epic plays that might suit the wide stage of the Sydney Opera House Drama Theatre, and urged writers not to be limited by considerations of staging and cast size. Balodis was one of three to be commissioned to develop treatment to script. He had in mind a series of plays which would combine Leichhardt's three journeys of exploration to Northern Queensland in

1845 with the experiences of a group of Latvian migrants in the same region some hundred years later. I found the idea 'interesting', but privately thought it no more than that, as I could not see how two such different stories could sit comfortably in the same play. The idea seemed too cerebral.

The play, with the working title of *Too Young for Ghosts*, was duly finished and presented to the STC. It had a cast of some twenty-four (huge by the standards of subsidised theatre in Australia) and a variety of settings. It did not excite much enthusiasm: the readers thought that the play lay too much in the realm of the intellectual. Worse: the company could no longer afford large casts—indeed, not more than eight. Balodis, nothing daunted, set about reducing his cast—to nine— by the only methods available to him: by eliminating characters and by mandatory doubling of those remaining. The STC's change of fortune was fortunate indeed for Balodis: in responding to it, he made a good play great.

The STC wanted to workshop the play but, being strapped for money, allowed Balodis to submit the play to the Playwrights Conference: which is how I, no longer artistic director but now director of script assessment, first came to read *Too Young for Ghosts* in its small-cast version. I was bowled over by it. Immediately on finishing it, probably imprudently, I rang Balodis to say what a wonderful play I thought it. Anne Harvey, artistic director of the 1984 conference, invited me to direct the workshop. With an intelligent and insightful cast— including Ailsa Piper as Ilse (a part she later played in the STC production) and Lex Marinos—and with the detailed dramaturgy of Philip Keir, considerable surgery was done on the play, but very little dialogue was lost or added. As that doyen of dramaturgs, Philip Parsons, had predicted in his report, 'it may need rethinking more than rewriting'.

I mention this because structural work, always the hardest, is, in my experience, that least attempted at the Conference: it usually proves too difficult for the inexperienced playwright in the limited time available. Indeed, major restructuring of plays does not often occur in Australia. It is a measure of Balodis' maturity, both as person and as playwright, that he was not threatened by the input of cast, dramaturg, and director. I give two examples. The main characters of the play are the migrants, but the draft submitted to the conference opened with the explorers. On the instant Balodis agreed to swap scenes 1 and 2. Again, the draft had Leichhardt doubled with Leonids and Gilbert with Edvards: the suggestion that Leichhardt and Edvards, being both outsiders, might make for a better double—the agreement was immediate. Other major work done at the conference included the splitting and interweaving of two long scenes in Part I.

The official guest of the conference in 1984 was the English playwright Howard Brenton. At the end of the presentation of *Too Young for Ghosts* Brenton, applauding warmly, leapt to his feet—so leading a standing ovation—with the words 'Australia has found its great play!' Allowance must be made for the emotion generated by the occasion, as I doubt that Brenton was acquainted with the canon of Australian drama; he was responding to the power of the play which, despite the nature of the presentation—no production values, the actors reading their scripts—was palpable. The play was successfully launched by the Melbourne Theatre Company in 1985 and produced by the STC later in the same year.

The play presents considerable staging difficulties. For the designer, both set and costumes pose problems, not least that of dressing a man to be both nineteenth century explorer and twentieth century migrant, for there is no time to change (a problem that continues throughout the trilogy). For the director the difficulties are as great. It is always a danger when a playwright puts information essential to a scene in stage direction rather than in dialogue, and so it is with *Too Young for Ghosts*. If I have a criticism of the play it is that time and place are not always sufficiently woven into the text for the audience to keep their bearings, particularly in the first few scenes. (To argue that in watching a play about people getting their bearings it is appropriate that the audience should have a similar difficulty is to stretch things a bit.) Balodis has a quick intelligence, and his writing flatters his audience in demanding of it an equivalent speed and concentration, for information is at times obliquely given and not repeated. This can be too demanding in places: flattery is in danger of becoming disdain.

In these multicultural times the *Ghosts Trilogy* must surely have a pre-eminent place. Balodis is a first generation Australian whose parents, finding themselves refugees at the end of World War II unable to return to their beloved Latvia, became assisted immigrants to Australia, by no special choice. Within a matter of hours of arrival in Sydney, speaking no English, they were put on a train to Brisbane, then to Tully in North Queensland, where they were met by a cane-farmer. Their new home was some distance from town, a corrugated-iron shed with no proper windows. (There still exist box Brownie snaps, tiny by today's standards, that show these sheds; the inhabitants look surprisingly happy.) This is also the experience of the play's migrants. I do not know of any other Australian play that treats this dislocation, let alone one that does it so well. The play speaks eloquently for the unheard thousands of migrants, reffos, displaced persons, DPs, New Australians, who arrived here in the wake of the war and, whatever their education, had to labour in the canefields, the Snowy Mountains, the steelworks and the sweatshops of the cities.

Balodis makes no special pleading, however: these people are lovingly rendered, yet quite unsentimentally; at times, indeed—Karl particularly—to the edge of mercilessness. They have, unsurprisingly, a European quality: they have come out the other side of a devastating war, yet their cynicism is tempered by hope—we have to keep reminding ourselves that they are still young, in their early twenties. Edvards' prevailing tone is sardonic, a quality more at home in Europe than Australia. Ilse stands with the great women of Australian drama, taking her place with Olive, Pearl, Aggie, Miss Siss, Coralie, and the others. She is tough, vulnerable, passionate, loving, selfish, intelligent, strong. She is at least the equal of men, and probably sees herself superior to them; this may be acknowledged an attitude more European than Australian, the more so in the Australia of 1946.

There is a deal of rawness, of ugliness even, in the play. Consider the greedy sex that Karl, just out of gaol, demands from Ilse, who is willing enough. Their stand-up coupling is at once sensual and animal, an expression both of love, or something like it, and need; it is quick, almost brutal. Balodis does not flinch from this: Man is both animal and angel. If he tends to dwell on the animal, he nevertheless shows us the angel, too: Man as lover and protector; Man with the aspirations that drive him to explore the unknown, to cope with the unknown. Exploring and coping may be seen as two manifestations of one concern: *Too Young for Ghosts* is for me the great play about coming to terms with Australia—the explorers physically, the migrants emotionally. This couple, and the angel-animal couple, draw attention to what distinguishes it from other Australian plays: a metaphysical theme that is so deeply embedded in the play that I doubt if Balodis himself is fully conscious of its constant presence. Again, this is seldom encountered in Australian plays, though quite frequently in European.

We might expect of the author of a play called *Wet and Dry* that he is drawn to pairs, in particular, pairs of opposites; indeed, there is the hint of one in the ironic title, *Too Young for Ghosts*. Such couplings abound in the play. The very conjoining of two disparate stories might alert us, as might the mandatory doubling of roles, to the importance of pairs to the play. The ability to dramatise is the distinguishing mark of a playwright: so in *A Midsummer Night's Dream* Shakespeare dramatises love at first sight with the flower love-in-idleness. How better to dramatise the very idea of pairs of opposites than by a man one half of whose face is perfect and the other man-made, a patchwork of imperfection? 'One face looks forward, one face looks back. Which is which?' So Edvards in the refugee camp at Stuttgart, a dead-and-alive man speaks to his young friends who stand poised between the horror of the past and the hope of the future. In his creation of Edvards, a man like no other in Australian drama, Balodis is a playwright writing at the peak of very considerable powers.

His invention and imagination are everywhere in the play, but most powerful in those scenes in which, in a sort of poetic and kinetic shorthand that is as thrillingly theatrical as it is original, he conflates events from past and present into one scene. Thus the rape of the aboriginal women and the prostitution of Ilse and Ruth to the GIs are presented simultaneously; thus, in the scene which has both the explorers settling for the night and Ruth seeking a moment alone with her lover while her husband gets drunk, the actor playing Leonids/Gilbert is, for a moment, both characters simultaneously, one hand holding the past, the other the present. This is playmaking of a very high order: the boldness is breathtakingly original, yet it is brought off with an assured ease.

Or consider Scene 6. This is a scene that I overlooked on reading, as it is apparently without dramatic action; I came to respect it in the rehearsal room. The man of action Leichhardt and the contemplative scientist Gilbert speak for their ways of exploring the new country, which may be inelegantly subsumed in the couple macroscopic/microscopic. Nothing happens, there is only talk, but the scene crackles with a rhetorical energy that is as invigorating and captivating as it is rare in Australian theatre. In a short scene Balodis dramatises a philosophical precept, that each of a pair of opposites takes its meaning from the existence of the other: without night we would have no concept of day, without evil, none of good. Leichhardt and

Gilbert need each other and their very different ways of seeing the world as surely as Edvards needs both sides of his face.

Further analysis from this metaphysical standpoint is beyond the scope of this introduction, but I assure the reader that the pairs are everywhere: blind/sighted, East/West, and many others. The mine is full of other treasure: Otto's sleepwalking; Ruth's imploring return to Ilse in labour, with its disturbing echo of folk- or fairy-tale ('there was once a woman who, about to be delivered of her first child, was visited by the ghost of her best friend: the ghost wanted three things'); and so on. If it is one measure of a work of the imagination that it withstands close and critical reading and repays rereading, then *Too Young for Ghosts* certainly passes the test. Many plays exhaust themselves after one production; some after only a reading. Since the Canberra workshop I have regularly included the play in courses of script analysis and have directed two student productions, and yet I know that I have by no means found all that there is to be found in the play.

Roger Hodgman, the Director of the Melbourne Theatre Company, was in the audience when *Too Young for Ghosts* was presented at the Playwrights Conference and immediately chose it for the MTC's program; indeed, he directed the world premiere. He had met Balodis when both were working for London's E15 Drama School in the 70s, and in 1987 appointed him associate director of the MTC, a position he held until his resignation in 1993. The liaison of director and playwright has been both unique in Australian theatre and uniquely fruitful: over a period of years Hodgman has encouraged Balodis, and has directed, since *Wet and Dry, Too Young for Ghosts, Heart for the Future*, and the two plays that complete the *Ghosts Trilogy*—*No Going Back* and *My Father's Father*. This despite the fact that Balodis is not an 'easy' writer, nor an obvious crowd-pleaser (though the night I saw *No Going Back* at the old Russell Street Theatre the house was full and the audience enthusiastic in its response).

Three Australian playwrights have each built a trilogy of plays on a successful first: Ray Lawler's *Doll* trilogy on *Summer of the Seventeenth Doll*, Peter Kenna's *The Cassidy Album* on *A Hard God*, and Janis Balodis' *Ghosts Trilogy* on *Too Young for Ghosts*. I have argued elsewhere that one at least of Lawler's plays is the equal of his first, but it is generally agreed that Kenna's latter two are less successful than the first. It is perhaps Balodis' misfortune, as it was Kenna's (but not

Lawler's), that the chronology of the sequence begins with the strongest play. I do not mean by this opinion disrespect to either of Balodis' two later plays, nor do I think that the quality of the writing is less (as I am inclined to think is true of Kenna's). The Sydney Theatre Company had asked for an epic play, and in *Too Young for Ghosts* they got one. The migrants live through events of epic scale: the aftermath of a horrific war, Edvards' return from the dead, the murder of the GI, dislocation, flood, the clandestine affair of Ruth and Leonids, their elopement ending in death, the birth of Karl and Ilse's first child. The explorers' events (all, incidentally, occurring on one day) are of similar scale: dislocation, the threat of starvation, insurrection put down, rape, aboriginal attack, death/murder (Balodis, or his play, inclines to the view that Leichhardt murdered Gilbert). The two later plays, however, as is perhaps fitting for people who have lost their ambition, are themselves less ambitious in scope and, possibly as a consequence, in technique. Both work a smaller, more domestic canvas; both deal with the migrants in middle to old age, their horizons shrinking—there is no Hollywood for Karl, no stardom for Ilse (did she ever want it?), just a small town in North Queensland, and, in the third play, a small town in Latvia.

By the time we come to *No Going Back*, Karl has had the stuffing knocked out of him; booze and sourness have taken over. Edvards has moved on to a desultory affair with Ilse; the possibility of a relationship with Otto's sister Lauma comes to nothing. The play's prevailing tone is one of sadness, of promise unfulfilled: did our friends live through the events of *Too Young for Ghosts*, which ends in such hope and heart for the future (in the play of that name the title is eventually not ironic), only for this? Otto and Lydia have escaped the oppression of North Queensland's comforts, Lydia regaining the life of the pampered bourgeoise that she so missed in *Too Young for Ghosts*—she alone seems fulfilled, or at least happy.

The critics agreed that the play was given an excellent production and were warm in their praise of it. 'A worthy sequel, and a fine play in its own right' (Chris Boyd, *The Financial Review*, 31.7.92). Helen Thomson (*The Australian*, 23.7.92) found it as 'dense, allusive and symbolically complex as its first part' and was aware of 'a series of parallels, ironies, flashbacks'; 'the play explores the mysterious intersection between physical place and personal identity'. Leonard

Radic (*The Age*, same day) wrote of a 'warm and touching work that uses the metaphor of the journey'—the play begins in an airport—'an experience built deep into the Australian psyche', and also commented on 'the preoccupation with identity, both nationalistic and personal'. John Larkin (*Sunday Age*, 9.8.92), acknowledging the presence of an aboriginal in the play, detected 'some analogy between the dispossession of the native people by the coming of the whites to Australia and the absorption by Russia of Latvia'.

Four years later the critics were less supportive, gently damning both production and play. There was general complaint that the two strands of the play, explorer and migrant, did not coalesce. In an essentially unsympathetic review, Helen Thomson (*The Age*, 7.3.96) yet granted that 'like the two earlier plays, this one is dark and multi-layered'. I do not understand the critical response. It is true that the mood of *My Father's Father* is dark, bleak even: the subject is death, the death of fathers. I have not seen the play in production, but on the page it moved me to tears: I can remember only three other plays that have had such a power. The migrants' territory has contracted, certainly, but it is not only mapped but mined. If the author of the first play of the trilogy is a Leichhardt unable to cover the ground fast enough, in the third he is a Gilbert, content to remain in one place for a time, the better to understand and record its emotional ecology. Balodis does this with devastating honesty and insight. The writing is as strong and striking as ever; stronger, perhaps, because of its concentrated focus.

It may be, however, that what the trilogy has to say about the nature of 'the Australian experience' is what has subconsciously deterred the critics, for it is not flattering. We do not often have the opportunity in our drama of comparing at some leisure the mature with their younger selves. The unstated subject that all three trilogies—Lawler's, Kenna's, Balodis'—have in common is time and what time works upon us. In the *Ghosts Trilogy* time shares the stage with Australia: what they have together done to Ilse, Karl and the others is sad to contemplate. Is this what Australia has done to all its migrants? A sort of reticence has kept me from writing about the next generation of the trilogy. In *No Going Back* we meet Karl and Ilse's son Armand, a photographer—an artist who observes and records in one way what a playwright does in another (and the scientist Gilbert does in his). Although the trilogy is neither biography nor autobiography, Armand may be seen as Balodis' doppelgänger (which may account for the fact that I find him less substantially rendered). Whatever Australia has done to its migrants we may rejoice that it has given us, not Armand, but Balodis, recorder and explorer.

The ghost that hovers over the trilogy is the Latvia that has nourished the migrants, to which they cannot at first return, and to which they will not return for years, some of them never. They must remain in exile so long as it is under Soviet control; they long for it the more. There is a poignant harshness to the young Ilse's certainty, 'I know I shall never see Latvia again': it seems an act of will, a decision to face the realities, as much as a feared truth.

If it is true that a play is not a play until it is produced and works on an audience, there is also a sense in which you do not know it, really know it, until you have spent weeks in the rehearsal room with it; that is certainly my experience, and, in that sense, I do not know the latter two plays. I have called *Too Young for Ghosts* great, a play that I believe will be performed and studied as long as there is an Australian theatre. I hesitate to make that claim for the other two plays in this volume. The Melbourne critics, uneasy about the presence of the explorers in *No Going Back*, were clamorous in their rejection of them in *My Father's Father*. I share their doubts. In the two latter plays, the explorers' stories are perhaps less interesting than in the first, and they are less imaginatively treated: the technical daring of *Too Young for Ghosts* is absent, and so the plays lack the stunning originality of *Ghosts*. Further: the two strands seem to me not dramatically interwoven in the latter two plays, and so not necessary to them in the way that they are to the first. It would be hard to conflate scenes from past and present in them: the explorers' drama continues, by its very nature, to be epic, whereas that of the migrants does not; the resonances dwindle. I cannot help thinking that, in killing the explorers off in the first play, Balodis intuitively knew that their useful life in his trilogy was over. He has said that he was committed to following Leichhardt's three expeditions: now that that is done he may reconsider.

Indeed, towards the end of 1996 he authorised a reading in Brisbane of *My Father's Father* which omitted the explorers; he said of the reading, laconically, that it worked. Perhaps there is a play to be made of those parts of the latter two plays that do not deal with the explorers. At the same time, I—for one—should like to know something of Karl, Ilse, and friends between their early adulthood and their middle age.

In writing the foregoing I am committing the critic's cardinal sin of reviewing the play I would like rather than the play written. I must immediately remind myself that Hodgman and two fine and intelligent casts have worked for weeks in the rehearsal room in the realization of these plays, and seem not to have come to the same conclusion; that Balodis is an assiduous reviser, and is particularly hard on himself, yet the explorers remain; and that the editors at Currency deem the plays worthy of publication as they stand, rather than as they might be.

And so, if I do not seem to contradict myself, do I. The trilogy is one of Australian theatre's most considerable achievements. I may be wrong in believing that Balodis is underrated in his own country: he is certainly underproduced here. It is a matter of shame that the Queensland Theatre Company, for whatever compelling reason, has never presented one of his plays. Since the unsuccessful production of *Too Young for Ghosts*, the Sydney Theatre Company has not touched a Balodis play, and the other state theatre companies, with the shining exception of the MTC, are silent, as are Belvoir Street and the Playbox. Yet the plays are superbly dramatic and theatrical, emotionally powerful, if uncompromising and at times uncomfortable; like all good plays, they play even better than they read. It was a surprise to me to discover, in preparing this introduction, that the plays of Janis Balodis are not only seldom produced but little studied in our universities. The trilogy has much to recommend it to the academy, as I hope I have suggested.

Let us hope that the present publication will act as a corrective: that our theatre companies, and others (the German theatre would surely respond to them), will produce them; that the academy will study them. And that audiences will be given the opportunity to discover what they have been missing.

March 1997

TOO YOUNG FOR GHOSTS

Too Young for Ghosts was commissioned by the Sydney Theatre Company under the Dead Authors Subsidise the Living Scheme and was later workshopped at the 1984 Australian National Playwrights' Conference, directed by Terence Clarke. The play was first performed by the Melbourne Theatre Company at the Studio, Victorian Arts Centre, on 4 July 1985 with the following cast:

ILSE	Pamela Rabe
RUTH	Mary Sitarenos
LYDIA / ANGIE	Robynne Bourne
KARL	Brandon Burke
OTTO	Geoff Revell
EDVARDS / LEICHHARDT	Denis Moore
LEONIDS / GILBERT	John O'May
MURPHY / G.I. SAM / BOURKE	Bill Fox
PHILLIPS / G.I. JOE / MCQUAIDE	Robert Essex

Designed by Eamon D'arcy
Lighting Design by Jamie Lewis
Directed by Roger Hodgman

CHARACTERS

ILSE, aged twenty-eight
RUTH, thirty-two
LYDIA / ANGIE, aged twenty-five and thirty-five
KARL, twenty-two
OTTO, twenty-six
EDVARDS / LEICHHARDT, thirty-four
LEONIDS / GILBERT, thirty-two
MURPHY / G.I. SAM / BOURKE, sixteen and twenty-three
PHILLIPS / G.I JOE / MCQUAIDE, forty-five

The doubling of characters is intentional and integral to the structure and meaning of the play.

SETTING

The action of the play takes place in North Queensland locations in 1845 and 1948–49; and in Stuttgart in 1947.

AUTHOR'S NOTE

There are fairly rapid switches in time and location and it is
important that the design should facilitate this movement and not
hamper the flow of action from scene to scene with unnecessary
blackouts or set devices. The minimalist approach to setting and
acting style is both necessary and desirable. Costume design is
probably the most critical problem. The actors are not given time for
elaborate changes so one costume must serve for different periods,
characters and locations. The solution most likely lies in the way the
action is framed: Leichhardt's journey and the D.P.s' time in
Stuttgart are like a 'dreaming' experienced by the D.P.s in Australia
in 1948–49. This leads to the entertainment of the idea of Leichhardt
exploring Australia in a 1940s suit, or the whole cast wearing a
uniform garb. The style of speech is also important. When the D.P.s
talk amongst themselves they speak fluently and without accent.
When they try to speak English to others their speech is accented
and halting.

*Left to right: Mary Sitarenos (Ruth), Geoff Revell (Otto), Brandon Burke
(Karl), Denis Moore (Edvards), Pamela Rabe (Ilse), John O'May (Leonids)
and Bill Fox (Murphy) in the 1985 Melbourne Theatre Company
production. (Photo: David Parker)*

PROLOGUE

The DISPLACED PERSONS *(D.P.s) in silhouette sing: "Blow Breeze"* *("Put Vejini").*

"Blow Breeze"

Blow breeze, set sail,
Blow breeze, set sail.
We are leaving our home
For a n ew land.

Blow breeze, set sail,
Blow breeze, set sail.
The past is the past,
A new beginning.

PART ONE

SCENE ONE

North Queensland. 1948. Cane barracks. Night.

BOURKE *enters carrying a lantern. He is followed by* KARL, ILSE, EDVARDS, RUTH, LYDIA, OTTO *and* LEONIDS. ILSE *wears a Latvian shawl.*

BOURKE: Well, this is it. Your new home, such as it is. Come the morning the cane growers will be thinking what to do with you.

They were reckoning on one married couple to a gang of single blokes; the woman to do the cookin'. You'll be finding a wood-burning stove through there; bit hot in summer, but warms up like a biscuit tin in winter. Mind you, it's not a scheme I fancy meself, one woman to half a dozen blokes. God never intended it.

KARL: There's only two beds.

LYDIA: There's seven of us.

ILSE: It's worse than the ship.

RUTH: We'll have to sleep in shifts.

OTTO: There must be more.

LEONIDS: Turn on the light.

EDVARDS: No electricity. No bulbs.

BOURKE: Thought you buggers was s'posed to talk English. No use makin' you gangers if you don't. How's a man to tell you what to do? You speak English, or not?

KARL: [accent] Yes. I talk.

   Pause.

BOURKE: That was it, eh? Not much to be goin' on with. You'll have to learn the language or me kids'll be throwin' stones at you and callin' you for all sorts of spies and wogs. Mind you, you'll confuse them for a while, not bein' Ities or Greeks.

   ILSE knocks on the wall. Some jump.

ILSE: Feel the walls. All iron. Tiny room, iron walls, iron roof, iron stove, like an oven.

BOURKE: Admiring the architecture, eh? Not bad, is it? Galvanised iron. The all purpose building material, put up a house in a week. What more does a man need? Just talk amongst yourselves, I can talk to meself all night.

   Pause.

ILSE: What do we do for food? He's the land owner. Do we have to buy from him? Go on, ask him.

KARL: I don't know. What are the words? [To BOURKE miming, putting his fingers to his mouth and speaking with an accent.] Ead! Ead!

BOURKE: You mean eat. Eat. You just had tea. There was even baked beans left in the tin. [*Suspiciously.*] You're not suggestin' I'm a mean man?

KARL: [*waving his hand to stop him, accent*] I show. [*Trying to take* BOURKE's *lantern.*] I buy.

BOURKE: Bugger off. You got a couple of bloody lanterns of your own. I'm not walkin' home in the dark.

LEONIDS: Show him some money.

The D.P.*s check their pockets.*

BOURKE: Bit over ten bob, eh? You're rich. You'll soon be making a quid if you bend your backs. Cane cutting is a cream of a job.

KARL: [*offering the money and trying to take the lantern, accent*] I buy. Eat.

BOURKE: [*refusing to hand over the lantern*] I told you once. Not much of a feed in it and you wouldn't want to drink the kero.

ILSE: He's stupid. [*Coming between them, accent.*] Me.

BOURKE: [*laughing*] If you give me a shilling and your missus, you can surely have the lantern.

He takes the shilling then gives KARL *the lantern.*

KARL: [*crowing*] You see. He understands.

BOURKE: [*winking at* ILSE] Couldn't ask for a fairer bargain.

RUTH: You just swapped Ilse for a lantern.

ILSE: Old habits die hard.

They laugh.

EDVARDS: OK. That's a fine piece of financial wizardry.

ILSE *gives the lantern back to* BOURKE *and takes the shilling.*

BOURKE: No deal, eh? Too bad.

ILSE *mimes falling asleep, waking and preparing breakfast.*

ILSE: [*accent*] Food.

BOURKE: Aha! Now I see. Breakfast. There's a box of stuff on the table. Bread, jam, eggs, tea.

ILSE: How much is?

BOURKE: [*speaking with an accent*] You keep. Pay later. Tomorrow. Domani. Shit! Now you've got me doin' it. Bedtime. [*Miming.*] Sleep. OK. Couple of you stay here, the rest follow me. OK.

He starts to go. The D.P.*s look confused.*

EDVARDS: OK.

BOURKE: Thank God someone speaks the lingo.

EDVARDS: I think he wants us to follow him.

They all pick up their bags.

BOURKE: Na, na, na, nah! Not all of you.

Separating KARL *and* ILSE *from the others.*

You two [*Speaking with an accent.*] stay here. Good night.

ILSE: [*accent*] Good night.

KARL: [*shaking* BOURKE'*s hand, accent*] Good night.

Much to BOURKE'*s discomfort* ILSE *shakes his hand.*

ILSE: [*accent*] Good night.

BOURKE: Good night. The rest of you come with me.

LYDIA: Where's he taking us?

EDVARDS: Don't worry. OK. There's only one of him, he has no gun
and it's too warm for Siberia.

LEONIDS: Edvards is full of joy as ever.

LYDIA *cries. They follow the disappearing* BOURKE. ILSE *and*
KARL *are left.*

ILSE: [*quietly*] This is our new home.

SCENE TWO

North Queensland. 1845. The explorers' camp. Day.

LEICHHARDT *takes a bearing with a sextant. He wears a coolie's hat.*
MURPHY *stands beside him with a book, pen and ink.* LEICHHARDT
reads the sextant, hands it to MURPHY *and prepares to write. He
checks the previous entry.* LEICHHARDT *speaks with a German
accent. In the camp,* GILBERT *crushes some leaves and bark which
he puts in a billy.*

LEICHHARDT: Ach! What is this? [*Re-reading the sextant.*] You have not fiddled this?

MURPHY: No, sir, Doctor Leichhardt.

LEICHHARDT: Then something is not right or we have gone backwards from yesterday. Impossible, no? With the sun over the same shoulder, it is so easy to say north, south, east and west. But north from where, or east to where that is a little more difficult. Ja?

MURPHY: [*hopefully*] Can't you take another reading?

LEICHHARDT: Not today. We know we are here so we cannot be lost.

MURPHY: Yeah, but where is here?

LEICHHARDT: We will see tomorrow.

> LEICHHARDT *takes the book, pen and ink and goes up to the camp.* MURPHY *tries to read the sextant.*

GILBERT: This morning as we crested that ridge, I thought I could smell the sea on the breeze. From the north-west.

LEICHHARDT: Sometimes I think I can smell my mother's back garden and fresh bread baking in the oven. But that is in Austria and my mother has been dead for some years.

GILBERT: I am suggesting we could be nearer to the Gulf than you think.

LEICHHARDT: In Austria we have a saying, "Take your eyes in your hand and your nose will show you." You think we should follow your nose?

> GILBERT *says nothing.*

Quite so.

Taking an axe and going off singing into the trees.

> Don't ask me, friend, why I rushed away
> And left you with a heart that's full of pain.
> Don't ask me why, why I said, "I love you",
> That's one thing now that I can't understand.

There is the sound of chopping, off.

MURPHY: [*showing* GILBERT *the sextant*] Can you read where we are, Mr Gilbert?

GILBERT: No, Johnny.

MURPHY: We're truly lost, then.

GILBERT: There's a line of marked trees all the way back to the Darling Downs waiting to be joined up like dots in a child's drawing.

MURPHY: It's a big country—bigger'n I can think—but I seen a lot of it in the past eight months. An' I'd like to see a whole lot more, so dyin' in the middle of nowhere ain't part of me plans. If we was to go home now, I'd be goin' home a man.

There is the sharp crack of a branch breaking.

[*jumps for his gun*] Halt. Who goes there?

PHILLIPS: [*off*] The Queen of Sheba, who yer bloody think? Put that gun down, you feeble minded idiot afore you shoot someone.

  PHILLIPS *enters.*

MURPHY: Sorry, Phillips.

PHILLIPS: Yer more damn skittish than an unbroken filly. Where's the gallant leader?

GILBERT: Carving his inspirational message into yet another tree.

PHILLIPS: "L eighteen forty-five"? Wonder who he reckons will be readin' 'em after we're gone. Last year it was "L eighteen forty-four", next year it'll be "L eighteen forty-six".

GILBERT: That's progress. What's the big hurry?

PHILLIPS: Blacks' camp, Mr Gilbert, about a mile away. Could mean nosh. He'll be wantin' to know.

GILBERT: If you want to be sure of a fair share you better be getting there before Doctor Leichhardt. You go too, Johnny.

MURPHY: Ain't you comin', Mr Gilbert.

GILBERT: I've work to do. I'll stay and inform the good doctor when he's done attackin' that tree.

PHILLIPS: Com'n, boyo, me arse is eatin' me trousers.

MURPHY: I'll bring some back for you, Mr Gilbert.

GILBERT: Thank you, Johnny.

  MURPHY *and* PHILLIPS *go.*

PHILLIPS: Mind where you're pointin' that damn thing.

  RUTH *enters opposite* GILBERT. *She stops and calls,* "Leonids". *Looks briefly, then turns to go.* GILBERT *turns in time to see her leaving. He stares.* LEICHHARDT *comes down into the camp. He carries the axe and mops his brow. He drinks from the billy.*

LEICHHARDT: Good tea. Like consommé. Probably quite medicinal.

He spits out some leaves and drinks some more.

GILBERT: Yes. Should be good for the bowels. It was a tanning mixture for my bird skins.

LEICHHARDT: Delicious! You must make some more. It will help sustain us on the road ahead.

GILBERT: Just now I thought I saw someone.

LEICHHARDT: Yes. It is me.

GILBERT: No. Before.

LEICHHARDT: So. Who was it?

GILBERT: I didn't see.

LEICHHARDT: [*gloating*] Who did you think you saw when you didn't see?

   Pause.

It is your language.

   He laughs.

GILBERT: Perhaps it was a native.

LEICHHARDT: Perhaps you are seeing viney-viney like the blacks.

GILBERT: We are the viney-viney to the blacks. I think they are right in believing that spirits roam this land.

LEICHHARDT: Perhaps you could collect them instead of birds. Spirit is lighter. The rate you are collecting, my trees will be devoided of life and your boxes will break the backs of the oxen before we reach Port Essington.

GILBERT: If we reach there.

LEICHHARDT: I will. Even if it kills me.

   He laughs and drains the billy.

Excellent brew, Mr Gilbert.

   Cooees are heard off.

KARL: [*off*] Hello!

GILBERT: It's the others. They found a natives' camp.

LEICHHARDT: Ah ha! You see! Just like the promised land, food lying on the ground.

GILBERT: Hardly manna from heaven.

LEICHHARDT: Depends on how you look. I will go see.

GILBERT: About a mile that way.

Hardly bothering to look, LEICHHARDT *goes.*

LEICHHARDT: Ja. Ja. My nose will show me.

GILBERT *is left in the camp alone.*

SCENE THREE

The refugee camp. Stuttgart. 1947.

KARL *enters carrying a large battered suitcase. He wears a cheap suit.*

KARL: [*calling*] Hello! Hey! Anyone home? For God's sake, Edvards, come on. I don't want you to get lost after all this time.

EDVARDS *enters carrying a wooden box of young chickens. He is dressed in standard refugee attire. American army uniforms dyed blue. His gait is awkward and one side of his face is scarred.*

EDVARDS: Okay. Okay. What do I do with these birds?

KARL: Put them down for a minute.

EDVARDS: You sure this is the right place?

KARL: It should be. I don't understand why there's no one about. Maybe they've been moved to another barracks.

EDVARDS: Can't we just leave this stuff here?

KARL: No, Stuttgart is crawling with thieves. All this is my livelihood, my future. I worked in the Yanks' Quartermaster Store before they put me away. And I made a lot of contacts so I could set myself up in business. What I haven't got I can get, for a price. You name it.

EDVARDS: How about a bottle of booze?

KARL: Later, after we've tracked down the others.

EDVARDS: Maybe they emigrated while you were in gaol.

KARL: I fell in with a good bunch. They would have let me know.

EDVARDS: You go, okay? I'll wait and keep watch over your precious future.

KARL puts his case down.

KARL: They can't be far away. What a lucky thing you bumped into me. I didn't believe my eyes. What a double-barrel surprise we've got for them.

EDVARDS: The self-made man and the man-made man.

KARL: Here, have a cigarette. Lucky Strikes, the best. You'll be fine.

EDVARDS: I'm a dumb ox some clown assembled in a butcher's shop for a joke. Who would believe a man was made of so many pieces? OK? After seeing corpses by the trainload, I'm not sure they're all mine. An arm off this one, leg off that one.

KARL: Dr Frankenstein did a good job on you. You look all in one piece now.

We hear the distant sound of people singing.

EDVARDS: OK. Some comfort.

KARL: Ssh! Come here and listen. Someone's coming.

The singing increases in volume as the singers approach.

"Don't Ask Me, Friend" (*"Draugs, nejauta"*)

Don't ask me, friend, why I rushed away
And left you with a heart that's full of pain.
Don't ask me why, why I said I loved you,
That's one thing now that I can't understand.
Don't ask me why, why I said I loved you,
That's one thing now that I can't understand.
Could it have been the madness of springtime
That set our hearts alight with burning love?
But autumn's wind has chilled my deep desire,
Don't ask me how, I'll never really know.
But autumn's wind has chilled my deep desire,
Don't ask me how, I'll never really know.

After hearing a few lines of the song, EDVARDS *stamps out his cigarette.*

KARL: Hey, you didn't smoke that. They're American, hard to get. [*Picking it up.*] That's the profit margin on a pack.

EDVARDS: [*agitatedly*] OK. OK. I need a drink. No. Better I don't stay.

KARL: Take another cigarette. There's plenty. You can't go now. You were given up for dead and here you are. A miracle.

EDVARDS: A mistake.

KARL: Wait and see Ruth. She never believed you were dead and she's been faithful. You want a beautiful woman like that to become a nun? Who would believe I'd seen you if you slip through my fingers like a ghost?

EDVARDS: OK. But I should have given her some warning.

KARL *steers* EDVARDS *into the room and leaves him with the case and the chickens.*

KARL: You leave that to me.

EDVARDS: Tell her first what to expect. OK?

KARL: Relax. It mightn't even be her. You're worse than a bridegroom. Wait.

KARL *goes out into the barrack square/clearing and joins in the singing. While* KARL *sings,* OTTO *comes on stage ahead of the others.*

OTTO: [*calling to the others*] Hurry. It is Karl.

LYDIA, RUTH, LEONIDS *and* ILSE *enter.*

What'd I tell you? Only one person sings like that. Karlo Caruso. [*Shaking* KARL's *hand.*] Look at that suit, for God's sake.

KARL: You've put on weight, Otto.

OTTO: It's that cow fodder they feed us. Spinach and oats. I'll be giving milk next.

The greetings are polite and restrained.

KARL: Lydia.

LYDIA: Hello, Karl. They let you out early?

KARL: Two months off for good behaviour.

RUTH: Good behaviour, lover boy?

KARL: You know me. You look a million dollars. Wait till you see what a surprise I've got for you. You'll be forever in my debt.

RUTH: [laughing] The big shot is back all right.

OTTO: Where did you get that suit?

LEONIDS: It's how they dress in American gaols. The gangsters, anyway. We've all seen the films. [To KARL.] Ruth has told me all about you.

RUTH takes LEONIDS' arm.

RUTH: Karl, meet Leonids.

KARL shakes LEONIDS' hand.

We're getting married.

KARL: Oh, well... you mean—but—what the hell.

ILSE: Have I become invisible?

KARL goes to her and swings her round.

KARL: Four months of dreams in the lockup when not once did you come and see me. Give me a kiss to prove you're real.

KARL tries to kiss her. She laughs and pulls away.

ILSE: You got yourself in there. Why should I worry?

KARL: Didn't you even miss me? I missed you.

ILSE: You're such a boy.

KARL: [saving face] A boy. How do you like that? Have a Lucky Strike.

OTTO: American tobacco. Seventh heaven.

Two G.I.s cross upstage. G.I. JOE whistles.

G.I. SAM: Hi, girls! How's about throwin' over those losers and showin' us a good time?

KARL: [waving and speaking with an accent] Hi, Joes.

G.I. JOE: I'm Joe, he's Sam and you gotta be the ugliest broad I ever seen. We was addressin' ourselves to the ones with the bumps on the front. Comprendy?

ILSE: They murdered Elmer Karklins.

KARL: Ssh!

ILSE: They understand nothing.

G.I. JOE: Ah! See ya later, girls.

KARL: [*accent*] See yous, Joes. [*No accent.*] It doesn't hurt to be polite.

RUTH: They're just a couple of unknown soldiers.

KARL: Unknown soldiers?

ILSE: Was there ever a soldier who gave a woman his right name?

The WOMEN *laugh.*

KARL: They murdered Elmer?

LEONIDS: Shot. Not by those two.

OTTO: When you were put away, Elmer took over your still. His last brew killed one man, blinded five and put a dozen in hospital. The Yank provos were taking him to gaol for manslaughter, but Elmer must've thought they'd hand him over to the Russians. That's how his brain worked, probably from drinking his own brew.

LYDIA: Otto.

ILSE: He ran and they shot him. Just like at the cinema. What happens to all crooks.

KARL: Silly bugger. The Yanks are good Joes.

RUTH: Elmer wasn't so bad.

ILSE: If you didn't drink.

OTTO *produces a flask.*

OTTO: Want to try his brew?

KARL: No thanks.

OTTO *drinks.*

LYDIA: Where'd you get that? Have you gone mad?

OTTO: It's one of his earlier brews. Not bad, but not as good as Karl's. [*To* KARL.] Try it.

KARL: Well, if you say it's OK.

OTTO *misses handing the flask to* KARL *and gropes about blindly.*

OTTO: Now where did he go? Karl? Anyone? I know you're all hiding.

The others laugh.

LYDIA: You're not funny, Otto.

RUTH: Before you all get blind drunk I want my little surprise.

KARL: Oh, well, yes, look. Give me a minute to set it up. Wait till I call you.

KARL goes into the room.

EDVARDS: OK. Is it Ruth?

KARL: In a minute she'll be coming through the door.

EDVARDS: Did you tell her?

KARL: There's been a slight hitch.

EDVARDS: OK. I'll give you more time.

He starts to go.

KARL: Look, it's not so easy to—

EDVARDS: The waiting is also hard. OK. Send her out to me. Then I'll know you told her.

He goes.

KARL: For God's sake come back.

RUTH: [*leading the others into the room*] Coming ready or not. Well, whatever it is, it doesn't exactly hit you in the face.

OTTO: Perhaps we're supposed to search for it.

KARL: Chickens. A box full of chickens. A surprise for everyone.

RUTH: I expected something more exotic.

ILSE: [*laughing*] A peacock at least.

KARL: The idea is you raise them till they're big enough to eat.

LYDIA: Someone else can have mine. I could never cold bloodedly choose one to die... ugh.

LEONIDS: They'll do it for you. When they sort out the pecking order you take the weakest, kill it and eat it.

LYDIA: Horrible creatures.

RUTH: What sort of man would surprise a woman with a batch of chickens?

KARL: A businessman. A farmer in gaol gave me some contacts in the chicken business.

RUTH: What's in the case?

KARL: [*opening it*] I'm glad you asked. My shop. Underwear, tinned food, cigarettes, chocolates, everything is for sale.

Taking out a bottle and some glasses for the WOMEN.

And some of my own vintage liquor I salted away. Four months old.

OTTO: You have to hand it to Karl. He goes to gaol, a small time bootlegger, and he comes back a big time businessman in a suit. I should be so lucky.

KARL: [*pouring drinks*] Where's the luck? I went to gaol to make the contacts. And the suit I paid for with a gold tooth.

LYDIA: Since when did you have gold teeth?

KARL: A year ago the ground was littered with teeth.

OTTO: You mean you pulled teeth from corpses?

KARL: It's easier. A live man will bite you. The dead have no use for teeth. They don't eat the worms, the worms eat them.

He laughs.

Try some of this, it'll take the bad taste out of your mouth.

They drink.

I'm back in business, so if there's anything you fancy to make life bearable while you're here…

LYDIA: We won't be here long so you can sell those horrid chickens. By the time they're big enough to eat, we'll be in Australia, thank God.

KARL: Australia?

OTTO: Yes. We're all going to Australia.

KARL: Who? All of who?

LEONIDS: Us here. Nothing's definite yet.

KARL: Why not America? Why not stay here? Australia?

RUTH: He's getting used to the idea.

LEONIDS: We've waited here two years for the Yanks to liberate our homes from the Russians. Why should they bother? We fought for the Germans. If we stick around here we'll probably end up in Siberia. Australia's a safe place to go and do a bit of honest work.

KARL: I have work here. For the first time since the war I can see how to make myself a bit of money. What's there? Light so bright you go blind.

ILSE: The same thing happens here from drinking bad booze.

KARL: Are you going?

ILSE: If they'll have me. They're asking for single women, so they must have work for us.

KARL: Single women, eh? Doesn't that make you wonder?

OTTO: They're only taking singles, men and women, but we'll pull a swifty by getting married when we get there.

LYDIA: A double wedding. Me and Otto, Ruth and Leonids. We don't mind making it a triple with you and Ilse.

KARL: What about Edvards?

RUTH: I've accepted he's dead, and I'm a widow. I won't regret leaving.

> RUTH and LEONIDS embrace.

KARL: Oh, well... Look, if you're so keen to be going to the jungles, you better look through my stock. You're sure to find some little luxury to make the journey more pleasant.

> KARL takes ILSE aside as the others look in this case.

I need you to do something for me. But first I have a surprise for you. Close your eyes.

ILSE: You're going to try to kiss me again.

KARL: Why not?

ILSE: I'm half a dozen years older than you.

KARL: I like older women.

ILSE: Yet you treat me like a little girl.

KARL: It's the only way I can stop you treating me like a son. Come on. Close your eyes.

> She does. KARL unfurls a Latvian shawl and drapes it over her shoulders.

LYDIA: Oh, Ilse. A shawl from Latvia.

RUTH: So beautiful.

OTTO: [whistling] That must have cost a whole mouthful of teeth.

KARL: You can open your eyes now.

LYDIA: Men understand nothing. You always want to look. She can feel it on her skin.

OTTO: It must be pinching her. She's crying.

KARL: It's just a gift, Ilse. Open your eyes, for God's sake.

ILSE: Oh, Karl.

RUTH: At least say thank you. I'll swap you any day. You can't wear a couple of chickens to a ball.

OTTO: No. A modest woman would need at least three.

LEONIDS: It's too beautiful to belong here—like sunshine in a nightmare.

The light changes.

SCENE FOUR

North Queensland. 1948. The cane barracks. Night.

ILSE: [*quietly*] This is our new home. Our ducks and chickens lived in more comfort. I thought these people came from Europe with knowledge that was hundreds of years old. There's no evidence of it. Perhaps we've fallen amongst exiles who have been sent as far from civilisation as possible. Is this the best they can do in a hundred and fifty years? They live as if they don't expect to stay.

KARL: I certainly don't. And while they're busy making up their minds, I can make a bit of money. When they don't know what they want, they can be sold anything. All I have to do is feel out the market.

ILSE: Does everyone who comes here have to start from scratch? There must have been some border crossing where knowledge and memories were wiped out. I escaped the treatment and remember too much.

KARL: We only have to stay till our contract is up. Latvia could be free by then and we'll go home and reclaim my father's farm.

ILSE: I don't believe for a moment I'll ever see Latvia again.

KARL: That's my only dream. I made a mistake coming here. A big mistake.

ILSE: Are you sorry you married me after only three weeks?

KARL: What a wedding, not even time to knock up a batch of grog. And I would've liked a proper photograph, just the two of us, instead of a piece of newspaper. I can't send this to my mother.

ILSE: We can buy a camera and have some real photos taken.

KARL: At least I made the papers. New Australians marry in triple wedding. We look confused, like smiling dummies, as if we didn't know what we were getting into. Too true.

ILSE: Why did you ask me to marry you?

KARL: Why did you say yes?

Pause.

ILSE: Two lost people together stand a better chance than one adrift.

KARL: A nice proposition.

ILSE: You shouldn't have asked.

KARL: You could have refused. You did last time.

ILSE: Circumstances have changed. Besides, I got the best of the deal. I know what I'm letting myself in for.

KARL: What's that?

ILSE: Knowing you can't be relied on. That's the one certainty in my life. A bad risk guards against complacency and seems a good way to deal with a strange country.

KARL: You really know how to make a man feel good.

ILSE: You got more than you bargained for. You were looking for a mother, I gave you a wife. I can comfort you if you like, the way a mother would.

KARL: No, keep away.

ILSE: Wives are harder to get rid of, especially when they give themselves so cheaply.

KARL: Not to me, you didn't. I'll be paying the rest of my life. I don't know what the hell I had to smile about in that photograph.

ILSE: I was squeezing your bum, remember?

RUTH *enters.*

We were just looking at the wedding photographs and remembering what fun it was.

RUTH: It's different for you. For me it wasn't real.

ILSE: Karl wishes it wasn't.

KARL: Where are you sleeping?

RUTH: With Edvards. In another iron shed just like this one, no better, no worse.

KARL: I'll go and take a look.

ILSE: He has to mark out his territory, like a tom cat.

    KARL *goes.*

RUTH: In the dark these places look awful and feel cold. Yet the iron sweats. Perhaps everything will look better in the morning.

    Pause.

Are you fighting already?

ILSE: Still.

RUTH: I didn't think it possible to share a bed with a man and not touch him. Even when you're asleep something watchful comes between you. Edvards doesn't seem to notice. One side of him feels nothing any more and in the other the nerves are twisted. All messages get confused. I lie there awake.

ILSE: What will you do about Leonids?

RUTH: Oh, Ilse, I'm so alone. When the train brought us here, stopping in the night in the middle of nowhere, I waited for the guard to come and put me off, beside the train, alone, with nothing. A worthless woman. The way the Russians put grandmothers off beside the track and saved themselves a bullet. And then the train would move off, and in the window, Leonids would be watching me as if I was a knife in his side.

ILSE: Tell him to go away.

RUTH: I'm going with him.

ILSE: Where to?

RUTH: We'll take the train and get off somewhere together, when we have enough money saved. Two people should be able to disappear in a country this size.

    LEONIDS *enters with his suitcase.*

LEONIDS: This seems to be where the extra bed is.

ILSE: I suppose that's where you'll have to sleep.

LEONIDS: Just for tonight.

    RUTH *holds out her hand to* LEONIDS.

There's another room, but it's full of fertiliser. Blood and bone. We'll clean it out tomorrow.

    RUTH *and* LEONIDS *embrace.*

ILSE: I'll leave you alone for a moment.

    KARL *enters.*

    KARL: [*to* LEONIDS] Oh, you're here. Thought we'd lost you.

    The light changes.

SCENE FIVE

Stuttgart. 1947.

EDVARDS: Ruthie?

OTTO: Someone's out there.

EDVARDS: Ruth.

KARL: [*in reply to* RUTH'*s look*] Yes, it's Edvards. But wait a...

    EDVARDS *walks away as* RUTH *goes out to him.* OTTO, LYDIA
    and ILSE *go to look.* LEONIDS *and* KARL *stay in the room.*

OTTO: Guess who's back from the dead?

RUTH: Edvards.

EDVARDS: Don't look, Ruthie.

    She comes round to him. He covers her eyes.

Don't look. OK?

LEONIDS: You should have told her straight away.

KARL: I tried... I was going to... She was all over you. What was I to
say in front of everyone: "Let that man go. Your husband has
come back from the dead with only half his face?"

LEONIDS: That should be me.

    Going out to the others.

That would be easier.

    RUTH *moves* EDVARDS' *hand away and gently touches his
    face.*

EDVARDS: It doesn't hurt, not to touch. OK. You are more beautiful
than ever, while I have been made by man, almost in his image.

RUTH: Don't talk like that.

    EDVARDS *turns to the others.*

EDVARDS: Are these your friends?

    LYDIA *can't look at him.*

RUTH: Yes. Lydia and Otto.

OTTO: I'm glad you pulled through. I always wanted to meet a real hero.

EDVARDS: You've got the horse by the dirty end, my friend. Heroes look like Karl. OK?

RUTH: This is Ilse, and Leonids.

ILSE: Hello, Edvards.

    ILSE *kisses his cheek and then takes* RUTH's *hand.*

LEONIDS: Pleased to meet you.

EDVARDS: [*to all of them*] Take a good look and don't pity me. Better yet, think of me as Janus the two-headed god. One face looks forward, one face looks back. Which is which? That is the riddle. It is not as you'd expect. This one [*his good side*] is my past. And this is my future. It doesn't look so good.

    EDVARDS *laughs. The others relax.* KARL *joins them.*

OTTO: It's not so damn good for anyone.

EDVARDS: OK. Here we all are, two years after the war, still in the uniforms of the victors. A displaced people. No past and no future. In that respect I am luckier than you.

LYDIA: Your future is no more stamped in your face than ours is and it doesn't mean we'll spend the rest of our lives with a jackboot on our necks.

EDVARDS: We are a problem. OK. No one knows what to do with us, but the Russians would find a solution, like the Germans with the Jews.

    He laughs.

OK. Look at you all. Waiting to be saved.

LYDIA: You do what you like. Otto and I are going to Australia.

EDVARDS: Go. Away. Anywhere. OK? Karl, I need that drink. The funeral is over. Don't worry, I will pay. OK.

KARL: [*going*] No, no. It's all right. On the house.

OTTO: [*to* KARL] This bottle is empty.

LYDIA: You've had enough. I want to go.

EDVARDS: Bring enough for everybody and I won't take charity. I insist on paying.

He takes a dental plate from his mouth and crushes it under his heel.

LEONIDS: Jesus Christ, what are you doing?

OTTO: His false teeth. Gold ones.

KARL *returns with a bottle.* EDVARDS *takes the bottle and gives* KARL *a tooth.*

EDVARDS: That should put me in credit.

KARL: [*trying to return it*] I can't take that. Not out of your mouth. Pay me later. I know a dentist who can repair that.

EDVARDS: [*refusing*] It didn't fit right and anyway it gave me a false smile.

He drinks.

A man only needs teeth to tear meat from bones or to hold onto his lover. OK. Already I've noticed all the cats and dogs have been eaten and I'm a married man again.

He embraces RUTH.

KARL: Ruth, take these. See if you can get them fixed.

EDVARDS: No. OK. [*To* KARL.] You want me to pay in cash? If I have to sell them on the black market, I won't get as good a price as you. You do me a favour by taking them.

KARL: It makes me feel like shit.

EDVARDS: A business man has no conscience. OK? And for the taste of shit there is an antidote. Let's get drunk. I have a lot to remember.

EDVARDS *puts his arm round* RUTH *and starts to go. All except* LEONIDS *follow.*

SCENE SIX

North Queensland. 1845. Day.
GILBERT *dissects a bird and makes entries in his journal.*
LEICHHARDT *enters carrying the carcass of an emaciated dingo.*

LEICHHARDT: I am back.

GILBERT: [*not looking up*] So I see. And smell. Where did you find that dog?

LEICHHARDT: Not find. I caught it on the path to the waterhole. It comes, panting, very slowly—

GILBERT: The maggots were carrying it off?

LEICHHARDT: I killed it with a stone.

GILBERT: Doesn't that nose of yours tell you it has an intolerably bad odour?

LEICHHARDT: Caused only by an insufficient diet.

GILBERT: Now that we're out of supplies, we must smell as rotten as that dog to the natives. No wonder they run off howling.

     Pause.

Have you given any thought to turning back?

LEICHHARDT: No!

GILBERT: My work on this expedition is finished. I have no blank pages left in my journal.

LEICHHARDT: Then you can no longer record my shortcomings.

GILBERT: I can no longer record my observations about my specimens.

LEICHHARDT: Good! I think you are sitting too long in the one place, looking into the gutses of chickens. Raise your head a little and look to the horizon. Have some vision, man, this country is more than one bush clearing and the next.

GILBERT: We merely see things differently and place different importance on what we see. You charge from one thing to

another and because you cover a lot of ground you think you have
seen a lot. Consequently, you make no sense of what you see or
how one thing is related to another. You want to see it all and yet
see nothing. Others will come afterwards and be astounded at the
things we missed. But sit still a moment. Notice this tree grows in
this soil, that this beetle is found on this tree and the bird feeds on
its berries. Look deeper still. Open up the bird, split the tree, dig
in the soil. That way you can steal nature's secrets. You can learn
so much just sitting here. Move fifty yards in any direction and
everything is different. My world is what is within my field of
vision. If I go to see what is there, I miss what is here. I build a
picture of this clearing by putting together the little things that
make it up. I build a picture of Australia by putting together the
clearings. I am happy, but for the knowledge that I won't see it
all. I can't cover the ground fast enough.

LEICHHARDT: I'm for covering it as quickly as possible. The further
the horizon the better.

GILBERT: So long as there's a tree you can head for.

LEICHHARDT: This is no ordinary adventure, Mr Gilbert. We are in a
new land in a new time. You look and you see specimens and you
see danger. You are not seeing the woods for the trees. I am
discovering the way for your "others" to follow and the trees I
mark will stand as monuments to our achievements. Thousands
will come from the stagnant civilisation of Europe where men kill
each other for a pocketful of soil. They will come with
knowledge that is hundreds of years old and cultivate this Eden.
The future is all around, larger than life, innocent and without
secrets. There are no ghosts in her closets.

GILBERT: Except for the natives and their whole host of spirits.

LEICHHARDT: Pah! Black men and their viney-viney. Thousands of
years they have been here and who can tell? They have hardly
marked the soil.

SCENE SEVEN

Stuttgart. 1947. Day.

KARL *and* ILSE *are walking together.* KARL *kisses* ILSE. *She draws away.*

KARL: I thought you would be glad to see me. I thought you were sweet on me.

ILSE: I did some thinking while you were away too.

KARL: And now a man can't even kiss you. Doesn't that shawl mean anything to you?

> *She gives it back to him.*

ILSE: You don't have to pay this much for a whore.

KARL: What do you mean? Don't put words in my mouth. I didn't mean that.

> *He moves to her. She doesn't resist.*

It's yours. Unconditional. I sat in my cell for four months just thinking of you.

ILSE: And tobacco and booze, black market deals and gold teeth. The only way I can fit in with such schemes is as a—

KARL: What the hell do you think of me? I like your company. It's natural. Blame God. Even Adam had his Eve.

ILSE: You'll have to play Eve because you've got the apple.

> KARL *returns the shawl to her.*

KARL: Here, please take it.

ILSE: If I bite, what is it that I'm supposed to learn?

KARL: [*laughing*] You want me to say I love you?

ILSE: Talk is cheap. Other men have loved me, as they loved other women.

> G.I. JOE *and* G.I. SAM *enter.*

G.I. JOE: She's still here with the jerk in the suit. Com'n, Sam. Don't go all shy on me now.

They approach.

KARL: [*accent*] Hi, Joes.

G.I. JOE: I'm Joe. He's Sam. How ya doin', Fritz? Nice suit. Must be doin' all right in the black market. [*To* ILSE.] You c'n do better than a two bit punk. Com'n, Sam, trot your stuff. I wanta do this very polite like.

G.I. SAM: While the suit's here?

G.I. JOE: Sure. Do it. He's a nice guy. OK, Fritz?

KARL: [*accent*] OK, Joe.

G.I. SAM: [*nervously*] Hiya, Ilsa. This is Joe Hallaran. Joe, this here's Ilsa.

G.I. JOE: Thanks for nothin', kid. As an icebreaker you could use a bit more steel in your pecker. [*To* ILSE.] Hello, Miss Ilsa. Sam here's been tellin' me a lot about you and I'm real happy to make your acquaintance. You're real pretty.

G.I. JOE *holds out his hand.* ILSE *doesn't take it.*

KARL: He wants to meet you.

ILSE: He wants a whore.

KARL: [*to* ILSE] All of a sudden you've got a one track mind. [*To all, accent.*] I think hers—

G.I. JOE: I get the picture, Fritz. She's shy. Look, why don't you two jerks give a man a bit of room?

He waves KARL *and* SAM *a few paces away.*

ILSE: [*to* KARL] Where are you going? He's the trespasser.

G.I. JOE: Now, Miss Ilsa, don't get me wrong. I'm not a bad sort of Joe. I'd like to get acquainted. [*Offering a small bottle to her.*] *Pour vous, ma'amselle.*

ILSE *doesn't take it.*

G.I. SAM: That's French, Joe.

G.I. JOE: So I came via Paree.

G.I. SAM: She ain't French, though.

G.I. JOE: It's the language of love, ain't it? *Parfum!*

Pause.

OK. So it's bloody American aftershave, but the German girls go
wild for it...

KARL: [*to* ILSE] He wants you to have that American cologne.

ILSE: Ask him when the American Joes will chase Joe Stalin out of
my home instead of signing a pact. The Yanks believe in one law
and one justice for all. When the Yanks sit down with the
Russians and make law, there's justice for no one. Horse shit!

KARL: I don't know how to ask that, luckily.

G.I. JOE: I think I made a breakthrough here. She said "Joe" twice.

G.I. SAM: Probably callin' us assholes.

G.I. JOE: [*to* KARL] Fritz? What *fraulein sprechen?*

KARL: [*accent*] She likes Americans plenty...

ILSE: [*accent*] G.I. Joes.

> She spits.

> Shits.

G.I. JOE: [*prodding* KARL] She don't like Americans, do she? Well,
you can tell her to go fuck herself on a barbed wire fence and
crawl back to Siberia. [*To* ILSE.] You think we wanted to fight
this bloody war? You got no sense of gratitude. A man could
practically screw his way from the beaches of Normandy. This is
the first time I come across this. Well, sister, I had my head in a
lot of laps and I ain't accustomed to such treatment.

> He forcibly kisses her. She bites him. He reels back as G.I.
> SAM and KARL step in.

She fuckin' bit me! Blood!

G.I. SAM: Come on, Joe.

KARL: [*placatingly, accent*] Sorry, Joe. She OK. Sorry.

> G.I. JOE struggles with G.I. SAM.

G.I. JOE: She OK! She's fuckin' crazy. She nearly took my lip off.
Goddamn cannibal.

G.I. SAM: Could a been your pecker.

G.I. JOE: You think that's funny. You think it's so goddamn funny?
You set me up.

G.I. SAM: I swear I never, I swear. I weren't the only one she had. You ain't missing anythin'. She'd just lie there while you ploughed a paddock.

G.I. JOE: Yeah! How come I hit the land mine?

G.I. SAM: Come on. Leave her to the suit.

G.I. JOE: [*to* KARL] You better watch yourself, Fritz, or she'll have you for fuckin' breakfast. [*To* ILSE.] Bitch.

They go.

KARL: What the hell did you have to do that for? He was just being friendly.

ILSE: They think any woman is theirs for the taking. The spoils to the victors. Why didn't you stop him?

KARL: I thought you knew them. That Sam knew you.

ILSE: That's one cock that won't be crowing tomorrow morning.

KARL: I don't think you were so clever. You drew blood. He'll never say you did it. I'll be blamed. If word gets to the Quartermaster, I won't get my old job back.

ILSE: You'll be in danger of becoming an honest man.

KARL: What I do is honest even if it's not legal. Let's not squabble. OK. Try to understand, just for a minute. Four months I waited for your visit. You didn't come. But every night and morning I said, I love you.

ILSE: As you looked in the mirror.

KARL: I was saying it to you. You must've heard me.

ILSE: No. I wasn't listening.

KARL: Oh, well. I'll say it now, then. I love you.

ILSE: Did you think that would bowl me over?

KARL: I'd need a tank for that.

ILSE: So you've used your biggest guns and I'm still standing.

KARL: I did hope for a slight crack.

ILSE: I'm broken already. My brother loved freedom and was killed fighting for one tyrant against another. As a child I played with him amongst the birch trees and now their shadows are crowded with the ghosts of the butchered. The fields have been fertilised with blood and bone. All for love. I'll never see my family again because they're slaves. At every gate and doorway there stands a stinking heavy booted Russian guard. He stands there for love. I run from it for my life.

KARL: Is it all right if I still like you? Tell you what, come to the United States with me. With your looks you could be in movies. Film stars don't have to love anyone. You could be a second Garbo.

ILSE: Would you really take me?

KARL: I'd have to send for you. That'd be best. I'd set myself up in a nice little business.

ILSE: And I'd have to wait here.

KARL: It wouldn't be for long. Anyone can be a businessman in America. In no time flat the dough will be rolling in. I'll wear a smart suit, smoke Havana cigars and drink bourbon out of crystal, no ice.

ILSE: You still sound like a bootlegger.

KARL: Prohibition's over. That went out with Al Capone.

ILSE: I heard he's dead, so there's plenty of room for another crook if you get into the country.

KARL: They've no good reason to refuse me.

ILSE: Except that you've just spent time in their gaols.

　　　KARL *gets his suitcase.*

KARL: I'm not a thief or murderer. I'd better go see about this job. Business depends on it. I'll see you tonight.

ILSE: If I'm not here, I'll be in Australia.

KARL: I'll take you dancing.

　　　He kisses her.

Don't go biting any more Americans, they're on our side.

　　　He goes.

ILSE: They're on your side.

SCENE EIGHT

North Queensland. 1845. A clearing. Day.

There is the sound of wailing in the distance. PHILLIPS *rushes on, puffing. He stops to listen. Silence, then the sound of someone crashing through the bush. A magpie calls. The wailing continues.*

PHILLIPS: Johnny! Johnny! This way, boyo. To your left.

MURPHY *enters carrying a rifle, very excited.*

MURPHY: Blast! I dropped Mr Gilbert's food.

PHILLIPS: Fuck the food. Where are the women?

MURPHY: I was right behind 'em, Phillips.

PHILLIPS: Yer reckon I've got 'em hid, yer daft monkey? They're probably up some bleedin' gum tree three miles back by now.

There is the sound of rustling in the bushes.

MURPHY: [*whispering*] That's them. They're here. Real close.

PHILLIPS: [*circling round*] You stay here and block the way. See if yer can't do somethin' right.

MURPHY: [*levelling his rifle*] Don't worry. I'll stop 'em.

PHILLIPS: Put that down. A dead woman's no good to anyone.

He goes.

MURPHY: I'll just wound them.

PHILLIPS *yells, off, and* RUTH *rushes on, clothes and hair awry, brandishing a shoe. She sees* MURPHY *and stops.*

[*hopping about*] Coo-ee! Coo-ee! We got one. We got one in hand.

PHILLIPS: [*off*] There was two in the bush so hang on.

ILSE *staggers on.*

MURPHY: [*hopping about*] Oh God. Oh God, look at 'em. Black as the devil himself.

ILSE *turns to go back but* PHILLIPS *cuts off her escape. The* WOMEN *should be near to exhaustion as should the* MEN.

PHILLIPS: [*to* MURPHY] Move slowly. We don't want 'em chargin' off again. [*To* WOMEN.] Easy now, easy. We aren't going to hurt you.

RUTH: The G.I.s are our friends.

ILSE: They think we're German women, that they can have us for nothing. [*To* MEN.] *Nicht Deutsche, nicht Deutsche.*

RUTH: *Freunden.*

MURPHY: Jabberin' away. They're frightened of us.

PHILLIPS: We aren't viney-viney, ladies, just white men with white cocks.

MURPHY: How's the two of us goin' to hold them down?

PHILLIPS: Do it right we won't have to. Put that rifle down. There's no pleasure in fuckin' a woman that's got shot.

MURPHY *puts the rifle down.*

Now back 'em into the trees. Gently now, gently.

KARL *enters with suitcase. Stops and watches as the* WOMEN *are herded back.*

MURPHY: Oh Jesus, those bosoms, can't we start yet?

PHILLIPS: Talk to 'em, calm 'em. Like a skittish horse.

MURPHY: Whoa there boy. I mean, thatta girl.

RUTH: He's only a boy playing with himself.

ILSE: [*holding out her hand*] Make them pay.

PHILLIPS: We got 'em now. Give 'em your buttons. Go on, rip 'em off.

MURPHY *frantically rips off his buttons and lunges for* RUTH. *They grab both* WOMEN *roughly to stop them running off.*

MURPHY: Oh God, oh God, oh noo!

PHILLIPS: Too bad boyo. You can watch me.

ILSE: [*as* KARL *turns to go*] Karl!

RUTH: Karl!

PHILLIPS: Karl karl karl! Like bleedin' crows.

SCENE NINE

North Queensland. 1948. The cane field. Day.

There is the sound of cane cutting. It gradually fades and then comes back and stops just before the MEN *appear.* ILSE *and* RUTH *enter carrying food baskets and a billy of tea.*

LYDIA: [*off*] Wait! Can't you? Wait. I can't keep up.

ILSE: [*stopping*] Wear something sensible on your feet.

LYDIA: [*off*] Like you're wearing? Oops! No thank you. I have never seen anything so ugly in my life. They make your feet look like a couple of flounders. I don't know how Karl can let you walk around like that.

RUTH: You mean Otto forces you to dress like that?

ILSE: Even in Latvia no one walked across a field in what you're wearing on your feet.

RUTH: Unless they were drunk and coming home from a dance.

LYDIA: [*joining them*] I didn't walk across fields. I left that to the peasants. I had a nice little shop in Madona and sold china and the most delicate glasses. Before the peasants came into the shop I made them take their boots off at the door and they had to stand in the middle of the room so that their coats and thick hands wouldn't bump the pieces. They could point to what they wanted to look at and I would hold it up before them.

RUTH *hands* LYDIA *half a dozen pannikins on string.*

RUTH: Then you must be the best person to take care of these.

ILSE: Now that you have to point for things in shops here, you're finding out how the peasants felt.

LYDIA: For iron. Everything is iron. Iron houses, iron cups, iron plates.

She drops the cups. They clatter.

They don't break. You can't even get rid of them.

RUTH: Don't drop them in the dirt.

LYDIA: We live in the dirt. My Otto had a responsible position as a book-keeper, and now he is breaking his back like a slave.

ILSE: There was always some clumsy peasant doing the slaving. The food on your table didn't grow in a nice little shop in town.

The WOMEN *put down a cloth and lay out the food.*

LYDIA: You can't call this... thing up the road a town. Half of it made of iron like our barracks. There is no respite. In Germany we lived in barracks. I could understand that. They were better than these tin drums. When it rains you can't hear. When the sun's out it's a sauna. At night it rains inside from the condensation. [*She is on the verge of tears of frustration.*]

RUTH: You'll get used to it. You got used to much worse in the war.

LYDIA: If this is peace, I'd rather be shot. I don't want to get used to it. Maybe it's all right for peasants.

ILSE: I'm no more at home here than you are. I don't like the jungles and stinking mud or blood sucking insects any more than you do. I don't understand this country and it doesn't understand me. I don't like the way men become raw boned and vulgar and I am afraid that I'll become tired and resentful like its women. But I can live in an iron shed and eat off an iron plate because it won't always be that way. I'll go back to a city and crystal and china. I don't fight it like you do.

RUTH: [*to* LYDIA, *keeping the peace*] It's not easy, but it's not as bad as you think.

LYDIA: You can say that because your biggest problem is how to get from one bed to another without anyone seeing you. Edvards must be blind.

RUTH: I know what you all think, that I wish Edvards was dead and you hope I will go away before anything unpleasant happens so you won't have to stand by and watch.

ILSE: Hush. You don't know what you're saying.

LYDIA: I'm sorry. It's my fault. I was looking for a way to tell you that I'm moving into town as soon as Otto can find me a little flat. There's electricity. It'll be better than out here.

ILSE: You're leaving us?

LYDIA: You can come with me.

RUTH: There's the men to take care of.

LYDIA: Let them fend for themselves during the week and on the weekend they can come to town.

RUTH: No. I'd never see Leonids except under your noses.

ILSE: A flat would be an extra expense.

LYDIA: Well, you'll come and visit me. We'll have coffee and cake off a linen table cloth with cups and saucers.

ILSE: That'd be nice for a change. But we couldn't come often. We have no transport. You'll be alone a lot unless you mix with the town women.

LYDIA: With them I'm a smiling idiot child who understands nothing.

RUTH: Learn English, Lydia.

LYDIA: I speak English, the way it is taught to us by a Dutchman, but no one understands it. I might as well be talking Dutch.

ILSE: Maybe we are.

LYDIA: [accent] G'day. Hows ares yous todays?

RUTH: [accent] Bloody crooks in za guts.

ILSE: That's not English, that's the bastard language. I will speak English. [Accent.] "Ziss is the chair." No? [Sitting down.] That's all there is to it. [Accent.] "Ziss is the floors."

LYDIA: [accent] "Zat is a doors."

RUTH: [accent] "Ze teas is on the tables." It doesn't help when you have to show the butcher you want some spicy sausages. You should have seen his face.

LYDIA: You should have done that Aboriginal dance for him. Then his eyes would really have popped out.

She sings with an accent and actions.

> You put the right hip in,
> You put the right hip out,
> You put the right hip in
> And you shake it all about.
> You do the hokey-pokey
> And knees-bend, knees-bend.
> That's what it's all about.

Robynne Bourne (Lydia), Mary Sitarenos (Ruth) and Pamela Rabe (Ilse) in the 1985 Melbourne Theatre Company production. (Photo: David Parker)

> ILSE *and* RUTH *laugh and join in. The dance becomes more risque and abandoned as they do frontside and backside, nearly collapsing with laughter. The dance is accompanied by the rhythmic sound of the approaching cane cutters. They enter during the last verse, black with soot and burnt sugar. Their eyes gleam whitely as they watch.*

EDVARDS: OK. You women are having a good time.

RUTH: And why not?

> *The* WOMEN *take the* MEN *damp cloths so they can clean their faces and hands.* LEONIDS *just sits and runs a file over his cane knife.*

KARL: Where did you learn such a dance?

ILSE: At English classes. You'd be surprised what you'd learn about your body.

KARL: My body teaches me all I need to know by how it feels and what it feels.

ILSE: So long as you're satisfied.

KARL: I'll let you know when I'm not.

> ILSE *goes to* LEONIDS. *She cleans his face.*

ILSE: You haven't cleaned your face. Let me. You'll feel better.

LEONIDS: You think the others would bother if you didn't do it?

ILSE: That's why we do it. To stop you living hand to mouth.

> *The* MEN *eat and drink, sitting on the ground. The* WOMEN *stand.*

OTTO: You should see this field. Twisted cane and stones as big as a man's head. It's murder. My hands are numb and I've got blisters again.

EDVARDS: Of the three farms we've cut, OK, this has got to be absolutely the worst. Bourke swindled you, Karl.

KARL: You've worked three farms and already you're an expert.

EDVARDS: It takes longer to teach an ox how to pull a plough than it does to teach a man to bend his back and swing a knife.

LYDIA: The price is too low if Otto has to pay with the skin of his hands.

KARL: Leonids and I aren't finding it so hard.

LEONIDS: Whichever way you cut it, it's money in the bank.

EDVARDS: OK. So it's two stallions against one clerk and a man of badly knitted parts. Explain to this dumb soldier, OK, why we aren't cutting the tonnage we usually do.

ILSE: Because you were drunk last night.

RUTH: Karl bought the booze, Ilse.

EDVARDS: [*to* KARL] You're the expert price fixer. Renegotiate. OK. You're the one who was swindled.

KARL: If that's what you think, then we've all been swindled.

LEONIDS: Maybe that's so. But maybe you're up to your old tricks and taking a bit off the top. You're not one to give beer away.

KARL: Remember that next time you drink it.

ILSE: Why don't you sort it out with Bourke. He's on his way. You better eat up or he'll be taking the food out of your mouth as well.

LYDIA: [*passing around the sandwiches*] Here, Otto. Make sure you have some.

> The MEN *take one or two sandwiches each. There are some they don't touch.*

EDVARDS: No, thanks. [*Accent.*] No cornered beef. OK. Pure salt.

OTTO: If that meat comes from a cow, it's a sea cow.

RUTH: We've roasted it, stewed it, fried it and grilled it. What else are we supposed to do with it? Boil it?

LEONIDS: Don't buy it again. It's our money you're wasting.

ILSE: Leave them for Mr Bourke. See what he makes of them.

BOURKE: [*off*] Hello there, missus.

ILSE: [*accent*] Yes. Good day.

> BOURKE *enters. He is carrying two bandicoots by the tail.*

BOURKE: G'day, boys.

> The MEN *eat.* KARL *waves.*

Ladies.

RUTH: [*accent*] Hows ares yous?

BOURKE: Pretty bloody good.

> BOURKE *holds the bandicoots up.* LYDIA *shrieks and hides behind* RUTH.

What d'ya reckon about these bandicoots?

LYDIA: Rats!

BOURKE: Always set a couple of snares when I burn off.

LYDIA: Rats! Look at the size of those rats. They'd carry off babies.

> BOURKE *advances.* RUTH *and* LYDIA *back off, squealing and laughing.*

RUTH: No. Take them away. Ugh! What a size. What kind of rat is it?

BOURKE: Bloody good tucker. One is enough for me. [*Turning to* ILSE.] What about you, missus? Game to try one?

> *He holds one out.* ILSE *backs away, shaking her head.*

ILSE: What does he want me to do with it?

LEONIDS: [*accent*] What to do with rat?

BOURKE: [*laughing*] Rat. No. Bandicoot. Fresh meat. Good to eat.

LEONIDS: [*accent*] No. No. Please.

BOURKE: Suit yourself.

> *He puts the bandicoots in the cane in the shade.*

ILSE: [*laughing*] He eats rats? We were lucky to get baked beans on toast the first night. We might have had rat. We wouldn't have got over it.

> *They all laugh.*

EDVARDS: And we thought we had it hard in the war eating cats and dogs.

LYDIA: The man is raving mad.

BOURKE: What's the big joke, eh?

> *The laughter subsides.*

ILSE: [*accent*] You eat rats!

BOURKE: Ha bloody ha. Bandicoots, yes.

> *The* D.P.*s laugh and shake their heads in disbelief.*

You don't know what you're missing out on. A man can live right off the land here.

RUTH: [*accent*] Yous like tea?

BOURKE: Ta. Wouldn't mind a cup.

> RUTH *pours him a cup.*

OTTO: Give him a sandwich now.

ILSE: No wait a bit. Eat. Make him feel hungry. When there's food he's just around the corner. If you want a new chimney for the stove or a new door hinge, he's not to be found.

LEONIDS: He overcharges for the barracks and we have to feed him as well.

KARL: What are you going to do with all the money you're saving?

LEONIDS: Buy nothing from you.

BOURKE: [*standing over them*] Speak English. Nattering away like monkeys. Bloody rude. So is eating in front of guests.

OTTO: The man's a miser. He'd squeeze a fart out of a dead man.

BOURKE: Just as bloody well I didn't sign you for the conversation. I reckon they made a mistake keepin' you all together. If they'd split you up amongst some Ities or Yugoslavs, you wouldn't be so chirpy. Still you work cheap. I got a real find in Karl.

ILSE: [*offering him a sandwich, accent*] Mr Bourke. Eat.

BOURKE: [*taking one*] Thought you'd never ask. Ta.

ILSE: [*accent*] Eat. Plenty.

He takes another.

BOURKE: Thanks, missus. Very decent of you. Greedy buggers.

They watch him.

Ah! Corned beef!

He bites heartily into the sandwich, chews, sucks in a breath, looks to spit it out and realises they are watching.

ILSE: [*accent*] Good? Yes?

BOURKE: [*pained*] Yes, good! Very bloody salty!

The D.P.s laugh softly. They eat and drink, watching.

RUTH: [*accent*] Eat! Eat!

BOURKE: I'm eating! See. Oh God. How did you cook this? With salt?

He gulps his tea.

ILSE: [*offering him another sandwich, accent*] You take more. Eat plenty.

BOURKE: [*taking another*] Very nice! I'll keep this one for later. Thanks. [*Thinking he has found a way out.*] Cheep-cheep, cheep-cheep. Pretty little birds, them.

He throws half a sandwich.

ILSE: [*accent*] No, no! You eat!

The D.P.*s laugh and encourage him. "Eat! Eat!"*

BOURKE: Think you're bloody funny, don't ya?

LYDIA: [*accent*] Your cane. No good.

BOURKE: Eh? What would you know, Princess Muck?

OTTO: [*knitting his fingers, accent*] Tangle up! Stones! Break hands. Look!

He shows his hands.

BOURKE: Yeah. Nice set of blisters. You hold cane knife too tight. Too tight. [*He clenches his hand.*] Best thing for 'em, pardon the French, is piss.

The D.P.*s look at each other, eyebrows raised.*

What'd I say now?

EDVARDS: [*accent*] Piss?

BOURKE: Yeah! Piss. I reckon you got the same bodily functions as us. A number one. You know. *Numero uno?* Ah. Come here, Karl.

KARL *comes to* BOURKE. *They face away from the group.*

Here! Hold this sandwich for a minute.

BOURKE *then goes through a charade of undoing his fly, taking out his penis and cupping his hands underneath. He whistles.*

KARL: He's washing his hands, Otto. Urinating on them.

The D.P.*s laugh.*

LYDIA: I've seen enough.

KARL: [*explaining quietly to* BOURKE, *accent*] Piss. My country. Mean fucks.

BOURKE: Fair go, eh? [*Shrugging.*] Maybe that works as well.

KARL *tries to return the sandwich.*

You keep the sandwich. You've had your little joke. Get 'em back to work. [*Pointing.*] Looks like rain building up over there.

They all look.

Rain. You cut cane faster. Presto, presto.

LEONIDS: [*accent*] No.

BOURKE: Eh? What d'ya mean, no?

> *They look to* KARL. KARL *shrugs.*

EDVARDS: [*accent*] Cane is bent. Plenty stones.

LEONIDS: [*accent*] Price no good.

BOURKE: Bullshit! You're getting a bloody good price. And there's bugger all wrong with the cane.

LEONIDS: [*accent*] Cane inspector comes.

BOURKE: No need. A couple of wild pigs might've got amongst the cane. Nothing more. I don't give a bugger if you have to work in the rain. Karl, sort these bastards out. Get 'em back to work. What the hell do I pay you for?

LEONIDS: [*to* KARL] You fixed the price. Renegotiate.

> *Pause.*

EDVARDS: How do you like that? Our crook won't deal with theirs.

KARL: I don't know what you expect. I don't speak the language any better than you. In Germany I could speak German and I traded on the black market which was German. It's time you all started looking after yourselves. I won't always be around to strike the bargains.

> *The group start talking all at once.*

LEONIDS: What bargains have you made for yourself?

ILSE: Ask him about the chimney for the stove.

OTTO: [*accent*] Price no good.

EDVARDS: The door hinge is broken. [*Accent.*] Door no good.

RUTH: [*to* LEONIDS] Ask him for a new mattress.

LYDIA: Otto. I want to go to stay in town as soon as possible.

LEONIDS: [*accent*] Money for barracks. Too much.

BOURKE: [*waving his arms*] All right! All right! Jesus Christ! You found them words quick enough. Karl is ganger, right?

> *The* D.P.*s nod.*

Together [*Putting his arm around* KARL.] we make price. Fair price.

KARL: [*accent*] You pay sixpence more a ton, OK?

BOURKE: Not on your bleeding life. [*Aside to* KARL.] If you're with them, Karl, you can forget our little deal.

KARL: [*to the others*] He says it's a fair price and I'm inclined to think it's not so bad. At the end of the season we'll want to go out on a good note. If we go along with him, we should be able to rent the barracks fairly cheaply in the slack.

LYDIA: I'm not staying one week more.

LEONIDS: [*accent*] Call cane inspector. We talk.

BOURKE: Too much bloody talk. Bloody Bolsheviks.

> LEONIDS *starts to go for* BOURKE. *"Bolshevik" is the supreme insult.*

EDVARDS: [*accent*] No Bolsheviks! We no work! Call cane inspector!

BOURKE: Your leadership isn't worth a pinch of piss, Karl. You've just done your bonus. From now on you get the same as them. You call me a cheat when I give you a good deal. The whole country opens their hearts to you and you rub salt into them. Well, make the most of what you've got. Next year you not so damn lucky. This good job, this good money. Go to Englishmen. Much as I hate 'em, at least they speak the same language. Understand? Next year. You no cut cane. No easy money. English migrant cut cane. You go to buggery.

KARL: [*accent*] We have contract.

BOURKE: You break. You give me word you cut. Now you no work.

KARL: [*accent*] We have two years contract.

BOURKE: Your contract's with the Government. Not with me. They can find you something else. Railways. Choo-choo. Timber cutting. Chop chop. You're getting it easy this year. Bloody good job. Thrown away. No wonder you lost the war.

> *He starts to go.*

KARL: [*accent*] We talk to cane inspector.

BOURKE: Get fucked.

EDVARDS: [*accent*] Hey! You forget. Rats!

> EDVARDS *tosses them off after him. There is some bitter laughter and a brief silence.*

ILSE: What did he say to you about a bonus?

KARL: What business is that of yours?

ILSE: It's everybody's business.

KARL: As we're not working we won't get one, simple.

LEONIDS: You said nothing about a bonus for us.

OTTO: It was never mentioned in the price.

EDVARDS: Because our little businessman was the only one to get one. OK? For the good deal he did for Mr Bourke.

KARL: [*shrugging*] You always got a fair price from me. See if you can do better. I get no thanks for my pains.

LEONIDS: Except what you could rake off the top.

EDVARDS: OK. We wait. The cane inspector will come and we'll get a better price. Bourke needs us to cut his cane.

KARL: This year, anyway. And next year?

LEONIDS: The sawmills are always looking for men to cut timber.

OTTO: Oh no. From cutting sticks to chopping trees.

KARL: This is what you wanted. Our name will be shit for cane cutting. But there's plenty of timber cutting.

RUTH: What happens to us?

EDVARDS: You'll stay in town. You'll like that. OK. We have to stay in a camp and come to town on weekends.

RUTH: While we sit and wait.

KARL: You're all good at waiting.

OTTO: If you hadn't tried to swindle us—

> KARL *goes.*

ILSE: Where are you going now?

KARL: I'll do my waiting at the hotel. When they fix a price, they can come and find me.

> *He goes.*

EDVARDS: I wait better with a drink. Come on, Leonids.

> OTTO *starts off with them.*

LYDIA: Otto.

OTTO: If I have a beer or two I'll make medicine for my hands.

> *The* MEN *go, laughing. The* WOMEN *sing:*

> Don't ask me, now, what makes love fade and die, friend:
> That's something I have tried to comprehend.
> Why was it that the summer spell was broken?

Ask no more, friend, there's no more that I know.
Why was it that the summer spell was broken?
Ask no more, friend, there's no more that I know.

The WOMEN *go during the last few lines of the song.*

END OF PART ONE

PART TWO

SCENE TEN

North Queensland. 1948. Night.
KARL *stands smoking a cigarette.* LYDIA *enters.*

LYDIA: [*calling softly*] Otto! Are you there? Karl!
KARL: Yes?
LYDIA: Have you seen Otto?
KARL: No.
LYDIA: I woke up and he wasn't there.
KARL: Don't worry yourself, he can't have gone far. I'm sure he will be back shortly. Stay here with me.
LYDIA: What are you doing? Stop it. Karl!

> *She backs away from him.*

KARL: You can't be happy with that weed.
LYDIA: Otto!

> ILSE *enters.*

ILSE: What's going on?
KARL: Lydia has lost Otto.
ILSE: How lost him?
LYDIA: He's gone; not in bed.
KARL: The blacks took him.
ILSE: Don't be stupid. We'll go and find him.

> ILSE *leads* LYDIA. KARL *shrugs and follows.*

LEICHHARDT: [*off*] Go on! Idiot! Go round further.

> OTTO *stumbles on. The sound of horses is heard.*

Cut them off. Cretin. You never saw horses before? Take a hold.
By the mane or by the tail.

> OTTO *advances, hand outstretched.*

OTTO: [*nervously*] There, boy. There you go. Come here. Time to go
to work. The fields have to be mowed. Can't stand idle all day
growing a big belly.

> *He stops.*

Hey up! Don't go.

LEICHHARDT: [*off*] Why are you standing? Idiot. You can wait all
day and it won't come to you. Run at them. Run now! Arrgh!

> *There is the sound of horses wheeling and leaping away. An
> old saddle comes flying through the air.* LEICHHARDT *enters
> bent double.*

You thick shithead! You caused me to be kicked in the stomach.
When you run, run. The animals are smarter than you.

OTTO: I don't know horses.

LEICHHARDT: That is painfully obvious to me. This time you will
take him round the neck and hold him till I put this saddle on. If
you flinch I'll see you walk across Australia with bloody
footsteps. Stand still and I will drive the horse to you.

> *He starts to run, swinging the saddle.*

Arrgh! Yah! Dumbest creatures on God's earth. Come on. Arrgh!

> *He throws the saddle off. The other* D.P.s *enter.* EDVARDS *and*
> OTTO *stand fast watching the horse shy away.*

EDVARDS: Horses.

LEONIDS: How come we no longer know the sound of horses?

ILSE: They are beautiful in the moonlight. Just like home.

LYDIA: Otto! Otto! Why doesn't he come!

RUTH: He is sleepwalking. We mustn't wake him suddenly.

EDVARDS: [*laughing*] I can bring him back. [*Calling like a drill
sergeant.*] Private Otto Bernhards. Attention.

> OTTO *snaps to attention.*

LEONIDS: Did you see that?

LYDIA: He's acting the clown again. Otto!

EDVARDS: Perhaps not. You wouldn't think that men at the front would sleepwalk but they did, OK. Up herding cows, gathering firewood, mowing fields. If they were lucky you could talk them back to the trenches. [*Calling* OTTO.] About turn! Quick march! Hup two! Hup two! Hup two! Right turn! Hup two! Hup two! OK.

KARL: I didn't know he could drill so well. Left turn! Hup two! Hup two!

>*The* MEN *laugh. They all give commands.* OTTO *grows frantic trying to follow them.*

LYDIA: Otto! Stop it! Come back. [*To the* MEN.] Stop it! Please stop!

EDVARDS: Halt! Surrender! You are surrounded.

>OTTO *puts his hands up.*

RUTH: Bring him back, Edvards. Leonids, for God's sake make them stop.

EDVARDS: Just having a bit of fun.

>LYDIA *goes to meet him.*

LYDIA: Otto wake up! The game's over. [*Slapping his face gently.*] Wake up!

OTTO: What! Are you—Where are the horses?

LYDIA: Where are the horses, indeed. Over there.

LEONIDS: [*laughing*] He was only fooling.

OTTO: I have to catch the horses for the German.

>*The* MEN *laugh.*

ILSE: Take him to bed. It was only a dream.

>RUTH *and* LYDIA *lead* OTTO *away.*

KARL: Nice act, Otto.

ILSE: [*to the* MEN] You should be ashamed of yourselves.

KARL: [*laughing*] Why? What did we do? He was only fooling.

LEONIDS: Tomorrow he'll probably be laughing at us.

ILSE: Of course that makes it all right. One of us has some trouble, the rest of us stand back and laugh. Because tomorrow the roles will be reversed. Who else can we turn to but each other? And when we do there will be a line of mocking faces. Mindlessly clucking hens.

EDVARDS: [*mocking* ILSE] OK. So let nobody call wolf. Hup two! Hup two!

SCENE ELEVEN

Both camps: North Queensland, 1845, and Stuttgart, 1947. Night.

PHILLIPS: [*off*] Hello, the camp.

PHILLIPS *and* MURPHY *enter.*

LEICHHARDT: So the hunters return. With empty hands.

PHILLIPS: [*sniffing*] What's cooking?

GILBERT: Dead dog.

MURPHY: Phew! What a pong.

PHILLIPS: It's putrid. Are you sure it wasn't ill, Doctor?

LEICHHARDT: You are not obliged to eat it and there is not enough for four men.

GILBERT: There's nothing else.

LEICHHARDT: Eat your specimens. Always teensy little birds. Half a mouthful. Why don't you find something the size of an elephant?

GILBERT: Elephant? So we're in Africa now? The way you use a sextant we'll be in London in a month. There has to be an easier way to Port Essington than strolling to the tip of Australia and turning left.

LEICHHARDT: You are not hungry, that is obvious. A hungry man always finds food.

PHILLIPS: Not if there's none to be found, sir.

GILBERT: It's about time you faced the facts: we're out of supplies, game is scarce and you don't know where we are.

LEICHHARDT: You hope to turn me back, but I am not so easily fooled. To a man you dream of sea coasts and ships and lust for the easy pleasures. But no man starves in paradise, so what are you afraid of?

GILBERT: Of stupidity and the senseless waste of life and work. What we've learned has no value unless we share it.

LEICHHARDT: If it's your bird skins you are worried about, strap them to your back and fly to safety. We will make better progress without your burden.

GILBERT: Phillips and John Murphy have the right to determine their own fate.

LEICHHARDT: A convict and a mere boy who joined me because they could not make good otherwise. What you are you owe to me. Phillips, you must go on to win a pardon.

PHILLIPS: A pardon won't profit me if I'm lyin' dead in a swamp, Doctor. I'm with Mr Gilbert.

LEICHHARDT: Shame them, Johnny. Show them how a boy can make cowards of men. Come beside me.

MURPHY: I'm not a boy any more an' I'm for followin' the marked trees back the way we came.

LEICHHARDT: The trees are not an avenue for retreat.

GILBERT: Three to one against. We go back, all of us.

LEICHHARDT: Thick headed louts. What pissy little lives in so vast a place. In the morning we go on. To discipline you I will not share my catch.

LEICHHARDT takes the dog and stalks off.

PHILLIPS: If yer want to discipline us, you'd make us eat that stinkin' dog.

MURPHY: We can't go back without him. They'll say we did him in.

GILBERT: We'll see in the morning. If you're hungry, there's some bird carcasses to make up a thin soup.

A shaft of light spills across the stage as from a doorway. An accordion plays a waltz. KARL and RUTH dance into the light. RUTH stumbles on the rough ground and stops. KARL holds her. GILBERT watches RUTH.

RUTH: I'm giddy. You certainly lost none of your flair for the dance while you were in goal. Who did you practise with? A G.I.?

KARL: With my pillow. No substitute for the arm of a warm woman.

How about a kiss?

RUTH: [*a peck*] There.

KARL: Is that all?

RUTH: I came out here for the air. Imagine if you had to pay for every breath.

KARL: I haven't been able to acquire the franchise. When I do, I'll make a killing.

RUTH: Several at your prices.

KARL: You'll always be good for a discount.

RUTH: Ka-arl! Don't, you're drunk.

KARL: So what? Did I step on your feet? No. I dance better when I'm drunk. I do most things better when I'm drunk.

RUTH: Stop it. Ilse's my friend.

KARL: I'm your friend too. Don't worry about Ilse. She blows hot and cold.

RUTH: Look, I'm not going to warm you up. I'm married.

KARL: Almost twice over.

RUTH: You're a pig of a man.

> RUTH *turns to go back inside.* ILSE *comes out into the light.*

ILSE: [*to* RUTH] Leonids is waiting over by the trees.

> RUTH *goes to* LEONIDS. *They embrace.*

KARL: Hey, where's she going?

ILSE: It's none of your business, businessman.

KARL: That's Leonids. Edvards is in there.

ILSE: Getting drunker and winning the war. He has several campaigns to fight before he looks for his bed.

KARL: Come inside and dance.

ILSE: I'm watching for Ruth.

KARL: She'll be a while.

> LEONIDS *and* RUTH *start to go.*

MURPHY: [*stopping them*] Mr Gilbert?

> KARL *and* ILSE *dance close in the light.* RUTH *waits.*

Mr Gilbert, I can't take your soup. I ate this afternoon at a natives' camp. I was bringing some back for you, but I dropped it.

GILBERT: Never mind. [*Sniffing.*] You smell different.

MURPHY: I had a wash.

GILBERT: That must be it.

MURPHY: In the lagoon. Took all me clothes off and had a right old scrub, all over.

GILBERT: And lost all your buttons in the process. You'll find some spares in my kit.

> LEONIDS *goes to join* RUTH.

MURPHY: Mr Gilbert… I'll turn down your bedroll.

GILBERT: Thanks, Johnny.

> KARL *and* ILSE *stop dancing.* LEONIDS *lies down on* GILBERT'*s bed,* RUTH *sits astride him. They make love.*

KARL: What a beautiful dress. I love the way the skirt swings below when you dance. But it's no good dancing out here. It'll ruin your shoes.

> ILSE *laughs. She kisses him quickly. He caresses her breasts.*

Lovely to touch. Peaches.

> ILSE *gently squeezes* KARL'*s balls.*

ILSE: Apples.

KARL: [*groaning*] You know what they're up to. Who knows how long they'll be there.

ILSE: You want to time them?

KARL: Not exactly with a clock.

ILSE: No. Not with a clock. [*Making* KARL *squirm.*] You could have been a cavalry officer. Your balls would sit well forward in the saddle.

> KARL *removes his jacket and puts it on the ground for* ILSE. *He kneels.*

If this ground will ruin my shoes, what will it do to my back? You lie down.

KARL: My back, your knees. You'd ruin your stockings.

> *He runs his hand up her leg.*

Did I give them to you?

> ILSE *turns her back to him and bends over slightly.*

ILSE: This way, standing. I can watch the door for Ruth.

KARL *undoes his flies and lifts her skirts.*

KARL: Hey, where'd you get this suspender belt?

ILSE: Look, are you taking an inventory or what?

KARL: No, no. But it's good stuff. High quality, like you. A man can't help noticing. High quality.

ILSE: Get on with it. Four months without and you want to chatter. Have you forgotten how to— [*Grunting.*] Wait.

KARL: Yes, no. Stop, go. Oh God!

By now, RUTH *rests beside* LEONIDS.

MURPHY: Mr Gilbert.

GILBERT: What is it now?

MURPHY: I'll repay you, Mr Gilbert. I owe you so much and to think when I dropped that food, I didn't even look for it.

GILBERT: When there's no food, it's best not to dwell on it. The same goes for beer, tobacco and women.

ILSE: [*to* KARL] It's no one. Go slowly.

MURPHY: I was lookin' out for meself, for me own pleasures... with some native women... I gave 'em the buttons... for... you know...

GILBERT: Cultural exchange.

MURPHY: It was me first time.

GILBERT: You're certain to remember it.

MURPHY: I didn't mean to hurt them.

KARL: [*groaning*] I can't...

ILSE: It's all right.

GILBERT: When you're in the desert you want water. At sea you pine for the shore. Completeness. God gave Adam a woman for that reason. Go to bed. Man. We have an early start.

MURPHY: G'night, Mr Gilbert.

LEONIDS *goes with* RUTH. *She leans back against a tree and they fuck standing up.* LEONIDS *has his back to us.* MURPHY *and* PHILLIPS *bed down.*

ILSE: Give me your handkerchief. What a flood.

KARL: Classy underwear.

ILSE: You still going on about that.

KARL: I didn't give them to you.

ILSE: I traded for them. You're not the only black marketeer in Stuttgart.

KARL: Too true. On the way over to get my job, I saw some G.I.s with two of our women.

ILSE: Lots of "our women" go with soldiers.

KARL: I suppose so. I never really noticed before.

ILSE: They learn some English, get a bottle of perfume and if they're unlucky, they get a baby as well.

KARL: You think it's a joke?

ILSE: Yes. A joke on all women.

KARL: It looked rough to me.

ILSE: The war isn't over for some of us.

KARL: I want to marry you, Ilse.

ILSE: No.

KARL: No? Why not?

ILSE: Men and women live separately in this camp and have to steal pleasures like thieves.

KARL: What's the difference? Man and wife or lovers?

ILSE: We're more like dogs in heat grappling in the dark under trees.

KARL: I really mean it.

ILSE: There's no point discussing it. I'm going to Australia and you're off to Chicago to drink bourbon from Garbo's shoe.

KARL: I've changed my mind.

ILSE: Why? Didn't you get your job back?

KARL: I didn't go. When I saw those two women with the G.I.s I had to turn away. I was afraid, for a moment, that one of the women was you, you and Ruth.

ILSE: What if it had been me? When that G.I. prodded me today like a cow in a paddock, you stood by hoping to profit from the exchange. When nothing comes of it, you ask me to marry you as if you owned the cow all along. "Our women". You work like a pimp.

KARL: Have you ever gone with them?

ILSE: You want to know how I came by this underwear? The same way I got this dress, the way you get cigarettes and razor blades and whisky...

KARL: I trade for them.

ILSE: With gold teeth. But a woman has to keep her teeth to keep her looks. If she keeps her looks, she can sell that soft part of her, even though men are sure it has teeth.

KARL: When I was in gaol?

ILSE: And before.

KARL: You needed food, clothes.

ILSE: I wanted for nothing.

KARL: They raped you, then.

ILSE: No. I went willingly.

KARL: I don't believe you.

ILSE: This afternoon you wanted to believe it was me and Ruth. You can believe it of me. Leave Ruth out of it.

KARL: What damn difference does that make when she's out there with Leonids?

ILSE: That's right. Shout. Tell everyone.

KARL: Everyone knows except Edvards.

Pause.

They all know about you too. All except me.

He slaps her.

Tell me they raped you.

ILSE: I raped them. I tried, anyway. I gave up. It was a losing battle. I wanted to break them on my body and all I did was confuse them.

KARL: [*slapping her*] Tell me!

ILSE: As mother, whore, mistress or wife? It's not easy to be a woman when boys become men by taking a life or two. They never know exactly what they want.

KARL: I'll kill you, you slut.

RUTH *and* LEONIDS *come back into the light.*

RUTH: Ilse, Karl. What's going on? Calm down.

KARL: You stay away from me. As if you don't know. "Lover boy". What a laugh, eh?

LEONIDS: [*from the shadows*] Go inside and have a drink before you wake the whole camp.

KARL: [*to* LEONIDS] You sure wouldn't like that, would you? Don't want to wake the dead, eh Ruthie? I'll fix them. I'll string their arseholes on a fence like dried apples. The bloody unknown soldiers.

> KARL *goes.*

RUTH: What on earth did you say to him?

ILSE: Not much.

> *The shaft of light snaps out. The dance music is replaced by the soft wailing of native women.* LEICHHARDT *comes from the trees.*

GILBERT: There's been some interference with the native women. I think we should have a guard on the camp tonight.

LEICHHARDT: Is it customary for a private soldier to make suggestions to his general?

GILBERT: I'm not in any bloody army.

LEICHHARDT: Bully for you or you'd be shot for desertion. I am still the leader.

GILBERT: Any man who can eat a rotten dog and then spend the best part of an hour vomiting in the undergrowth is no longer fit to lead.

LEICHHARDT: It is my destiny and you will not cheat it from me.

GILBERT: As you have clearly gone mad, we are restoring some sanity to proceedings—

LEICHHARDT: By molesting the native women. What a fine beginning you have made.

GILBERT: I said nothing about molesting.

LEICHHARDT: If I am mad, how is it that you see the nightmares? I wish you sweeter dreams, Mr Gilbert.

> LEICHHARDT *beds down.* GILBERT *does so on the other side of the fire. As the* MEN *settle, dark figures carrying pieces of timber approach stealthily from the trees. The attack begins. It is as though a spear had been thrown into camp.* MURPHY *screams and tries to roll away. The attackers disperse.*

Native attack! Gun caps! Quick. Gun caps. Attack. We're being attacked.

> *They all grab for their rifles. There is confusion and mayhem.*

MURPHY: Me rifle's not loaded.

GILBERT: Load it, for Christ's sake.

GILBERT *gets between* MURPHY *and the attackers and tries to bring his rifle to bear.* LEICHHARDT *fires at the attackers.*

LEICHHARDT: Fire! I hit one.

GILBERT *drops to his knees clutching at his chest.* LEICHHARDT *and* PHILLIPS *fire after the attackers.*

KARL: Provos! Run—Get out of here.

OTTO: The others—

KARL: Forget them! Move!

GILBERT: Here, Johnny. Take my gun. The bastard killed me.

He laughs. MURPHY *takes the rifle, follows attackers. Then all is quiet.* GILBERT *lies by the fire. He coughs.*

G.I. SAM: Come back and fight! Chicken livered bastards.

MURPHY *returns to* GILBERT'*s side.*

LEICHHARDT: [*snapping*] Keep from the light, donkey. You want to die?

MURPHY: Mr Gilbert's dead.

LEICHHARDT *bends over him.*

LEICHHARDT: He can't be dead! I must bleed him. Give me a knife.

PHILLIPS *gives* LEICHHARDT *a knife.* MURPHY *cradles* GILBERT. LEICHHARDT *slashes* GILBERT'*s wrists. He tips* GILBERT'*s head back and slashes a temporal artery.*

No blood. Too late. His heart is stopped.

MURPHY: Poor Mr Gilbert.

PHILLIPS: What happened? Was he shot?

MURPHY: Me rifle wasn't loaded.

LEICHHARDT: A spear. It must've dislodged as he fell. I didn't see.

MURPHY: Me rifle wasn't loaded.

LEICHHARDT: There is nothing more we can do. We pack up and strike camp now. Work quickly or you will be massacred too.

PHILLIPS: Where're we goin'?

LEICHHARDT: Port Essington.

PHILLIPS: Oh no we ain't. Just tonight we decided to go back. We still outvote you two to one.

LEICHHARDT: Just tonight Mr Gilbert was killed by natives. Something made those natives upset. I say we go now.

MURPHY: Don't argue, Phillips.

> MURPHY *starts to drag* GILBERT *off.*

LEICHHARDT: What are you doing? It's too late for him.

MURPHY: I'm not leavin' him. I'll bury him in the mornin'.

> *He goes.*

LEICHHARDT: [*to* PHILLIPS] Take only what is necessary. And Mr Gilbert's specimens.

SCENE TWELVE

Stuttgart. 1947. Night.

KARL *waits. He watches* OTTO *tip-toeing in the dark.* KARL *grabs him and throws him down.*

KARL: Come here, clown.

OTTO: It's you!

KARL: Don't wet yourself again. What'll you say to Lydia about your trousers?

OTTO: I'll say I was walking home drunk and I fell in a puddle.

KARL: It hasn't rained here in Stuttgart for weeks. I hate to think what kind of a husband you'll make. You can't even lie convincingly. What'll you do if we wind up in court on a murder charge? Spill your guts?

OTTO: You should've stopped Edvards kicking that Yank when he was down.

KARL: Where are the others?

OTTO: We decided to make our way here separately so we'd be less conspicuous.

KARL: If they're tippy-toeing round the place like you were, we'll be behind bars in no time.

LEONIDS *enters. He says nothing.*

OTTO: We're just waiting for Edvards.

KARL: [*to* OTTO] Go and see if you can't find him. He's probably out starting World War Three.

OTTO: You started it. Yes, all right, what the hell.

He goes.

KARL: What are you going to do about Ruth?

LEONIDS: What business is that of yours?

KARL: Edvards is a friend. I don't like it when someone gives his wife a good fucking under a hedge when he's not been back a day.

LEONIDS: Some friend you are to tell him the Americans had been taking advantage of his wife when it wasn't true.

KARL: Can you be sure of that?

Pause.

I've done you a favour, see. Putting it bluntly, you can get out from underneath.

LEONIDS: I was going to marry Ruth. Who knows? If Edvards killed that Yank, maybe he'll disappear again.

KARL: Don't even think it. If he goes down, we all go with him.

EDVARDS *and* OTTO *enter.*

OTTO: Here we are. I don't think anyone saw us.

EDVARDS: All quiet on the western front. OK.

LEONIDS: The war is over, Edvards.

EDVARDS: After one little skirmish. Then let's go home. OK.

OTTO: Did you kill that G.I.?

EDVARDS: The Latvian divisions take no prisoners, Otto.

KARL: Oh good! We go to teach some clever Yanks to keep their hands off our women and because you get carried away, we could end up on a murder charge.

EDVARDS: The way I see it, OK, if you're going to give someone a hiding, you do it properly.

KARL: I can't afford another stretch in gaol on any count.

OTTO: What if they shoot us?

EDVARDS: You die. OK. It's permanent.

KARL: All we have to do is keep our mouths shut and go on like before. We know nothing. We went to the dance, got blind drunk and returned to barracks. That's easy enough to remember.

LEONIDS: [*pointedly at* KARL] And then one night some drunk will start shouting—

KARL: Who cares? We'll be in Australia by then.

OTTO: Are you coming too?

KARL: I'll put my application in tomorrow.

LEONIDS: What about Ruth and Edvards? They're not taking married couples.

KARL: I'll get Edvards some false papers to say he's single.

LEONIDS: Ruth will be a widow again.

KARL: Not for long. She and Edvards can remarry in Australia.

OTTO: A fresh start with a new wife. Like me and Lydia.

EDVARDS: I think Ruth would like another wedding. So that's the future. OK.

KARL: All we have to do is see what can be done about finding a wife for Leonids.

SCENE THIRTEEN

North Queensland. 1949. A clearing surrounded by a river in flood.

LEICHHARDT *stands facing the sunrise.* GILBERT *enters during* LEICHHARDT's *speech and crouches behind him.* LEICHHARDT *is unaware of* GILBERT's *presence until* GILBERT *speaks. They are the ghosts of* LEICHHARDT *and* GILBERT *for the rest of the play. They should not be played 'ghostly'.*

LEICHHARDT: The loveliness of morning just before and after sunrise. The air so clear and transparent. The promised land lies always to the east. Walk to the west and you walk into the hottest fire. With the sun on my back, I walked away from each morning. I saw where each day ended. At night I fell on a soil as unyielding as stone. When I lifted my head my skin was scorched to the ground. My eyes saw nothing. The red of day and black of night. Blinded. The horses fell down and died. Their tongues bloated so large they choked. My body dried out and my mouth filled with sand. Before a man dies, his breath whistles round his ribs as if he were already a skeleton hung in an exotic garden. A wind chime. I have heard my own bones sing.

GILBERT: You deserted me in such a wilderness. You shot me and left me lying in a burnt clearing.

LEICHHARDT: I lit a fire over your grave so the natives would not see the earth had been disturbed.

GILBERT: I was scoured out by a flood. Some natives found me after the flood receded. Not having had so tame a spirit in their clutches before, they opened me up, as I would have liked, to learn my innermost secrets. How disappointed they were to learn the viney-viney was like them. They washed and wrapped my organs in aromatic leaves, filled my body and laid me to rest on a platform in the branches of a tree. Light and airy and warm. A kind of heaven. But the birds gave me no peace and my bones were carried off by wild pigs. I live in dread of rain and floods. At night to get warm, I sit in warm ashes until the sun rises.

LEICHHARDT: Fire and flood! That is the singular character of this remarkable country, extremes so often meet. The coast is luxuriant green. The interior is burnt red.

GILBERT: I've heard all this before. No doubt it was part of your victory speech in Sydney. But did you tell them how you shot me and left me to rot?

LEICHHARDT: That is why I've come, to lead you back to Sydney. But first I must drink. Is there a river nearby?

There are sounds of people wading through water.

GILBERT: A great flood, an inland sea.

LEICHHARDT: It was promised to me. Wait here. I have logged your position.

GILBERT: With your usual precision. Is there a tree on your horizon?

LEICHHARDT: [*gazing off*] Now that you mention it, yes there is.

GILBERT: [*going*] It's one of yours.

ANGIE: [*off*] Are you sure we're going the right way?

MCQUAIDE: [*off*] It's the only way to go. Uphill. Downhill is under water.

ANGIE: [*off*] We've been walking in water for half a mile. Uphill is under water as well.

> *There is a louder splash.*

Shit! I walked into another hole.

> MCQUAIDE *laughs.*

Let me ride in the boat.

> LEICHHARDT / EDVARDS *looks off, towards the approaching walkers.*

MCQUAIDE: [*off*] It drags on the bottom. Won't be long now. It's getting shallower.

EDVARDS: [*calling, accent*] Hey Doctor! Where yous go?

MCQUAIDE: [*off*] Eddie! We're getting closer than we thought. Go through the trees.

EDVARDS: [*laughing, accent*] You go fishing?

> MCQUAIDE *and* ANGIE *enter.* MCQUAIDE's *trousers are rolled up.* ANGIE's *skirts are tucked up and wet.*

MCQUAIDE: Yeah, we go fishing for men in a timber camp.

EDVARDS: [*accent*] We go to town?

MCQUAIDE: No need, mate. Town is very boring. Angie and me thought you must be dry out here so we brought you something to wet your whistle. You can't be cutting much timber in this weather.

> MCQUAIDE *carries a carton of rum and beer.*

EDVARDS: [*accent*] Hello Mrs McQuaide.

ANGIE: Hello Eddie. Your lot are the best drinking company he ever had. No one else drinks heavily enough.

EDVARDS: [*accent*] Water comes up. OK.

MCQUAIDE: Yeah, terrible drink. Can't keep it down, myself.

> OTTO, KARL *and* LEONIDS *enter carrying sandbags. They dump them. The* MEN *look very dishevelled.*

KARL: [*accent*] Good day, Doctor. And Angie.

KARL *shakes her hand then kisses her.*

ANGIE: Quaint foreign custom.

OTTO *and* LEONIDS *smile and nod.*

MCQUAIDE: [*laughing*] He's the only one practising.

KARL: [*to* ANGIE, *accent*] You are wet.

ANGIE: Very. [*Looking down at her legs.*] Oh, Doc! I've got leeches on me. Doc!

MCQUAIDE: Karl will take care of them.

ANGIE *lifts her skirts.* KARL *squats and picks the leeches off her legs.* MCQUAIDE *opens a fresh bottle and passes it around.* MCQUAIDE *sits and drinks heavily.*

EDVARDS: Look at him. A woman lifts her skirts and he dredges up the old charm from some stinking pit. No pride.

OTTO: Leave him alone. He doesn't get much chance to practise these days.

ANGIE: Ooh! You're very good at that. So gentle.

LEONIDS: [*accent*] Water comes up. Big flood.

MCQUAIDE: No need to worry. It won't come any higher.

KARL *squeezes water from* ANGIE's *skirt.*

KARL: [*accent*] Come. We make you dry.

ANGIE *gets a bottle from* MCQUAIDE.

ANGIE: Karl's going to dry me out.

MCQUAIDE: Be right with you.

ANGIE: Don't hurry on my account.

LEONIDS: [*to* KARL] Will you bring more sandbags?

KARL: What's the point digging out the hill on the other side to bring it over here? We're not gaining anything.

LEONIDS: What if we're washed out?

KARL: I'll climb a tree.

LEONIDS: I say we need sandbags. I'm still in charge of this camp.

KARL: That means you get to stay here while we go off in the boat. Get sandbags for yourself.

KARL *and* ANGIE *go.*

EDVARDS: He's right. We have a boat now. OK.

OTTO: How come he has all the luck?

EDVARDS: Think of it this way, the worst you'll end up with is a hangover. He could get the pox. Pass me that bottle. OK.

LEONIDS: Are you two going to bring more sandbags?

EDVARDS: I'm going on sick parade. My joints are playing me up.

> EDVARDS *uses some of the rum as rubbing alcohol on his shoulder.*

OTTO: If the water rises, I'd rather leave. They're not paying us to sit here.

> LEONIDS *goes.*

MCQUAIDE: I've never seen much in the way of war wounds. Nothing as impressive as that. Shrapnel?

EDVARDS: [*accent*] English bomb. [*Pointing to his face, chest and stomach.*] Here. Here. Here. [*No accent.*] It smashed this shoulder and the skin was hanging off my face and arm. I pull the skin back. I can see with one eye, but the view is from above. [*Accent.*] I float. Outside. See myself. OK. Medic comes. [*No accent.*] He finds some small holes. Puts on a dressing. And he gets up off his knees, his trousers are soaked in blood. OK. [*Accent.*] My blood. On knees. [*No accent.*] He sees my back. Big hole. He stuffs his shirt into the hole. And then I feel my body filling up with blood. It filled my throat. [*Accent.*] I drown. In blood. OK. [*No accent.*] I see myself. Peace. Sleeping on a stretcher. A team of doctors stole me away, with masks and bloody hands. [*Accent.*] They give me life. Full sentence.

> *During the last part of the speech, there is the distant sound of a chugging motor.* LEONIDS *enters with more sandbags.*

LEONIDS: [*accent*] Listen. Boat.

> *The motor dies.*

MCQUAIDE: Someone making deliveries to the farms. The sound carries a long way over water. From farms. Down below.

OTTO: [*to* MCQUAIDE, *accent*] You are doctor. No?

MCQUAIDE: Yes.

OTTO: [*accent*] We find bones. Old bones. From man, or womans.

MCQUAIDE: You don't say?

OTTO: [*accent*] And tree. Datum on tree.

MCQUAIDE: A blind man could find a tree here.

> OTTO *scratches in the dirt.*

"L one-eight-four-five". You don't say, eh? Could be quite a find, that.

OTTO: [*accent*] I show.

MCQUAIDE: Later, later. Let's have a drink first.

> OTTO *goes.*

LEONIDS: The water is still rising.

EDVARDS: We are only men, OK. We can't turn back the tide. Let's go back to camp where there are chairs to sit on. The least we can do is have a drink, OK, while we watch our ship go down.

> LEONIDS *shakes his head.*

Suit yourself.

MCQUAIDE: Hang on a minute, Eddie. Don't leave me with this bloke. He doesn't drink.

> *They go.* LEONIDS *looks off. We hear the sound of people approaching through the water.*

BOURKE: [*off*] You coulda stayed in the boat, missus. No need to go exertin' yourself now. Don't want you droppin' the kid on me.

ILSE: [*accent, off*] Is all right. Thanks. I can walk.

BOURKE: [*off*] Ahoy the camp.

> ILSE *and* RUTH *enter, skirts pulled up.* ILSE *is very pregnant.*

RUTH: [*to* LEONIDS] Look at you. What have you been doing? Two weeks away from civilisation and you're a wild man.

> OTTO *enters to see* RUTH *and* LEONIDS *embrace.* BOURKE *enters.*

OTTO: Well, look who's here in time for the party. [*Accent.*] Good day, Bourkie.

BOURKE: G'day, Otto. Brought some supplies for you fellers. Your women talked me into it when I saw them in town.

> OTTO *takes the bag of food.*

OTTO: [*to* ILSE] Better call Karl to check for leeches. [*Calling.*] Karl! Lydia didn't come up?

ILSE: No. She thought it was too dangerous.

OTTO: Oh, that's a new one. Usually everything is too dirty, too small, or too rough. Now it's too dangerous for her.

He goes.

BOURKE: If the water keeps rising we all go back to town.

KARL *and* ANGIE *come from the trees, laughing, unaware of the arrivals.* ANGIE *now wears one of* KARL's *shirts. It is long enough and baggy enough to be a dress on her. When they see the others, they walk apart guiltily. A brief silence.*

Hello, Mrs McQuaide. Get caught with your pants down?

ANGIE: [*evenly*] How's the farm, Ollie?

BOURKE: Pretty damn wet. Like your backside.

KARL: Hello, Ilse. You shouldn't be here in your condition.

ILSE: There's nothing wrong with my condition, but you look a bit red in the face.

KARL: It isn't how you think—

ILSE: I know.

KARL: I was showing Angie this tree.

ILSE: Grown a bit lately, has it? Last time you showed it to me it was a drooping twig.

KARL: [*accent*] I show Angie tree.

ANGIE: That's right, all very harmless, missus. There really is this tree. Eighteen hundred and something carved in it.

BOURKE: [*steering* ANGIE *away*] Let's get out of here before the hair and teeth start to fly.

They go.

ILSE: You think I'm stupid. When you married me, I made sure you knew what you were getting and you've hardly spoken a civil word to me since. That didn't surprise me. Nor did the nights when you would lie on me, drunk, vent your spleen inside me and roll off. Snoring. I'm carrying your child, born of a whore, you think, and fathered by a pimp. I know you. But you come laughing from the bushes with that woman wearing a shirt I washed. And you can stand there, in front of people, and tell me you were showing her a tree.

KARL: That's right.

ILSE: I'm ashamed for you.

> LEONIDS *and* RUTH *start to go.*

KARL: Don't go. You don't have to be embarrassed for me.

LEONIDS: [*shrugging*] Lying only makes it worse.

KARL: [*angrily*] Don't you preach to me. You've worked and eaten and drunk beside a man for two years now, and all that time, right under his nose, within reach of his ears, you are rutting with his wife.

RUTH: No, Karl. Stop.

> *She cries.*

KARL: You even helped him murder that Yank to deceive him.

LEONIDS: I never lied to his face.

KARL: No. You lie in shadows, under a tree, against a wall.

> EDVARDS *and* MCQUAIDE *enter.*

You steal from his bed in the dark while he sleeps on. Unknowing.

LEONIDS: Shut up. Shut your filthy mouth.

EDVARDS: I know. OK. I knew from the first night. I am man made. With all his imperfections. Half crazy. Half beautiful. Half ugly. And impotent. But not blind. [*To* LEONIDS.] You made Ruth happy. When she left your side the warmth would steal back into my bed. From the first night you had my blessings. If you deceived yourself, you have never deceived me. If ever we killed a Yank that night in Stuttgart, we did it for Karl. For that he won't forgive his wife. He is only a small hero, our petty thief and gangster. I love him for all that. That we can stand alongside him.

> RUTH *is crying.* EDVARDS *goes to her and takes her off.* LEONIDS *goes off towards the boats.* BOURKE *enters carrying a native bark coffin.*

BOURKE: [*excitedly*] There really is a tree. "L eighteen hundred and—"

MCQUAIDE: Yeah, I know. Otto told me.

BOURKE: What happened?

MCQUAIDE: I don't know. I reckon one or two of them will be rocking a bottle tonight.

BOURKE: Say, what'd ya reckon this is?

MCQUAIDE: Some old blackfeller's bones wrapped in bark. Let him rest in peace.

He tosses the bones off into the flood. They go.

Now we got a reason for a wake.

BOURKE: I'll drink to that.

ILSE *and* KARL *are left alone.*

KARL: Well? What are you waiting for?

ILSE: For you.

KARL: You're suffocating me.

ILSE: I'll go.

KARL: Not only you, the whole damn lot of you, the whole damn place. Leonids has had me by the nose for so long. If he hadn't been riding me, none of that would've come out.

ILSE: No one has to hide any more, not even you. We women don't have to pretend we don't know what happened to that G.I. in Stuttgart.

KARL: Don't you talk to me about Stuttgart.

ILSE: It's not Leonids, it's me you want to hurt. [*Crying.*] And I won't cry. Not for you.

KARL: Look, I'm sorry, I'm sorry.

ILSE: That you were caught.

KARL: I didn't know you were coming up here.

ILSE: Everybody here knew what you were up to. It's only you who thinks you're the only one in the know, and you're usually the only one who isn't. It's time you grew up, I have a baby to look after.

KARL: Why don't you just throw me out?

LEICHHARDT *enters carrying* GILBERT *on his back.*

ILSE: That's what you'd like. To be free. No responsibilities. You think you'd be better off on your own. If that's what you want, you'll have to stand on your own two feet and walk. I won't carry you any more.

KARL: There's nowhere to go. I'm… I'm lost in this country. I'm afraid to go and I'm afraid to stay. My luck has deserted me. I don't know what to do.

ILSE: Stay alive like you did in Europe.

KARL: It was easy when I was by myself.

ILSE: I didn't marry you to make your life miserable or mine, and that isn't why I came to this country. I need you now, Karl.

KARL: Do you love me at all, Ilse?

ILSE: No. Not today. Maybe tomorrow I will, or in twenty years.

KARL: I never thought it would be like this. You'll drive me crazy, Ilse.

ILSE: If I came easily to you, you'd only abuse me. I'm tired now, I'm going to the camp.

KARL: Take my arm, the ground is slippery. You shouldn't be up here at all. What if you have the baby in the bush?

ILSE: The baby might feel right at home. The doctor is up here.

KARL: He's a drunk. I'll have to take you back to town.

They go to the camp.

GILBERT: Find my bones.

LEICHHARDT: You said the wild pigs took yours.

GILBERT: The pigs did take mine, but these others gave me comfort to sleep near. These intruders threw them into the flood.

LEICHHARDT: Pah! Some dried up old black woman.

GILBERT: Why have you brought me here?

LEICHHARDT: I want you to show me my tree. You are my eyes now.

GILBERT: All I see is water. Put me down. What are you up to?

LEICHHARDT: I am as innocent as when I embraced you for the last time.

GILBERT: That was just after you shot me dead. Put me down.

LEICHHARDT: Your time had come. There were no blank pages left in your journal. That is past. These migrant peoples have found my marker tree. The last one. That's what I want you to show me. It is a sign of hope.

GILBERT: Of portent. They'll make no sense of it.

LEICHHARDT: Their dreams are troubled by the horrors of Europe. But they have escaped and they will forget. They are young and strong, the treasure of this country, the nucleus of a nation. And at the centre, my tree.

GILBERT: They are disaffected and wretched, not at home on this soil. Not seeing what is here, pining for what is not.

LEICHHARDT: My journey was successful.

GILBERT: The second was a failure. You died of thirst on the third. You wander still as I do. The unknown soldiers of a fruitless battle, inevitably lost.

LEICHHARDT: What could you be but a pessimist, forever gazing into the gutses of dead things? Show me my tree. There is life, and then I will find your bones.

GILBERT: I will find them myself.

LEICHHARDT: I will carry you through the water.

GILBERT: I don't trust you.

> GILBERT *walks into the flood.*

LEICHHARDT: Wait, wait.

GILBERT: Don't worry. Your position is firmly mapped in my mind.

> *And he's gone.*

LEICHHARDT: You can't desert me now. Come back.

> RUTH *enters. She is drawn to the boats.*

RUTH: [*calling softly*] Leonids.

EDVARDS: Ruthie.

> RUTH *goes to him.*

I am so tired.

RUTH: You work too hard. Lie down. Put your head in my lap.

> *He does.*

EDVARDS: Leonids is not a bad man.

RUTH: Hush!

EDVARDS: You won't ever leave me?

RUTH: Go to sleep.

EDVARDS: We all work hard. We are all good men, in our own way.

> LEONIDS *enters.*

RUTH: He's asleep.

LEONIDS: It won't be the same now. I can't stay.

RUTH *nods.*

Come with me.

RUTH: Back to town? That's nowhere. They'd follow.

LEONIDS: We'll take one of the boats. Go down river. I have everything we need. I've saved a lot of money. We can start afresh together.

RUTH *gently lowers* EDVARDS' *head. She goes with* LEONIDS. EDVARDS *stirs.*

EDVARDS: [*as though in a dream*] Can't touch her. Can't stop her. I can only watch her go. I could scream.

He wakes as the boat's motor starts and sits up.

Ruth! Leonids! Wait! Wait! Take me with you. You can't desert me now. Come back. Come back!

ILSE *and* KARL *come running.* KARL *drags him back.*

KARL: Edvards, what the hell...

EDVARDS: She s gone. Let me go.

The others come.

MCQUAIDE: Is he all right?

KARL: [*accent*] The boat. Leonids and Ruth.

MCQUAIDE: My boat's gone. They took my boat. [*To* BOURKE.] Go after them.

EDVARDS: [*taking* BOURKE *towards his boat, accent*] Ruth. Take me. Find Ruth. Take me.

BOURKE: Stop him. There's only enough petrol to get back to town.

KARL: No petrol, Edvards.

EDVARDS: [*accent*] I work contract. Work hard. No pay. You find Ruth.

EDVARDS *charges off.*

BOURKE: Where's he goin' now? We'll all have to go back to town. They'll send out a search party.

ILSE: Ruthie.

KARL: Leonids. Don't be stupid.

The sound of chopping starts, off. Full blooded swings with an axe.

BOURKE: What is he doing?

OTTO: [*accent*] Edvards working.

KARL: [*accent*] He cutting down old tree.

BOURKE: Bloody hell. We gotta stop that.

LEICHHARDT: [*off*] Stop! Stop! Are you mad! Crazy swine!

> *All go except* ILSE.

ILSE: Ruth!

> *The chopping continues.*

SCENE FOURTEEN

North Queensland. 1949. Night.

ILSE *is in labour.* RUTH *enters. By this light she looks much as she did in the last scene. Her hair is a little wilder.*

ILSE: Ruth! You've come again tonight.

RUTH: I said last night I would.

ILSE: Where have you been?

RUTH: I walked until it grew too windy. It's still flooding. Does it hurt, Ilse?

ILSE: Yes. Horribly. Sometimes. [*Talking through a contraction.*] I have hurt worse before and I know that this will pass. At times I think the pain will never end and I will die. How cold your hand is.

> RUTH *draws her hand away.*

RUTH: My hands used to be soft and supple. Now they are stiff and puffy and white. I use a cream, but I've run out. Lend me yours.

ILSE: You know my hands. Like slabs of meat. I don't use a cream. And it shows.

> *An owl calls.* RUTH *starts.*

RUTH: Look what's happened. My hair is a mess. Lend me your brush.

ILSE: I can't.

RUTH: I'm going away, Ilse, with Leonids. I have nothing to wear. The moths have eaten my clothes. What isn't eaten, green mould grows on, like moss. Give me your shawl.

ILSE: No.

RUTH: You'll never wear it again. You'll have more children, settle here and never go back home. You don't need the shawl. Give it to me.

ILSE: No. Please go.

RUTH: Can't you see how unhappy I am? I have a pain in my heart, Ilse.

ILSE: [*crying*] And do you think I don't?

RUTH: I'm not asking for much. A tiny silver spoon will do.

ILSE: It's for the christening.

RUTH: There will be others. A keepsake, Ilse.

ILSE: I'll always remember you. I love you.

RUTH: Help me! Ilse, I can't catch my breath. Help me!

ILSE: No, too late. Far too late. I can give you nothing. To give you something, however paltry, is to take from the life of my child. [*Moaning.*] He is kicking and butting to get out. I love you, Ruthie, I love you.

    KARL *enters.*

KARL: The doctor is coming. You're crying. I'll make him hurry.

ILSE: No! Stay with me.

    KARL *sits on the bed. A brief pause.*

KARL: [*to* ILSE] They found the boat. Washed up. Miles away. That's all. They must have drowned.

    He puts his head on the bed and cries.

RUTH: Goodbye, Ilse.

    She goes.

ILSE: Ruth was here.

KARL: [*lifting his head*] Another dream. You're a real peasant, you are.

ILSE: [*taking his hand and putting it on her stomach*] Feel! Don't look so afraid. He's just anxious to see this country of his.

KARL: Or hers. Could be a daughter. I'll try to do the right thing. For once.

SCENE FIFTEEN

North Queensland. 1950. Day.

LEICHHARDT: It is believed in Sydney that I have been murdered long ago, or that I have starved to death. I am curious what people will say when I appear suddenly, resurrected from the grave, with a heap of mountain ranges and rivers in my pockets.

GILBERT: People will be astonished at my beautiful collection. Never before will they have seen skins got up in such style.

LEICHHARDT: I fear I will be so affected in finding myself again in civilised society, that I will scarcely be able to speak. In my throat the words will grow big with tears and emotion.

> LYDIA *and* ILSE *enter, separate from* KARL *and* OTTO. LYDIA *holds the child wrapped in the shawl.*

ILSE: Hurry now. You don't want to miss your train.

LYDIA: Come with us. Come to Sydney. Life will be better. I don't know how you can stay…

> *She trails off.*

ILSE: In the city I'd think of Ruth and Leonids more. I'd see them in the streets, believing they got away safely.

> KARL *and* OTTO *join* EDVARDS. RUTH *stands with* LEONIDS.

KARL: We're brothers. We ate together, got drunk together, slept with women—

EDVARDS: And we killed men together. Joined by blood.

OTTO: Ssh! You'll get me into trouble. If ever you come to Sydney—

KARL: I'd like to be going now.

OTTO: What will you do?

KARL: Become a peasant. Scratch a living from the ground. I'll always wonder if I made a mistake. I was making a nice living in Germany and maybe I should have gone to America.

EDVARDS: Poor Karl is still in shock about not going to Hollywood. OK. He has Australian nightmares instead of American dreams.

LYDIA: There's nobody left for you to talk to, except Karl and Edvards.

ILSE: I'll talk to the people who live here.

LYDIA: An outsider can't hope to understand this society. It's different if you're born here. You'll only be welcome at the bottom.

ILSE: [*not unkindly*] And you will go to Sydney and collect in pockets with other Latvians. You'll be a crutch to each other and dream for ever of returning home.

KARL: I still do. Don't you?

ILSE: I dream. But this place is so unlike home, I can make a new life.

> *She takes the child.*

See, I've started—

LEONIDS: The train is coming.

RUTH: At last we are going.

LEONIDS: In those last few days before we left Stuttgart, I imagined that at any moment an American provo would take me away and you would all leave without me.

ILSE: I won't go to the train. It'll disturb the baby. Goodbye, Lydia.

> *They embrace lightly.*

LYDIA: I'll write. You must come and see us. Goodbye.

OTTO: [*giving a handshake and a kiss*] Goodbye, Ilse.

KARL: I'll come over with you.

> *The train comes to a halt. Doors open and close. The guard's whistle blows. The train pulls away.*

RUTH: Oh Leonids. We're truly lost then.

LEONIDS: I'd just hoped we'd catch the train and get off somewhere, just as we'd planned.

RUTH: We'll never get away now or find any peace.

LEONIDS: I'm sorry Ruthie.

> ILSE *softly sings "Blow Breeze" to the baby.* KARL *walks back from the train.*

LEICHHARDT: All has passed before me now like a vivid dream. The remnants are only a few impressions, satisfied vanity, and the memory of some graceful girl.

KARL: I won't be able to call this place home. Not for a long time.

ILSE: Don't drink too much and save your money. You have a daughter to take care of. I will work too.

THE END

NO GOING BACK

No Going Back was first performed by the Melbourne Theatre Company, at the Russell Street Theatre, on 16 July 1992 with the following cast:

ILSE	Joan Sydney
LAUMA	Deidre Rubenstein
LYDIA	Maggie Millar
RUTH	Nina Landis
KARL / BUNCE	Peter Adams
EDVARDS / LEICHHARDT	Simon Chilvers
OTTO / BOEKING	Tom Considine
TIM / HELY	Bradley Croft
ARMAND / MANN	Paul English
DARTZER / BROWN	Philip Charles

Designed by Tony Tripp
Lighting Design by Jamieson Lewis
Directed by Roger Hodgman

CHARACTERS

ILSE, mid-fifties
LAUMA, mid-fifties
LYDIA, mid-fifties
RUTH, early thirties
KARL / BUNCE, mid-fifties and mid-thirties
EDVARDS / LEICHHARDT, sixties and mid-thirties
OTTO / BOEKING, mid-fifties and mid-thirties
TIM / HELY, thirties and mid-twenties
ARMAND / MANN, thirty
DARTZER / BROWN, thirties, Aborigine

The doubling of characters is intentional and integral to the structure and meaning of the play.

AUTHOR'S NOTE

The action of the play takes place in North Queensland in 1846 and the summer of 1979–80.

There are fairly rapid changes in time and location and it is important that the design should facilitate this so that scene flows into scene without unnecessary blackouts or set devices.

The style of speech is important. When the Latvians talk amongst themselves they speak fluently and without accent. When they speak English their speech is accented. There is a variation on this, when Ruth or Armand speak Latvian to their parents their speech is accented and halting.

Deidre Rubenstein (Lauma) and Joan Sydney (Ilse) in the 1992 Melbourne Theatre Company production. (Photo: Jeff Busby)

PART ONE

SCENE ONE

Provincial airport. ARMAND *waiting outside with a large, much travelled suitcase, camera case, battered artist's portfolio. The light on him is very bright. Initially he is stunned by its weird intensity. In a heightened way we hear the garbled sounds of the public address system and of arriving and departing traffic. In the ghostly spill of light other* TRAVELLERS *collect their luggage.* ARMAND *composes shots through the lens of his camera, occasionally taking a photo. Under the other sounds the* TRAVELLERS *are singing softly, in Latvian.*

"Put Vejini" *("Blow Breeze")*

Put, vejini, dzen laivinu,
Aizdzen mani Kurzeme;
Kurzemniece man solija
Sav' meitinu malejinu.

As ARMAND *focuses on this group through the camera, their singing grows louder and they form up with their bags as if for a photograph:* KARL *with* ILSE, OTTO *with* LYDIA, EDVARDS *with a shadowy figure,* (LAUMA).

RUTH *comes. She takes no special notice of the* TRAVELLERS *nor do they react to her. She sees* ARMAND.

RUTH: Armand?

She falters when he appears not to see her, his concentration still on the TRAVELLERS. *She comes to him.*

Armand.

> *Now the spell is broken. The singing stops. The lighting changes. The* TRAVELLERS *disperse.*

ARMAND: [*embracing* RUTH] Hello Ruthie.

RUTH: You didn't seem to recognise me. You had me wondering if it was you.

ARMAND: I'm sorry. It's me all right. Playing an old eye game with the light. You forgot how bright it is. I was just trying to make things... kind of blur out, soften... the way everything has these hard edges, the shadows and the light. God, I'm raving. It's so good to see you. Let me look at you.

RUTH: This is the modern lady lawyer.

ARMAND: Mum told me you got your articles while I was away. Congratulations.

RUTH: Well. Shall we go?

ARMAND: I'll just take your photo first.

RUTH: No, please.

ARMAND: So I can remember.

RUTH: My hard edge?

ARMAND: I didn't mean you.

RUTH: Oh no. Legal practice does that.

ARMAND: You look great. [*Expertly takes several shots of her.*] I assume you and Tim are still married.

RUTH: What made you say that?

ARMAND: Nothing. I'm just trying to catch up.

RUTH: He's fine. He's given up teaching to sell houses.

ARMAND: Real estate?

RUTH: No, houses. Logan homes, the ones you put together with a spanner.

ARMAND: You must mean Lego.

RUTH: Better not be. He sold one to Mum and Dad.

ARMAND: You mean she finally talked Dad into it?

RUTH: You've come back just in time to help put it together.

ARMAND: I'm not going.

RUTH: I was joking. That's enough now. [*Photos.*] We should go. I hate driving at night.

ARMAND: I'm serious. I'm not going.

RUTH: What do you mean you're not going? You have to. What'll they think? You haven't seen them in three years. They'll have killed the fatted calf and everything.

ARMAND: I know, I know. I will go. I just can't today.

RUTH: They're expecting us for the weekend. Tim's already up there wielding his spanner. And they've got Otto and Lydia turning up from Sydney.

ARMAND: Otto and Lydia? From the wedding photograph?

RUTH: That's right. The triple wedding. It's their first time back in thirty years. It'll be some party. You have to be there!

ARMAND: You go. I just can't. I have to stay here. A couple of days, that's all. [*Suddenly close to tears.*] I can't explain. Maybe it's crazy, but I'm scared. Don't ask me what of.

RUTH: Three years in London haven't left you unchanged either. You were the one who was hard edged, so certain of everything.

ARMAND: Coming from London, to Sydney and then here, it's so far from... everything. I need time to... get my bearings. It's no good looking at me like that. I just can't.

RUTH: OK. You're quite welcome to stay at my place, but you phone them, and you explain. Is that all your luggage?

ARMAND: That's my whole life.

RUTH: I meant to ask, how's Mary?

ARMAND: She's fine. I suppose. Considering.

RUTH: Have you split up?

ARMAND: No, not exactly. I don't know. Maybe. That's not why. It's coming back here. It's really made me wonder what it must've been like for Mum and Dad.

RUTH: Except that you've been here before.

ARMAND: That's what's strange, seeing things you know are exactly the same but it's like you're seeing them for the first time.

They go.

SCENE TWO

House block. A slightly sloping site. An established garden. A galvanised steel garden shed that serves as a tool room and general store room. It is the end of day and the light is fading. There is power to the site and some lights strung between a tree or pole and the shed. The sound of lawn mowing at the extremities of the block.

A concrete slab has just been poured and its surface levelled and finished. EDVARDS *is cleaning his tools. One side of his face is scarred and he has a slight limp.* TIM *is writing names in the fresh concrete and occasionally drinks beer from a stubby.*

TIM *does not speak Latvian. When the Latvians speak to him their English is accented. When they speak Latvian amongst themselves they speak fluently and without accent.*

TIM: Fifteenth right? That the date, Eddy? OK. December already. 1980 in a few weeks. Where does the time go?

EDVARDS: It goes in asking questions no one can answer.

TIM: There's no point going on at me in Latvian. You know I don't speak the language.

EDVARDS: [*accent*] I just finish there. What you mucking round?

TIM: Leaving our mark.

EDVARDS: [*accent*] Don't put my name. OK.

TIM: What is it you say? We'll never be so young again. It's a day to remember, Edvards.

EDVARDS: [*accent*] Yes, Tim. How you make mistake with concrete.

TIM: I should have left it to you, I know.

EDVARDS: [*accent*] I tell you last week you no order enough, but you expert.

TIM: "X", an unknown quantity, spurt, a drip under pressure. You just looked at it. I used a calculator and everything.

EDVARDS: [*accent*] Next time better use brain.

TIM: Well, it's in the ground now. Set in concrete as they say.

EDVARDS: [*accent*] Forever. In wrong place. OK.

TIM: Come on Eddy, you're a builder. It was easier—

EDVARDS: [*accent*] Easier yes.

TIM: And cheaper—

EDVARDS: [*accent*] For you. Because you forget cost of slab in price of house.

TIM: Karl and Ilse are happy.

EDVARDS: [*accent*] Because you family.

TIM: What's best is a matter of opinion.

EDVARDS: [*accent*] Easy and cheap is matter of business. OK.

TIM: I'm sorry you feel like that.

EDVARDS: [*accent*] I sorry you don't.

> *He crosses with a trowel and wipes out the names and date.*

And I say don't put my name.

TIM: Hey! Go easy! Christ you don't have to wipe them all out.

> ILSE *enters from the garden shed where she has been changing her clothes. She puts cream on her face and hands.*

ILSE: [*accent*] What happens here? I thought you finish. Nobody can dress without some trouble. You worse than kids.

> EDVARDS *goes back to putting his tools away and covering them with a tarpaulin.*

TIM: All I'm doing is writing our names, except Edvards, in the concrete. [*To* EDVARDS.] OK?

ILSE: [*accent*] Everything be OK. Don't make trouble.

TIM: It's no trouble. It's the form, how things are done.

> ILSE *leaves* TIM *to his scratchings and goes to* EDVARDS. *They speak to each other without accent.*

ILSE: I can't believe what the cement has done to my hands.

EDVARDS: I told you to wear gloves.

ILSE: I did, at first. Then I took them off and they got buried when the cement started coming at such a rush.

EDVARDS: So we could see how much concrete was needed for Tim's extra mix.

ILSE: It's done now.

TIM: [*calls*] I bet Eddy's still going on about how I stuffed up the concrete order.

EDVARDS: [*accent*] You want to know what I talk, learn Latvian. You marry Latvian girl.

TIM: Ruth won't teach me. She hardly speaks it herself.

ILSE: [*accent*] Tim, you shut up. Don't drink too much before visitors come.

TIM: Just celebrating Mum. Your first house, and my first house in this town. If things take off for me here I might have to set up a branch office.

EDVARDS: [*accent*] First finish one house, then talk.

TIM: Yeah, yeah. I better put Ruth's name because she brought us lunch. I won't put Armand's because the bugger didn't turn up. Mustn't ruin his surgeon's hands.

EDVARDS: Why couldn't you see that the house would be better located if it was turned through ninety degrees and the driveway came in at the bottom of the block?

ILSE: I could.

EDVARDS: I don't understand you.

ILSE: It was easier, and cheaper.

EDVARDS: For Tim's company.

TIM: Nearly finished.

ILSE: For Karl and me as well. It's Tim's new venture. And while he and Ruth are having some problems, we thought—

EDVARDS: You put your house in the worst place to save their marriage? In twenty-five years as a builder, I've never heard that one.

The sound of the lawn mower approaching.

ILSE: You don't want me to build this house.

EDVARDS: I built a house for you years ago. You refused to live in it.

ILSE: I wanted my own house.

EDVARDS: Or you didn't want me.

ILSE: We've been over all this. I thought you understood. When I couldn't afford to build, why did you help me buy this land, make this garden?

EDVARDS: To spend time with you.

ILSE: Please. Not tonight.

>   KARL *pushes the lawn mower all the way up to them before he*
>   *switches it off.*

KARL: What kind of grass did you plant? It grows while you watch
it.

ILSE: Did you have to mow it now?

KARL: I would've needed a tractor tomorrow.

ILSE: Ruth will be back with Otto and Lydia soon and you're not
even ready.

KARL: What would you have said if the grass wasn't cut when you
showed them the garden?

ILSE: There's soap and water in the shed, and clean clothes.

>   TIM *comes with beers, and a glass for* ILSE.

TIM: Ready for a beer Karl? Need I ask?

ILSE: [*to* KARL] I don't want you drunk before they arrive.

KARL: I hope they get here before midnight or I'll have to mow the
lawn again.

>   KARL *goes, taking a stubby and the mower.*

TIM: Eddy?

EDVARDS: [*accent, to* TIM] We all ready.

TIM: Mum?

EDVARDS: [*accent*] Ilse too.

ILSE: [*accent, to* TIM] OK. Just to keep company.

>   TIM *hands a stubby to* EDVARDS *and fills a glass for* ILSE.

[*to* KARL] Karl. There's still the chairs and tables to set up—

>   KARL *crashing around in the shed.*

KARL: [*off*] Just found them.

ILSE: [*to* KARL] Ach! Blind man! If you'd taken your eyes in your
hand, your nose would've shown you.

TIM: Don't get in a state, Mum. You stay here. I'll sort it out.

>   TIM *goes. A couple of safety lights come on.*

ILSE: I don't suppose you're going home to change?

EDVARDS: For Otto and Lydia? We cut cane together for two years
and we haven't seen them in thirty. We hardly know them.

ILSE: I heard they'd done very well for themselves.

EDVARDS: They made a point of telling us, OK? Is that why you're like a cat on hot bricks?

ILSE: Oh what are you talking about?

> ILSE *begins to move the chairs about under the lights as* TIM *brings them out.*

EDVARDS: This show of prosperity, building this house.

ILSE: Why won't you understand? I'm building this house for me, because I have to, to feel I belong, not to Karl, not to you, but to this place. I just never imagined it would take me thirty years but Karl said he would never move from that flat.

TIM: You want them under the lights? What about the bugs and...?

> [*He shrugs.*]

EDVARDS: Karl's paying for the house.

ILSE: Over the years I've earned every cent.

EDVARDS: And over the same years, OK, most Friday nights Karl and I drink together at the pub. He stays, drinking, getting drunk. I leave to take you out, to the pictures or for a drink at a different pub. The next day I get drunk with him and on Sundays we all go fishing or have lunch together. He knows, we know he knows and he knows we know and we all go on pretending. What are we playing at?

> KARL *comes from the shed looking quite dapper and wheeling the barbecue.*

KARL: [*accent*] Hey Mum, where you want this?

ILSE: [*accent*] You doing cooking. Put where you like.

KARL: [*accent*] Oh no. Not that simple. If I do that I know it be in wrong place. Tonight I do everything by book.

ILSE: Don't ask me. You're not a child any longer. Use your brains. [*accent*] Who's the stupid put chairs under lights? With bugs in clothes we dancing all night.

> ILSE *starts moving the chairs again, angrily.*

KARL: [*accent*] Calm down. I do it, I do it. Get food ready is your business.

> ILSE *goes off.* KARL, TIM *and* EDVARDS *move all the chairs.*

TIM: She put them here herself.

KARL: [*accent*] Then don't move far. Tim you go set up table for Mum.

TIM: No bloody fear. You go do it.

The MEN *laugh.*

EDVARDS: All this fuss because Otto wants to show his sister, just arrived from Latvia what a pioneer he was in the old days.

KARL: [*accent*] We better go help or we be in more trouble. You too, Edvards.

The MEN *go.*

SCENE THREE

MANN *comes with his personal belongings and swag. He is ill and tired, drops his gear and begins to search through the other packs (under the tarpaulin covered tools).*

LEICHHARDT *comes staggering with his swag. He lowers it and anxiously takes his pulse. He is not aware of* MANN *who watches him.*

LEICHHARDT: Ticka ticka ticka. Is going like a rattle with the least exertion.

MANN: Dr Leichhardt?

LEICHHARDT: Aargh! Is the devil!

MANN: Are you all right?

LEICHHARDT: Till you frighten me to death, Mr Mann.

MANN: You looked as though you might faint.

LEICHHARDT: My pulse was going from the day's exertions. For what are you looking there?

MANN: I need something for my eyes.

LEICHHARDT: You won't find. There is only soap for preserving birds and plants if ever we find new specimens. All medicines I have in safe keeping. The silver nitrate I have here.

MANN *goes to* LEICHHARDT *who tends his eyes.*

MANN: My sandy blight is much worse. I can barely see.

LEICHHARDT: Ja, ja. But you crossed the river, Mr Mann. That is good.

MANN: You left us little choice. You moved the camp and all the stores to this side.

LEICHHARDT: Now they all must come.

MANN: The others are far too ill. The exertion will only cause a relapse of the fever.

LEICHHARDT: When three weeks lying down brings no improvement perhaps moving will. And the promise of suet pudding.

MANN: Then at least send Bunce to help.

LEICHHARDT: Bunce is helping sheep and goats to settle. It was quite an ordeal for them to be thrown into a flooded river.

LEICHHARDT *takes* MANN'*s pulse.*

MANN: I can well imagine from my own crossing. You might like to know I happened upon one of the trees you marked on your last expedition. "L 1845".

LEICHHARDT: Ja. History. The cruel reminder that two years ago it only took two months to make the same progress as we have made in five.

MANN: None of us can help being ill.

LEICHHARDT *takes his own pulse.*

LEICHHARDT: Is still running. You have my watch?

MANN: Yes. Though it's somewhat out of order I'm afraid.

LEICHHARDT: How out of order?

MANN: I've been waiting for the opportunity to show you.

LEICHHARDT: I need to count my pulse.

MANN: Don't pull.

LEICHHARDT: Quickly.

MANN: My hand won't open. It seems to have locked.

The watch spills to the ground. LEICHHARDT *picks it up.*

LEICHHARDT: The only working watch. Stopped.

MANN: Some days ago.

LEICHHARDT: My watch I entrusted you when you broke your own? Completely stopped.

MANN: It fell when I was recalculating our position.

LEICHHARDT: What is there to recalculate? We have not moved in three weeks. We have hardly made forwards progress in two months.

MANN: I thought it important to check over my figures.

LEICHHARDT: For what? We are still only following the path of my last journey.

MANN: It is essential practice. It is so easy to be wrong.

LEICHHARDT: And with no clocks is even easier. No lunar reading can be accurate. Was my humiliation not enough that your figures showed how the map of my last journey is wrong? Am I not reminded every day by our painful inching over the exact same path?

MANN: I meant I could be the one who is wrong. Consistently misreading, miscalculating.

LEICHHARDT: With the result that every clock is calculated into oblivion. How can we now do correct mapping when we venture into unknown territory?

MANN: We know where we are, and using your map and a compass I believe I can chart our course easily enough.

LEICHHARDT: Easily is not enough. Must be accurate as well. This journey cannot be wasted. Now is going like a hammer.

MANN: Perhaps you should sit down. It could be serious.

LEICHHARDT: Is nothing. Only a small affection of the heart from the heavy work of crossing. [*Sitting down slowly.*] Once I rest...

ILSE: [*accent, off*] Karl, watch what you do. You breaking my flowers.

TIM: [*off*] Go straight ahead, Dad. Now I'm getting tangled up.

ILSE: [*accent, off*] Bloody mens! Put table down here!

MANN: Sounds like the others have crossed after all. I'll go and help them.

LEICHHARDT: No! [*Checks himself. Takes care not to excite himself further.*] They must come themselves. Otherwise we cannot get on, discover new country. That is the cure for all our ailments.

SCENE FOUR

A continuation of Scene Two.
The headlights of the car hit KARL *and* TIM.

TIM: Hey Dad, you expecting a Mercedes?

EDVARDS: [*accent*] Otto the millionaire, OK.

KARL: [*accent*] Mum. Come on. They here. Ilse.

ILSE: What are you shouting for? Do you think I'm deaf as well as blind?

KARL: Take a look at the car.

ILSE: What did you expect, a horse and cart?

KARL: Otto in a Mercedes...

ILSE: [*taking* KARL*'s arm*] Stay here. You won't be able to see them out there. I wish Armand was here.

KARL: Yes, well, we're only family.

EDVARDS: [*calling*] Otto. Aren't you ashamed to turn up here in such a jalopy? What will Karl's neighbours think?

OTTO: [*taking* EDVARD*'s hand*] It's OK, I stole it. I'm sure Karl can get me a good price on the local black market. [*Pumping his hand.*] Edvards.

EDVARDS: Welcome, friend, welcome.

   ILSE *can no longer restrain herself. She breaks from* KARL.

ILSE: Lydia. Lydia.

LYDIA: Ooh Ilse.

   The two WOMEN *hug and kiss and laugh and cry and look at each other and do it all again.* RUTH *comes and hugs them both. The three of them stand in the embrace. Meanwhile* KARL *has moved to greet* OTTO.

KARL: Otto, you look so well, so prosperous.

OTTO: Life's been good to me. It hasn't been too bad to you either. You have the glow of a publican about you.

KARL: I'm keeping one or two in business.

    OTTO's *sister,* LAUMA, *has been forgotten in the flurry of greetings.*

EDVARDS: I didn't know you married again, Otto.

OTTO: What? Come on. This is my sister, Lauma. Edvards. Karl.

    They shake hands more formally with her.

She's been out from Latvia for only a week and a half so be good to her.

KARL: Not only a Mercedes but a beautiful sister?

EDVARDS: [*to* LAUMA] Karl always did have an eye for quality.

LYDIA: [*accent*] Oh Ruthie, your mother and me and…

RUTH: Ruth, who I'm named after. Edvards' wife.

LYDIA: [*accent*] We were like sisters. You were a baby…

RUTH: I wasn't even born when she died.

ILSE: It's true. How old we've all got.

LYDIA: And now my make-up has run.

ILSE: Welcome, Otto.

OTTO: Ilse.

EDVARDS: Lydia.

LYDIA: Hello Edvards.

EDVARDS: Who could forget such beauty, OK.

LYDIA: I look a mess, OK. Still, you never said anything like that before.

EDVARDS: I always had my good side.

LYDIA: Someone has tamed you.

EDVARDS: Old age slows us all down.

LYDIA: A woman knows. Ilse will tell me. Yes I like you better like this. And Karl, as roly-poly as a publican.

OTTO: That's what I said.

ILSE: He's keeping a couple in business.

KARL: And that's what I said. Ilse this is Otto's sister, Lauma.

ILSE: [*taking her hands*] You are very welcome. I hope you enjoy your stay.

LAUMA: Thank you. I've heard so much about you all I already feel like I belong.

EDVARDS: And we've only been together two years in the last fifty.

LYDIA: And in the D.P. camp in Stuttgart.

EDVARDS: What's another year here or there, OK. [*Accent.*] Let's drink to the next fifty. Together, OK.

RUTH: You still haven't met Tim, my husband.

TIM: Hi everybody. Think I've caught all the names. Lydia, Lauma, Otto. I'm Tim, your barman. What would you like to drink?

ILSE: Come and see the garden before it gets completely dark.

KARL: Take particular notice of how neatly the lawn is mowed.

TIM: [*handing* KARL *a beer*] At least I know what you have.

> *Before* OTTO *can take one.*

LYDIA: Garden first, Otto.

> EDVARDS *presents* LAUMA *with a rose he has plucked.*

EDVARDS: From my very own garden.

LAUMA: "For him who has his flowers / For whom the flowers bloom / He lives in expectation / For him there's always hope."

EDVARDS: If that's true I'll take up gardening immediately.

ILSE: If your ploughing's as rough as your harvesting I think you've plucked your last flower.

LYDIA: Ilse!

LAUMA: Stolen flowers always smell sweeter.

OTTO: Coming Lauma?

EDVARDS: You lot run along. I'll take care of Lauma.

OTTO: That's what I'm worried about.

> ILSE, OTTO *and* LYDIA *go.*

EDVARDS: [*to* LAUMA] If anyone's name should be set in concrete, OK, it's yours. Proof that you actually got free of the Russians.

> EDVARDS *scratches her name in the cement.* KARL *and* RUTH *sit.* TIM *watches* EDVARDS *warily.*

TIM: What you doing there, Eddy?

EDVARDS: [*accent*] Don't you worry. We always remember who do this. People know from road is your work.

TIM: Yeah, yeah.

KARL: Did you get down to the TAB?

RUTH: I almost forgot. Here's your winnings, or should I say what you didn't lose?

KARL: Is that all?

RUTH: Dad, you picked the horses. I just placed the bets and collected the money.

KARL: Don't tell your mother.

TIM *brings* RUTH *a drink. Gives her a kiss.*

TIM: You look lovely as ever tonight, dear.

RUTH: Phew! Wish I could say the same for you.

TIM: Very busy day wasn't it, Dad?

RUTH: Dad's scrubbed up pretty well.

TIM: Edvards—

RUTH: Has always made his own rules. Why don't you go have a shower and change? You won't miss anything.

TIM *takes his beer and goes over to* EDVARDS *and* LAUMA.

EDVARDS: [*accent*] Hey what you do now?

TIM: Just wiping out Ruth's name.

TIM *goes.* EDVARDS *and* LAUMA *laugh and move off into the garden.*

RUTH: He's a child at times that man.

KARL: Maybe we all are when we're hurt.

RUTH: It'd be good if Lauma and Edvards hit it off, wouldn't it?

KARL: You think so?

RUTH: Yes I do. He's lived alone too long.

[*Pause.*]

Dad. I don't understand why you put up with—

KARL: [*gently*] No you don't understand. And I'm not asking you to. You know I often forget how much your mother's daughter you are.

RUTH: I've always thought of myself as my father's daughter.

KARL: I know, darling. You have my interests at heart but you must live your own life. And be careful. What you disapprove of in her I see more and more in you.

RUTH: What do you mean?

KARL: A tone of voice. Like you're angry at the world when it isn't the world to blame.

ILSE: Karl! Why are you just sitting? Everyone will be hungry.

KARL: [*laughs*] You see. It's me. Try to understand Tim. Try to be
    happy.

SCENE FIVE

Continuation of Scene Three.

BOEKING *and* HELY *stagger on, half carrying, half dragging a
bundle in a piece of canvas.*

HELY: In the middle of the camp will do.

> HELY *drops his end.* BOEKING *collapses under the weight.*

LEICHHARDT: What is that you have brought?
BOEKING: The fat calf.
MANN: What happened to it?
HELY: I shot it.
LEICHHARDT: You shot the calf?
BOEKING: Ja, we save him.
LEICHHARDT: By killing?
BOEKING: He lose his mother. Nothing for suck.
HELY: It was bawling itself to death and driving us all mad.

> BROWN *slips into camp.*

LEICHHARDT: Couldn't you wait for Brown to bring up the cattle?
BROWN: I couldn't find 'em, boss. They gone wild. And I was that
    crook I couldn't hardly stay on me horse.
LEICHHARDT: And now I suppose you eat calf?
HELY: It'll be a welcome change from boiled sheep and goat.
BROWN: Sheep and goat good tucker. Easier to catch than kangaroo.
    Easier than cattle too. More stupid, eh?
BOEKING: We promised suet pudding when all safe to this side.
MANN: Bunce isn't here yet.
HELY: He was the first one over.
BROWN: He's gone back to get his swag.
LEICHHARDT: Bunce was the only one to help with crossing. When I

announce plans to proceed you all fall into the grip of fever. Now you ask for pudding.

MANN: Because you promised.

LEICHHARDT: When all safe across. Where are cattle?

HELY: Where we'd still be if you hadn't moved the stores.

LEICHHARDT: I move deliberately so you move.

HELY: Only because we have to eat if we're to get better.

LEICHHARDT: Eat the calf. Bad flour is the worst thing for sickness.

All end up talking at once.

MANN: We've had no flour for weeks—

HELY: And we're all still sick.

BOEKING: You promise.

LEICHHARDT: Always sick except for eating.

BROWN: Mr Bunce comin' and he's yellin'.

BUNCE: [*off*] Thief! Thief! Who's the greedy thieving pig?

MANN: What's he yelling?

LEICHHARDT: Natives! Guard the camp! To arms! Must be native attack. We must save Bunce!

A flurry of activity as they dive for rifles and guns. LEICHHARDT *brandishes his sword.* BOEKING *blows a bugle.* BUNCE *is still yelling.*

MANN: This way, Bunce, over here.

HELY: Get out of me line of fire.

BROWN: I didn't see any natives.

BUNCE: [*entering*] Own up the thief amongst us. Own up. Who's the wretch who—

He stops dead as the rifles come to bear.

HELY: Get down Bunce we have you covered.

BUNCE *gets down.* BOEKING *stops blowing the bugle.*

BROWN: I don't see any natives.

LEICHHARDT: Don't shoot.

BUNCE: It was only me.

LEICHHARDT: Then why you cause excitement?

LEICHHARDT *checks his pulse again. Goes into decline.*

BUNCE: Someone stole my cress. I went back for my possessions and I remembered the plot of cress I planted on the riverbank and it's been severely weeded. Some villain stole—

LEICHHARDT: No one stole. I eat it.

BUNCE: But... but... it was to be shared, honourably, equally. I meant to cut it for the sick.

LEICHHARDT: I was sick when I ate. Whoever wants cress let him cut for himself as I did.

HELY: Doesn't look like it did you any good.

BROWN: I seen that little grass. Thought it was for cattle.

BOEKING: Is better we have suet pudding.

BUNCE: Yes. As we're all here safely now.

MANN: It seems there's to be no flour while the cattle are still lost.

BUNCE: Lost? They're standing around in the old camp across the river. They could be fetched over before dark.

HELY: It was Brown who lost them.

BROWN: I still too crook.

BOEKING: With flour to strengthen our stomachs we can fetch in the morning.

LEICHHARDT: Pudding will be only for those who can work to bring cattle across.

BUNCE: If I had some help...

BOEKING: Ja, I can give hand.

BROWN: If they that close, might as well finish the job.

HELY: Less chance of them escaping if we all go.

MANN: And we'll be able to make an early start tomorrow.

HELY: To hell with tomorrow. Can you taste that first morsel? Joy, oh joy.

BOEKING: Soon be little dumplings singing in the pot.

All except LEICHHARDT *have gone.*

LEICHHARDT: Bad flour will only make you worse.

SCENE SIX

The house block a few days later.

ILSE: Edvards, I've brought you some lunch.

EDVARDS: Needn't have bothered. OK.

ILSE: No bother. Every meal is a party down there. I'm glad to get away from it. Besides I wanted to see what you were doing.

> EDVARDS *comes and sits while she lays out the food.*

EDVARDS: Removing the formwork. Not too many holes in the finish. Not that anyone will ever see it. It's a good job, OK.

ILSE: Don't sound so surprised.

EDVARDS: Not because of you but that useless Tim. He used to be a sensible young man.

ILSE: While he and Ruth were both teaching he was fine. It was when she moved into law that... well...

EDVARDS: This is only the third business he's tried to set up.

ILSE: Come on, eat up.

EDVARDS: Did you leave Karl to get his own lunch?

ILSE: Lauma offered to take care of him.

EDVARDS: I don't know if you can trust that Lauma. You know what they say about merry widows.

ILSE: What? That they poisoned their husbands?

EDVARDS: And you let her get Karl's lunch? OK.

ILSE: What do you think of her?

EDVARDS: She seems very intelligent.

ILSE: And?

EDVARDS: And she's certainly no older than you.

ILSE: And?

EDVARDS: Why aren't you eating?

ILSE: Perhaps I poisoned your lunch.

> *They laugh.*

And?

EDVARDS: You want more? OK. She's available.

ILSE: What makes you think she'll have you?

EDVARDS: Because you won't and because my Ruth preferred to drown in another man's arms?

ILSE: Forgive me. I shouldn't have asked that.

EDVARDS: No, no. It's a fair question, supposing I was to pursue her.

ILSE: Are you going to?

EDVARDS: Might be third time lucky.

ILSE: I won't play this game, Edvards.

EDVARDS: [*shrugs*] OK.

    ARMAND *has arrived with his suitcase and camera case.*

ARMAND: Mum.

ILSE: [*startled, accent*]] What now?

ARMAND: It's Armand, Mum.

ILSE: [*stands*] Armand.

    They embrace awkwardly. Kiss.

What are you doing here? No I mean... what do I mean? Welcome home, well this isn't home yet, and yes, what are you doing here?

ARMAND: Hello Edvards.

EDVARDS: Welcome back.

    The MEN *shake hands and kiss.*

ARMAND: I got into Vince's taxi at the station, to go home, and he said you were up here.

ILSE: [*accent*] Busybodies know everything and we worry about KGB.

ARMAND: ASIO here Mum.

ILSE: [*accent*] You worry about ASIO, let me worry about KGB.

ARMAND: Speak Latvian, Mum. I mightn't speak it but I still understand.

    Pause.

ILSE: I know what that look means.

ARMAND: [*laughs*] What? I haven't seen you for three years.

ILSE: No. You were thinking, "Who is this little old woman? Is she my mother?"

ARMAND: Well, yes. I was.

EDVARDS: At least you could lie, OK.

ARMAND *takes a few quick photos of them.*

ILSE: Oh no Armand. Really.

ARMAND: All done.

EDVARDS: Modern cameras. Didn't even have time to smile.

ILSE: You've got thin.

ARMAND: Airline food, Mum.

ILSE: There's plenty to eat here. Sit down. Have something.

ARMAND: No thanks.

ILSE: Armand, don't be silly.

ARMAND: I'm not hungry. Really.

EDVARDS: How was Europe?

ARMAND: All right.

EDVARDS: [*after a pause*] That's all?

ARMAND: It was pretty good, really.

EDVARDS: Sounds enthralling, OK.

ILSE: Give him time to draw breath.

ARMAND: So this is going to be the new house?

EDVARDS: If you take the word of "Spanner-in-the-Works".

ARMAND: Who?

EDVARDS: Tim. That's my new name for him.

ILSE: Let me show you around.

ARMAND: I'll find my own way. You stay in the shade.

ILSE: [*as he goes*] See, he's even treating me like an old woman.

EDVARDS: She's sensitive about it at the moment.

ILSE: Don't you think he's got thin?

EDVARDS: Maybe he's in love.

ILSE: Is that why you haven't eaten much?

EDVARDS: I've had plenty, OK.

ILSE: I'll leave you some for later. Do what you like, I won't be made jealous.

EDVARDS: Maybe you don't know how to be.

ILSE: It's probably just as well.

EDVARDS: Maybe you have to love first.

ILSE: I've said all I'm going to say. But consider Lauma's feelings when you carry on like you were the other night.

EDVARDS: Like what?

ILSE: Hanging on her every word.

EDVARDS: She quotes poetry.

ILSE: Other people's.

EDVARDS: OK. It's still a novelty round here. Armand's had a university education and he can barely speak.

ARMAND: [*rejoining them*] I know it's too late, but wouldn't the house have been better positioned if it'd been turned through ninety degrees and the driveway—

EDVARDS: Anyone with half a brain can see that.

ILSE: Especially after the thing's been done. That's usually when the experts know best and talk loudest.

ARMAND: I'm sure it'll be all right.

ILSE: If we hurry, Armand, we might just catch Dad before he goes back to work. He was upset you didn't come home with Ruth last weekend. When he was your age he was exactly the same. He never wrote to his mother, I had to do it. The same way Mary had to write for you from England or we'd never hear anything.

ARMAND: She said to give you her love. All of that.

ILSE: You should've brought her with you.

ARMAND: I didn't want to.

ILSE: Oh well, I'll mind my own business.

ARMAND: I might as well tell you first. I didn't come up with Ruth… I was trying to sort something out. I've decided I'm going to give up medicine.

ILSE: Decided? What will you tell Dad?

ARMAND: The truth.

EDVARDS: Why couldn't you bring the boy up to lie, OK? It's the only way to keep peace at home.

ILSE: What will you do?

ARMAND: I don't know. Paint, maybe.

EDVARDS: Aah! Dangerous things, hobbies. Destroyed many a good career.

BROWN *comes*.

BROWN: How you goin', Doc? Long time no see. Missus.

ARMAND: G'day Dartzer.

BROWN: I come to look at you mob puttin' up some new fangled house with a spanner.

ILSE: [*accent*] You come look for work?

BROWN: Can't work missus. Broke my back.

ILSE: [*accent*] How you do that?

BROWN: Too many girlfriends, eh. [*Laughs.*]

ARMAND: He fell off a roof at the sugar mill.

BROWN: Just goes to prove, eh, work buggers you up for life. I can still lift a spanner but, so I might come back when you're putting up the house, if that's OK?

ARMAND: Yeah sure.

BROWN: The Department owes us some houses. If it's dead easy, we can put 'em up ourselves.

EDVARDS: [*accent*] Putting houses up with spanner is unnatural, OK.

BROWN: Maybe puttin' up houses at all is what's unnatural. Blackfellas did without for thousands of years. See you again.

ARMAND: See you round.

    BROWN *goes.*

ARMAND: From what happened to his back, he has to be in pain but I couldn't ask him about it. I don't want to spend my life with sick people.

ILSE: What will you do? How will you live?

ARMAND: I haven't decided completely yet. All I know is I had to come back, sit on the beach a few months, think it through.

EDVARDS: He already talks like an artist.

ILSE: I wouldn't tell your father that.

EDVARDS: If you want to eat you have to work, OK. It's one of nature's laws.

ARMAND: I bought a secondhand Mercedes overseas. I'll sell that when it arrives, buy myself some time.

ILSE: I don't know what to say. Good luck. Take a sandwich, you could be sitting for a long time.

SCENE SEVEN

A light comes on. EDVARDS *and* LAUMA, *both partly undressed.*

LAUMA: Why did you turn on the light?

EDVARDS: So you could see who you were dealing with.

LAUMA: Dealing with? We were making love. You stopped.

EDVARDS: Making love?

LAUMA: Well whatever you call it. Those first movements of discovery before you forget yourself. So who are you that I should see? Or is it what? Are you your scars? Not only. You show me these to keep me out. I'm not so easily frightened.

EDVARDS: I'm the one who's shaking, OK.

LAUMA: What is this fever?

EDVARDS: Resistance, holding back. Against the inevitable.

LAUMA: Not if you hold out.

EDVARDS: I am only a man.

LAUMA: What more should I know? I've seen your body scars. I know who tends your hearth, who feeds the fire.

EDVARDS: Who?

LAUMA: You do. So who would you betray by making love to me? The dead?

EDVARDS: No. Not after all these years.

LAUMA: The living?

EDVARDS: Yes! OK?

LAUMA: OK.

She begins to go.

EDVARDS: No. It is not OK. Who do you think you are?

LAUMA: I am only a woman.

EDVARDS: You poke around in my life and lead me to the edge and leave me there?

LAUMA: You don't have to say.

EDVARDS: Myself! That's who! My solitude!. Waiting alone for years! OK? You think I don't know that's what I'm risking?

LAUMA: I'm not asking for your life. We have tonight and perhaps tomorrow night as well. We haven't time for romance or happy-ever-after.

EDVARDS: Are you a witch?

LAUMA: I merely asked why you turned on the light. And now you can see me as well. Where I sag, my stretch marks. Is that who I am? Not only. In the darkness was I someone else?

EDVARDS: Never. You were only you, OK, and I was me. And perhaps we were beginning to discover who we are. Inside the flesh.

LAUMA: Beyond the flesh. Shall I turn off the light?

EDVARDS: Let's go into this with our eyes open. OK?

The light holds briefly on their love making which becomes noisy and playful. As the light fades we dimly see RUTH *watching them and* TIM *sits up.*

The sounds of laboured breathing in the darkness.

HELY: John Mann! John, wake up! Wake up!

MANN: What is it?

HELY: Can't you hear?

BUNCE: Down by the river.

MANN: It's probably some old man koala on the rut.

HELY: Then why is Dr Leichhardt's bed empty?

MANN *goes to* LEICHHARDT. RUTH *goes.*

MANN: [*shaking him*] Dr Leichhardt? What are you doing down here?

LEICHHARDT: Mann. [*Embraces him.*] John Mann. [*Kisses him.*] Mann.

MANN: Have you gone mad? [*Spits.*] What have you been eating? It's sugar!

LEICHHARDT: I find I cannot get on without it. It agrees with my stomach.

LAUMA *goes.*

MANN: Your handkerchief is full of it.

LEICHHARDT: I have had a vision, of my death. Abyss upon abyss. Misfortune on misfortune. Men all sickening, cattle scattered, mules and horses lost.

MANN: That isn't a dream, but our lot exactly.

LEICHHARDT: I cannot survive long. I have offended Providence. Why has he deserted me? On my last journey my luck was with me always. Except for Mr Gilbert's death.

MANN: It was a great mistake to set out with insufficient medicines and now we all suffer.

LEICHHARDT: My last journey was wasted in miscalculation. How will I be remembered if this one ends in failure? Where is my boat? Sturt took a boat to the desert. How will I be remembered? Damned coast hugger! All my journeys I am practically wading at the sea shore.

MANN: This is fever talk. Can you rise? I'll help you back to camp.

LEICHHARDT: I go down, down, down.

MANN: If you will not help I cannot lift you.

LEICHHARDT: When I am gone mark a tree for my passing, but not too close to the river. In case of flood.

MANN: Once we get into the high country we will be all right.

LEICHHARDT: I will die for Australia in Australia. It is my destiny. Promise me you will go on.

MANN: We are all with you.

LEICHHARDT: Promise me.

MANN: It is our great wish to go on, push ahead.

LEICHHARDT: If I have not died, there will still be fame and fortune enough for me.

MANN: I'll have to leave you here.

LEICHHARDT: That is my wish.

MANN *sits a little way off, watching* LEICHHARDT.

Mr Gilbert's name was also John. Poor John Gilbert died on my first journey and now I go to meet him. Down and down and down.

SCENE EIGHT

RUTH *at the beach.* ARMAND *at the beach, taking photos.*

ILSE: [*off*] What are you mincing about for?

KARL: [*off*] The water's cold.

EDVARDS: [*off*] It's the middle of summer.

KARL: [*off*] It'll stop my heart.

ILSE: [*off*] Since when did your heart hang that low?

KARL: [*off*] Ooooh! I don't want to lose them either.

RUTH: We used to come to the beach practically every Sunday.

ARMAND: Yeah.

ILSE: [*off*] You don't need them any more.

KARL: [*off*] Maybe you don't, but I do.

RUTH: They would fish and we'd swim and play and just talk. We haven't had much chance to talk, have we?

ARMAND: No, not much.

RUTH: I miss it. Well, at times I do. Tim and I don't seem to have much in common any more.

ARMAND: Did you ever?

RUTH: What's that? Another of those "Still married?" lines? Of course we did. We must've. We've been together, what?

ARMAND: Nine years. When you were both teaching here.

RUTH: Yes. Nine years. Half my property work is from divorce settlements. You'd think I'd know what keeps people together.

ARMAND: I don't know either.

> OTTO *comes carrying a fertiliser bag.* LYDIA *follows.* ARMAND *takes photos.*

LYDIA: Otto, wait.

OTTO: They'll want the bag for the fish.

LYDIA: Are you going to say anything to Lauma?

OTTO: No. Why?

LYDIA: She's your sister.

OTTO: She's a grandmother for Christ's sake.

LYDIA: No need to blaspheme. Why didn't she come back to Ilse's last night?

OTTO: Maybe she finds their flat a bit cramped.

LYDIA: Didn't she say anything to you?

OTTO: Good morning, little brother.

LYDIA: I'll drown you.

OTTO: "I am afraid of early spring / Let it come slowly / Let it come and stay a long time." Or words to that effect.

LYDIA: What does it mean?

LAUMA: [off] Otto! Come on, we need the bag.

OTTO: Coming! [Going.] They were both smiling a lot this morning.

LYDIA: No one else was. Wait.

> OTTO *and* LYDIA *go.*

RUTH: Edvards gave Tim and me his bed. He was going to use the spare room. We left him talking to Lauma and I thought he was going to take her back to Mum's. Then in the middle of the night the funniest thing happened. I woke up and I heard these odd noises. For a moment I didn't know where I was and then I thought, "My God, Edvards is having a heart attack." So I leapt out of bed and headed for the other bedroom in the dark. All the doors were open because it was so hot and the noise was getting louder, more urgent. His light was still on and I was about to charge into the room when I realised what it was. They were making love, really fucking. And I watched them. I stood and watched them. I don't know how long but Tim lead me back to bed and I just cried. I don't know why but I cried and cried. I've started again. Silly isn't it. [Laughs.] Jesus, what right have they got to be so happy?

ARMAND: "When you're in love you only need a single bed."

RUTH: Who said that? Lauma?

ARMAND: Dad used to say it. Don't you remember?

RUTH: Did he? You seem to remember everything.

ARMAND: I just take a lot of photos.

RUTH: You're serious, aren't you?

ARMAND: What about?

RUTH: Painting. I stuck my nose into your studio up at Edvards'. I hope you don't mind.

ARMAND: Hardly a studio.

RUTH: There was a picture. I assumed it was of me, the photos you took at the airport were pinned up around it. Well it looked like my dress.

ARMAND: It isn't really you. Well, not if you only recognised the dress.

RUTH: Oh that's a pity. I'd rather hoped it was.

ARMAND: It can be. If you want it to. You're in it.

RUTH: I thought it a good likeness.

ARMAND: Of your dress.

RUTH: No, no. That blurry figure, no hard edges, that's me, exactly. There was another figure, sort of ghostly with some sort of measuring instrument.

ARMAND: It's a sextant, of sorts.

RUTH: Is that what you're doing? Measuring us up? Is that why you came back? To assess our usefulness for your art?

ARMAND: Yes, I suppose that's one way of looking at it.

RUTH: Mercenary sort of business.

ARMAND: It's the only way I know to try and make sense of things. How we came to be here. Why here and not somewhere else. What we're doing, to ourselves, to each other, to the world.

RUTH: How come you didn't photograph me before? When I was crying.

ARMAND: I wanted to.

RUTH: Jesus!

ARMAND: Out of the blue, one day, I thought, I knew, I had to come back here and paint. Now, I think it's because I was feeling cornered and I had to get out. Why I left.

RUTH: Left Mary?

ARMAND: Someone else. Who I worked with.

RUTH: And Mary found out.

ARMAND: She never said. But things weren't right between us, so she came back to Australia three months before I did. And when I saw Mary at Sydney airport I thought, "I've made a terrible mistake."

RUTH: Does she know now?

ARMAND: About Jessica? Yes. I have to decide.

RUTH: But you know.

ARMAND: Jessica offered to keep me, if I wanted to paint. She offered to come out here, and I said, "No." I didn't want to be showing her, I wanted to see for myself. And wherever I look I'm thinking, "How would she see this? Would she belong here? Do I? Is this what I came back to see? Or is it just part of the same mistake?"

The FISHERFOLK *return.* ARMAND *photographs them.* ILSE *and* LAUMA *have their skirts tucked up.* EDVARDS *and* KARL *and* TIM *are wet. They carry the drag-net between them.*

OTTO: If you look along the beach with the pines and the low grasses, it's exactly like Jurmala in Latvia.

LYDIA: Except for the mountain.

KARL: And they're she-oak not pines.

ILSE: And the sand at Jurmala is purest white, not yellow.

EDVARDS: Ask Lauma, OK.

LAUMA: It couldn't be more different. There are no microphones in the trees and I'm not surrounded by thousands of jabbering Russians and the fish don't stink of pollution.

LYDIA: What fish? Karl scared them off with his complaining.

KARL: Edvards and Tim didn't do any better. We'll try in the estuary and it can be your Otto's turn to get wet.

LYDIA: Don't be silly Otto. There's probably crocodiles.

OTTO: Think of the insurance you'll collect.

ILSE: And widows have more fun. Ask Lauma.

They go. TIM *stays.*

RUTH: Did you have to get yourself wet?

TIM: Getting wet is what you do at the seaside. It's the form.

RUTH: Not with your good clothes on.

TIM: It's the stinger season. Big box jellyfish. Wham! Dead in fifteen seconds. Still, think of the insurance you'd collect.

RUTH: We just did that joke in Latvian.

TIM: [*shrugs*] I don't know what they're saying but it has the makings of a good party.

RUTH: Just go please.

TIM: You really want to know how I got wet? There's this little thunder cloud that follows me around and if I'm having a good time it dumps on me.

   He goes.

RUTH: I've married a man like my mother did. How did that song go? I don't know. About Tim. And me.

ARMAND: I always thought you adopted him, like a stray.

RUTH: What do you mean?

ARMAND: When he transferred here after Vietnam, he was kind of lost.

RUTH: I love Dad but I don't want to be like Mum. She should've left him. Years ago.

ARMAND: Maybe in her own way she still loves him.

RUTH: Oh come on. You know what's been going on.

ARMAND: No I don't. Nor do you, not really. Speculation. And Dad must still love her. I mean, it's not as if they stayed together for us.

RUTH: Unless it's habit. [*Shudders.*] I can't bear to contemplate that. I've applied for a job in Canberra. Well why not? I work harder and bring in more than anyone else in my firm but they're never going to give a woman a partnership.

SCENE NINE

Early morning. BROWN *comes.*

MANN: Aren't you watching the cattle.

BROWN: I watch 'em all night. Then they go bush.

HELY: You mean you lost them?

BROWN: Something spooked 'em. And they not lost, eh? They know where they goin', back the way they come.

HELY: Perhaps it's time we followed their example instead of always having to drive them on.

BROWN: When we go back, I take you back straight, quick, not wrigglin' all over the country like snake.

MANN: When we go back?

BROWN: This country makin' everyone sick. He don' know us. This country don' want us here. Cattle knows. He can go anywhere but he always goes back.

MANN: That's just what cattle do.

BROWN: They not stupid, eh. What's cookin'?

BOEKING: Goat head soup. Mr Mann won't give flour.

MANN: I haven't talked to Dr Leichhardt this morning.

BROWN: He's down by the river, washin'.

BOEKING: If only eat meat, meat, meat all time, that make very sick.

HELY: He cuts our rations and helps himself to sugar and who knows what.

BROWN: I seen him takin' tapioca in his hat.

BUNCE: He is in a very bad way himself.

HELY: Which one of us is not? All the more reason not to go on.

BUNCE: If we had more rations I'm sure that would make a difference.

MANN: If we were to maintain rations at their current level they wouldn't last us to the end.

BOEKING: If not go on then no reason to save rations.

BUNCE: The last expedition lived high off the land. Surely we could do the same.

MANN: I know you intend to make your name writing up our adventures, Mr Bunce, but surely you've thought of going back?

BUNCE: There is no honour in returning sick and defeated.

HELY: What honour is there in being dead?

BUNCE: John Gilbert's glory was hard won. And ill as I am, I will go to the end or die in the attempt.

HELY: Only because there is no fame or fortune to be earned on a journey where everything was discovered two years ago.

MANN: Dr Leichhardt is prepared to sacrifice himself to that end.

HELY: Sacrifice himself!

MANN: His heart is affected by fever and he cannot travel, but it is his wish that we push on though it kill him.

    LAUMA enters. A chill ripples through the camp.

LAUMA: Edvards? Edvards!

    After she has gone.

HELY: If we let him die while we are still within reach of safety, we'll surely be famous then.

BUNCE: I would not return if I could help it, but as Dr Leichhardt is too ill to go on...

HELY: It'd be hopeless, Mr Bunce, to maintain this expedition should continue.

BUNCE: Yes, quite hopeless.

MANN: So long as we're all resolved it's our best course of action.

BROWN: I hear Dr Leichhardt singin' to the land all night that he comin'.

BOEKING: Ja, was like the opera. Over and over he dies.

BROWN: But he don't know the right singing.

HELY: He probably spooked the cattle.

BROWN: It was blackfellas. I seen where they dancin' on me tracks.

HELY: What? Why didn't you say?

MANN: Dr Leichhardt's still down by the river. He could be in danger.

BROWN: No danger. They comin' for makin' friends.

    The camp begins to rally to save LEICHHARDT. BOEKING *on the bugle.* OTHERS *searching for guns. It is much less urgent, organised than the last time.*

BUNCE: Dr Leichhardt!

BROWN: The wommins comin'.

MANN: Don't shoot. Just scare them off!

OTTO: It's Lauma. Let's hide.

    LAUMA returns.

    Lauma! Here we are! [*Ducks from view.*]

LAUMA: Otto, is that you?

KARL: Lauma! [*Ducks from view.*]

LAUMA: Come on out!

OTTO: Lauma! [*Ducks from view.*]

KARL: Lauma! [*Ducks from view.*]

LAUMA: Edvards!

ARMAND: [*with his camera*] You're scaring her now. Lauma…

> LAUMA *starts to go and runs into* BROWN *carrying a fishing spear. She freezes.*

BROWN: You lookin' for someone missus?

EDVARDS: Lauma? What are you doing?

> *She grabs* EDVARDS. BROWN *goes.*

BROWN: Looks like you found him.

LAUMA: Did I really see him?

EDVARDS: I did.

LAUMA: What was that…?

EDVARDS: A spear for fish.

OTTO: Lauma! [*Ducks from view.*]

KARL: Edvards! [*Ducks from view.*]

OTTO: Edvards! [*Ducks from view.*]

KARL: Lauma! [*Ducks from view.*]

LAUMA: You clowns! You can come out now.

> *They don't. And she is still holding on to* EDVARDS *making him uncomfortable.*

EDVARDS: Where are the other women?

LAUMA: They were going to clean the fish. I came looking for you.

OTTO: Watch out Lauma. He's not to be trusted on his own.

EDVARDS: You couldn't get lost here.

LAUMA: You weren't so standoffish last night.

ARMAND: Smile for the camera.

> ARMAND *takes a photo.*

EDVARDS: They're all watching, OK?

LAUMA: Let them. I'm not ashamed. They're only jealous that we found a little happiness. I'm only here one more night.

EDVARDS: Yes I know.

LAUMA: I can see you're not interested. What do they say? "By the cruel light of day."

EDVARDS: Look you mustn't think—

LAUMA: I don't but clearly you do.

> *She goes, leaving* EDVARDS *grasping at the air.*

EDVARDS: My heart is pounding. I'm too old. This shouldn't be happening to me.

MANN: Dr Leichhardt?

LEICHHARDT: Ja, speak. I listen.

MANN: I have been asked... I represent the party... it is a matter of some delicacy. With all the sickness and so on, the state of the medicines—

LEICHHARDT: And so on and so on. I hear this catalogue many times.

MANN: You yourself claimed to feel weaker every day, fearing you could not go on.

LEICHHARDT: That was my foolishness. But I exorcised some demons in the night.

MANN: The party is resolved upon returning.

> *Pause.*

LEICHHARDT: It can't be I am dreaming. This is not my last journey. You are not John Gilbert. He is dead. I must pinch myself that I am not hearing you.

MANN: I am to convey to the party your opinion—

LEICHHARDT: No! My opinion is no! Simple no! I will give my opinion to party but yours is not the only voice I want to hear. I will hear the opinion of every man.

SCENE TEN

At the beach. ILSE *and* LAUMA *are cleaning fish.* LYDIA *watches.* RUTH *comes with a bottle of kummel and a small glass. The* WOMEN *will drink by turns from the same glass during the course of the scene.*

RUTH: I thought you might be able to use some of this.

ILSE: What is it?

RUTH: Kummel. A taste of the old Europe. I bought it especially for us women.

LYDIA: Do you think we should?

RUTH: Oh come on, Lydia. Loosen your stays. Have you never had a drink without Otto's permission?

LYDIA: I don't need Otto's permission to do anything.

RUTH: Good. Lauma first.

ILSE: Speak Latvian, Ruthie.

RUTH: My bread and butter Latvian? I murder the language.

ILSE: Try.

LAUMA: Yes, try. We're all friends here.

RUTH: [accent] OK. Don't talk that you not be warning. [Pouring a drink.] First, Lauma, our... celebrated, I know that isn't correct, guest.

> Some polite encouragement for RUTH.

LAUMA: Very good. [Takes the glass, sniffs.] Mmmm.

RUTH: [accent] I believe that go very well with fishes.

LAUMA: To us and to fish. Strange animals that they are. Their scales may be hard, yet their flesh is sweet. [Drinks.]

ILSE: From ode to a fish, Lauma?

LAUMA: [laughs] I was going on to say like a woman in her prime.

ILSE: One minute she's swimming free, then along comes a man dangling his bait and zzzt, she's in the pan.

LYDIA: Ugh! Horrible.

RUTH: [pouring for LYDIA, accent] This one helps you.

ILSE: It depends on the man, and the pan. Hey I'm a poet myself.

LAUMA: You just have to admit these fish are beautiful.

LYDIA: If I looked like that I'd be lining up to have myself scraped.

ILSE: Well here's to fish, they are our distant ancestors, the scientists say. And here's to us. [Drinks.]

LAUMA: And smell the sea, and blue air and sunshine. I feel like a girl again.

LYDIA: I don't think I want to hear this.

LAUMA: What?

LYDIA: Little girlie things. They're unbecoming to women of our age. Go ahead and say them if you must, I won't listen.

LAUMA: Forgive me for saying so, Lydia, but you're being stupid.

LYDIA: I wasn't born yesterday.

LAUMA: I was thanking Providence for my good fortune.

LYDIA: If you couldn't be discreet, at least you can spare us the details. I'm sure Ilse doesn't want to hear them either.

ILSE: I wouldn't mind hearing them.

RUTH: It's really none of our business, Mum.

LAUMA: If I was in Latvia it would be cold and grey with muddy snow and empty shops and defeated people. But to my delight, I'm here amongst straight backs and plenty. It's summer and it's free. It's free. The last time I knew this I was still a girl. I never expected to feel like this again.

RUTH: [*accent*] That is our luck that we have like that, freedom always. But we forget.

ILSE: It isn't luck that life is as it should be. It's our right.

LYDIA: I'm sorry, Lauma. I thought, well what does it matter?

LAUMA: You thought I was such a dry old stick that one night with a man would get my sap running? Well let me tell you that it's because my sap is still running that I can not only contemplate such a thing but do it.

RUTH: [*accent*] Well spoked, Lauma. I drink on that.

LAUMA: It must be the same for you and Ilse? Even Ruth. None of us believes it's men who make us young.

LYDIA: I know that doesn't work. But I wish I knew what did.

ILSE: Sleeping with toads. I'm sure I can organize that for your last night with us. For you too, Lauma, if you like.

LAUMA: Perhaps I should warn you, Edvards and I will probably spend one more night together.

LYDIA: You know what will happen? You'll fall in love and ruin the rest of your holiday.

LAUMA: In eight weeks I'll be teaching school back in Latvia and you'll all be part of a cherished dream.

RUTH: [*accent*] That you come so far and staying such little time. If you give to me your papers, perhaps I can help stretching your time.

ILSE: [*accent*] You say yourself, Ruth, is not our business.

RUTH: But if Lauma would like to stay longer—

ILSE: [*accent*] I think you are last person to play matchmaker.

RUTH: [*accent, to* LAUMA] Think about it. I help.

> BROWN *enters along the beach. He is dressed in the same clothes as when he is an explorer and he carries a hand spear made of steel.*

BROWN: G'day missus. Not many fish round, eh?

ILSE: [*accent*] What you say?

BROWN: Not many fish.

ILSE: [*accent*] Plenty more if you look.

BROWN: I been lookin', and looks to me like you caught them all. You get that house up yet?

ILSE: [*accent*] House still in factory, till New Year.

BROWN: Yeah, well, Rome wasn't built in a day. I heard you talking funny. Wasn't Itie or Greek. You're not Russians are ya?

ILSE: [*accent*] I give you Russian.

RUTH: Oh Mum! [*To* BROWN.] We're Latvian. Well they are.

BROWN: Russians went into Afghanistan, eh? They're taking over the world.

ILSE: [*accent*] What rubbish you talking now.

BROWN: Was on the news yesterday. Don't you listen to the news?

RUTH: We must've missed it.

BROWN: Never know what's going to happen, eh? The world could end. Not that it makes that much difference. When the fish are gone so are we. And the fish are gone. I didn't see one in the water. Don't s'pose you could spare one, eh? Could be me last supper and all that.

ILSE: [*accent*] You lazy. You catch.

RUTH: Give him one, Mum. We've got plenty.

> *Gives him two of the fish.*

Hope you enjoy them.

BROWN: Thanks missus. I will. I know you, eh. Well I know your brother, the Doc. Hey, didn't you used to teach round here?

RUTH: Used to. I'm a solicitor in Townsville now.

BROWN: Yeah. I could use a good lawyer. See you all later. [*Goes.*]

ILSE: You could have given him ones we hadn't cleaned.

LYDIA: You never see them in Sydney, you know? And he spoke English. On the television they're always subtitled.

LAUMA: His skin was so black.

ILSE: When I first came here, they used to be blacker. He's probably half white. But then I was told they were cannibals.

RUTH: [accent] Then it's good that I gave him some fish instead.

LYDIA: [to LAUMA] He said that the Russians marched into Afghanistan. Yesterday.

LAUMA: What? Is it war? How will I get home?

RUTH: [accent] Maybe you have to stay. Tomorrow I will phone Immigration Department.

ILSE: Crazy Russians. Always sticking their noses in where they're not wanted.

LYDIA: Will you look at that blackfellow. Now he's begging from the men.

SCENE ELEVEN

Explorers' camp.

BOEKING: Soup is ready. You want eat?

HELY: Boiled goat again. Meat morning, noon, and night. We are indeed a set of fools. We are nearly mad for want of flour but not one crumb can we get.

BUNCE: Perhaps we should wait till Mr Mann returns from talking to Dr Leichhardt.

HELY: It is shameful to deny sick people their natural food. A real Doctor would not let us touch meat.

BROWN *comes with the fish.*

BROWN: Look what I catch.

BOEKING: Where you get?

BROWN: Off them wommin you chase. They think you ghosts, viney-viney. I tell 'im you only men, you yellow 'cos you plenny crook.

*Nina Landis (Ruth) and Paul English (Armand) in the 1992
Melbourne Theatre Company production. (Photo: Jeff Busby)*

*Left to right: Paul English (Mann), Simon Chilvers (Leichhardt),
Tom Considine (Boeking), Philip Charles (Brown), Bradley Croft
(Hely) and Peter Adams (Bunce) in the 1992 Melbourne Theatre
Company production. (Photo: Jeff Busby)*

They laugh 'cos you go walkabout without wommin. They very
  friendly. We can all go meet 'im.

BUNCE: I don't think we'd better.

BROWN: When the men gives their wommin' to lay down with then
  you belong here.

HELY: We are gentlemen, Brown. We find your suggestion quite
  repellent.

BROWN: They waitin' for us.

BOEKING: Yesterday I can go, but today I am escalated to gentleman.
  Also Mr Bunce?

  LEICHHARDT *charges into the camp, breathing raggedly.*

LEICHHARDT: Good, we are all here.

  He takes the pot off the fire, and begins eating greedily. The
  OTHERS *are momentarily stunned.*

BUNCE: Except for Mr Mann.

LEICHHARDT: I believe I am going too fast for him. My appetite has
  improved as well.

HELY: What about the rest of us?

LEICHHARDT: Cry louder then you get mother's milk. Can you smell
  bad odour? From illness in the party? Or rather is the stink of
  your proposal. A mule is more faithful, a dog is not so low.

  MANN *comes.*

  I had just started to give my opinion. Is disgrace. Shameful.
  Highly insulting. Despicable, scandalous, unheroic. To use a few
  simple words. If you go back, you will never live down the sneers
  and the slurs, never escape the laughter of those who waited for
  us to fail. My opinion is better you die now. I own this
  expedition. I pay for everything. I will not return. I am going to
  Swan River as planned with whoever has courage. My question,
  for your opinion, one by one, is, "Do you wish to go forward or
  back?" Mr Bunce?

BUNCE: All I wish, is for some increase in rations.

LEICHHARDT: How much?

BOEKING: Double flour I go forwards.

LEICHHARDT: Who else wants flour?

BROWN: I take the flour, boss.

LEICHHARDT: Easy to grant. [*To* MANN.] You see. No catalogue of miseries. No party proposal. You are free now to represent yourself.

MANN: Forward, is my wish, but I feel sorry to think I can hardly load a mule.

LEICHHARDT: Double flour will double strength and halve the load on the mule. [*To* HELY.] And now the ringleader of complaints and underhand schemes.

HELY: What am I supposed to have said or done?

LEICHHARDT: Exactly nothing. That is the trouble. Now I am saying. You want to go back, take a horse and double rations, triple. I am glad to be rid. We rest can make a fresh start.

HELY: Mann?

    ILSE *comes.*

ILSE: Why are you all sitting and waiting to be served like kings?

EDVARDS: It's my fault, OK. I suggested we have lunch here.

ILSE: Then you could have brought everything over, not only the beer.

KARL: We didn't dare until we had it ratified by a higher authority and now you're here.

ILSE: What are you blathering on about?

KARL: [*trying to dance her round*] Thirty years of marriage to you my love.

ILSE: Oh stop it. In May it will be thirty-two.

KARL: I should have known you'd keep count.

ILSE: I knew you wouldn't. Now move.

OTTO: Just like the old days. Scratch and bite. I wouldn't miss this.

ARMAND: I'll send you tapes, Otto.

KARL: [*pulling* ARMAND *to his feet*] It's how your mother and I show our love for each other. [*Accent.*] Tim. We have to bring lunch.

TIM: Righto.

BROWN: [*to* ARMAND] I'll see you later mate.

ARMAND: Stay for lunch of you like. We won't be long.

    As the MEN *go.*

ILSE: Edvards?

EDVARDS: Her mistress's voice. If four of you can't carry it come back and tell me, OK?

HELY: Mr Mann, you were supposed to tell him we were going back, not ask his opinion. Bunce is happy. Must be worth an extra chapter. A few extra sales.

BROWN: Hello again missus. I'll just sit here, keep out of the way.

EDVARDS: [*offering from the pot*] Prawn.

ILSE: [*taking one*] Why here?

EDVARDS: It's a nicer spot than near the tables. More secluded.

ILSE: This used to be our special place.

EDVARDS: [*accent, to* BROWN] What you think? Here is, how you say it, sacred place?

BROWN: Sacred site? Maybe. I don't know. Not for me. Or if you look at it another way, the whole of Australia is.

EDVARDS: Pick an answer. He covered them all.

ILSE: There are many good memories attached to this place. But not after today.

EDVARDS: Why not?

ILSE: You know why.

EDVARDS: [*shrugs*] Last night. You think you can't change what once was? It was and that's it? No, OK. Memory will always play you tricks. What was once good can be remembered as either a better experience or a worse experience. Or you can forget altogether. Why clutter up your mind?

ILSE: Why are you doing this?

EDVARDS: I embarked on a journey with companions and now I find I must go the last leg alone. I must cast off anything that holds me back.

ILSE: Cast off or kill?

EDVARDS: They are often the same thing. We both learned that through the war.

ILSE: We survived.

EDVARDS: Better on our own.

ILSE: How did we ever love each other?

EDVARDS: How could we?

ILSE: Don't. You think you'll break me.

EDVARDS: No. You would break me first. I'm no match for you. But at least I understand that now.

The OTHERS *return with containers of food which is put out on rugs.* ARMAND *takes photos.*

KARL: Ilse, do you know what Otto just said? He wonders how you and I lasted so long together. Apparently Lydia thinks the same.

LYDIA: When will you learn to keep your mouth shut, Otto?

ILSE: I've wondered it myself once or twice.

KARL: For me the answer's simple. I couldn't imagine life without you.

RUTH: You mean you couldn't manage your life without her.

KARL: I admit it. She's made me happy.

ILSE: I've made you happy?

RUTH: Mum.

KARL: I know it's hard for you to believe because at times you try your best not to. But today I am. We're among friends. Do your worst.

ILSE: I won't have to. One or two more drinks and you'll be crying in your beer. Now what have you done for me?

RUTH: Mum, leave it.

ILSE: No, no. I've never heard this before.

KARL: Haven't I ever made you happy?

ILSE: Perhaps once or twice. I don't remember.

KARL: She doesn't remember! Now what the hell can I do about that? It wouldn't matter if I had or hadn't. I might as well have a drink. [*Accent.*] Tim, a stubby.

TIM: Coming right up.

OTTO: Thirty years ago they were at each other like this.

LYDIA: Otto and I are happy, aren't we Otto?

OTTO: Are we? Right, then we are.

LYDIA: Don't joke about it. I was serious.

OTTO: So was I. If you say we are—

KARL: Why wouldn't you be? You've got your importing business. You drive a Mercedes.

OTTO: I worked damn hard for them.

LYDIA: We both did.

OTTO: Right, Lydia pushed me all the way.

LYDIA: We always thought Karl would be the one to make money.

ILSE: I held him back.

KARL: I have never said that. Not even when drunk. Have I Edvards?

EDVARDS: I can't be expected to remember that. When you were drunk so was I most likely.

ILSE: We know you've worked hard for what you have.

LYDIA: You have to work smart as well.

KARL: That makes us stupid as well as poor.

OTTO: You've put your foot in it this time.

LYDIA: I didn't mean it like that?

KARL: How did our children get to be so clever?

ILSE: That had nothing to do with you.

KARL: Oh really, who was it then?

ILSE: You're either born with brains or not.

KARL: Fortunately both our children were. Except that Armand took up surgery and removed his brain. He's gone back to smearing paint on walls.

LAUMA: Latvian society always used to revere its artists.

EDVARDS: And most of them starved the way they do here, OK.

ARMAND: It's much more enlightened here. At least they don't encourage you.

KARL: A perfectly good career in medicine thrown away. Is that what I worked for?

ILSE: No. You only worked to drink beer and bet on horses.

ARMAND: I do have a Mercedes.

KARL: At least that's a doctor's car.

ILSE: A car is a car.

KARL: Tell Otto and Lydia that.

LYDIA: Oh shut up about it. Why can't you leave us alone? We're sorry we made money. We're sorry we didn't have children. We're sorry we drive a Mercedes. And we're starting to feel sorry we came up here for a holiday.

    Pause.

OTTO: You don't mean that, Lydia.

LYDIA: You know I do. This trip was Otto's idea.

OTTO: We've been having a good time.

LYDIA: I wanted to go back to Latvia.

OTTO: We were there only eighteen months ago...

LYDIA: When will we be able to go again? With the Russians in Afghanistan all the borders will be closed. On the radio they're talking of sanctions. Most of our stock is imported from behind the Iron Curtain.

OTTO: For God's sake, Lydia, have some regard for Lauma's feelings. You can at least count your blessings you don't have to go back.

RUTH: [*accent*] If Lauma want stay. I'm sure that that can be fix.

LYDIA: That will make sure all the doors are slammed against us.

LAUMA: I've lived nearly forty years under the Russians. I'm not worried for myself. Here, "I have filled myself with blue mornings / And the midday sun. / Now I climb serenely / Towards sunset with a slow and lingering tread. / I have been blessed with great fortune, / This earth's gravity / That holds me in firm embrace / And will in time embrace me for life." I would not have missed this, even at the cost of good friends falling out.

ILSE: Perhaps we aren't such good friends.

LYDIA: We never kept in touch.

KARL: We took up where we left off thirty years ago.

OTTO: That has to mean something.

EDVARDS: If Ilse had married Otto and Karl had married Lydia, then Karl would be rich and, I don't know Otto, you could just be happy. At least things would be different. OK.

LYDIA: You've always got something clever to say. Why have you never remarried?

EDVARDS: Australia is a single man's paradise. Plenty of work, plenty of money and women hanging from the trees.

ILSE: By the neck.

   Pause.

TIM: Any one for another beer? [*Gets drinks.*]

ARMAND: I'm as bad as they are. I keep forgetting. You can't have understood any of that. Or Dartzer.

TIM: You'd be surprised at what I can pick up.

RUTH: Like what?

TIM: Some of it was funny but it wasn't very happy. Right?

KARL: [*accent*] Right, right. Very good.

TIM: I'm always on at you to teach me.

RUTH: I can barely speak it myself.

ARMAND: I can't speak it at all.

ILSE: [*accent*] Our clever childrens.

EDVARDS: [*accent*] Now we all speak English. Even Lauma, OK?

LAUMA: [*accent*] OK.

RUTH: Are you happy, Tim?

TIM: [*suspicious*] Can't complain. Why?

RUTH: Why not? Everybody else has.

TIM: Santa came. My brain's out to lunch. All's right with the world.

LYDIA: [*accent*] Have you never thought of going back to Latvia?

KARL: [*accent*] I have. I want to but Ilse won't go.

ILSE: [*accent, to* KARL] You go if you want but not me. Never! Bastard Russians. I never forget. I never forgive. I see what they do.

BROWN: What'd they do, missus?

ILSE: [*accent*] What you think? Take country. Take farms. Kill animals. Send peoples to Siberia to concentration camp. Kill and rape and waste everything. Everyone.

BROWN: Did them Russians reckon they discovered Latvia?

ILSE: [*accent*] Aach! You talk rubbish. Discover!

OTTO: [*accent*] Latvia and her peoples have been there thousands of years. Not like here.

BROWN: I dunno. This was all here a few thousand years when them explorers reckon they discovered it. We were livin' here.

EDVARDS: Latvia was the most civilised nation in Europe. We had social reform long before the Swedes.

OTTO: [*accent*] English, must speak English.

LAUMA: Sorry. I can't. That Latvia where we grew up doesn't exist.

LYDIA: [*accent*] But when I am there I can still remember it, the smells and the colours. I know where things used to be. You do remember and your blood sings. I don't know this place but Latvia I still know in my bones.

OTTO: No we don't. Not any more. When we got back to Australia, I got down on my knees and kissed our doorstep. I almost kissed the asphalt at the airport except that I thought people might mistake me for the Pope.

ARMAND: I don't understand that, and I was born here. I look around, I remember things but I don't know them, not in my bones. But I'm not Latvian either. I know some stories, I know some snatches of songs, but I don't know... Maybe it's that it's still so new, so alien, that it has to be discovered and rediscovered, generation after generation before it's in our blood, in our bones.

LEICHHARDT: My first expedition to Port Essington is the longest journey yet accomplished in Australia, yet it has been no more than a rehearsal, a preparation for the real task—the journey to Swan River.

LYDIA: [accent] I am sorry, what I said before. This place gives me too many bad memories of the heat and flies, dirt, small town thinking. And Ruth and...

EDVARDS: Leonids, OK? Ruth and Leonids.

LYDIA: Drowned in that river.

OTTO: [accent] Well, we're leaving tomorrow. For a week in paradise on Lizard Island. I wish you were coming with us.

KARL: [accent] You pay Otto and we come.

EDVARDS: And after, we can all take a journey together, for Lauma's sake, OK?

OTTO: We had plans to go inland and see the country anyway.

LYDIA: We should go back to Sydney. The business.

OTTO: We can't stop the world. We'd have to wait for things to settle down.

LEICHHARDT: The journey is an end in itself. And one should always be accompanied by men influenced by ideals. Mr Mann?

ARMAND: I will gladly go.

ILSE: If everyone is going...

KARL: I'll still be on holidays.

RUTH: [to TIM] You have three houses to put up so don't you even think about it.

TIM: I don't know what you're talking about.

BROWN: Are you the one I have to see about the houses?

TIM: You can help me put them up.

LAUMA: Where will we go?

EDVARDS: A few days in the bush, OK. Probably discovering what none of us would have seen if you hadn't come here.

ILSE: Who knows how long it would be before we saw each other again.

OTTO: We can't wait another thirty years.

KARL: Not when we took up where we left off in younger days.

LYDIA: That has to mean something.

> *They sing "Jauniba".* KARL *starts.*

"Jauniba"

Mile dzel un mile glasta
Atver sirdi tai.
Nes ta tevi prieka brizos
Preti jaunibai.

Jauniba jauniba
Sartais vina trauks,
Dzer no ta, lidz rudens salnas
Novist dzives lauks.

Lai ko liktens plecos veltu
Tas mus nesaliec.
Cauri visiem dzives erkskiem
Izvedis mus preiks.

Jauniba jauniba
Sartais vina trauks,
Dzer no ta, lidz rudens salnas
Novist dzives lauks.

LEICHHARDT: Life is short. I have no time to lose. I shall hasten to explore more, that I have done enough when my time comes.

END OF PART ONE

PART TWO

SCENE TWELVE

Explorers' camp. Slabs and strips of bullock hung up on lines and poles to dry. Boiled and roasted bones lie around the place. A few black puddings hanging from a tree.

The sound of retching, off. BOEKING *and* LEICHHARDT *listen anxiously for the retching to stop, quelling their own internal disturbances. The mules grow restless. The retching stops.*

BUNCE: [*off, spits*] Aaah! Aaaaahh!

LEICHHARDT: The meat must be turned over again today. We cannot risk fly blowing.

BOEKING: Ja. Two more days warm and will be ready for packing. Lucky is good climate.

LEICHHARDT: The climate is most delightful.

BOEKING: One has to ask how is possible that anyone can be ill here?

BOEKING *rushes off. The sound of vomiting, off.*

LEICHHARDT: The simple reason is that after the long attack of fever, not one makes the least exertions after hearty meals, for good appetites have all but only lay down on backs all day or if any walking about is only from the couch to the fireplace. But I bite my tongue lest I offend.

BUNCE: [*enters*] The mules are restless.

LEICHHARDT: They are tired of being tethered so long but I dare not let them wander.

BUNCE: No sign of Brown or Mr Hely.

LEICHHARDT: No.

BUNCE: Eleven days they've been gone now.

LEICHHARDT: I count.

BUNCE: They only took six days' provisions.

LEICHHARDT: I count that too. Worse is they were not strong and if anything should have happened there is none here who could go after them. They would be lost people.

BUNCE: Who knows how far they had to go to find the cattle?

BUNCE *groans with stomach cramp. Goes for food.*

LEICHHARDT: Only Providence. He will help me through. He has been always ready to my prayer and has been merciful in the case of need. Do you think it is wise, Bunce, to be eating again so soon?

BUNCE: I suffer less when my stomach is full.

LEICHHARDT: But when we are waiting so idle and little but sleeping is done, such a quantity of damper cannot agree with the stomach.

BUNCE: Perhaps you are right. I'll have some black pudding instead. There's one left from this morning.

MANN *comes, a bag of flour on his shoulders.*

MANN: That belongs to Dr Leichhardt.

LEICHHARDT: I cannot eat.

MANN: It's the last one.

LEICHHARDT: Out of thirty?

BUNCE: We had to eat them, they were going off.

LEICHHARDT: Is too rich for my stomach.

BUNCE: I'll cut it into three then.

MANN: Not for me either.

BUNCE: I might as well just eat it.

Before he can, MANN *who has crouched to slip the flour bag off his shoulders crashes to the ground with its weight. He doesn't let go of the bag because he can't.* BUNCE *goes to help him.*

His joints have locked up again.

They have to prise his fingers open to release the bag. This particularly interesting symptom which only MANN *manifested, meant that when he was afflicted he was literally stuck until someone came and straightened him out.*

LEICHHARDT: Why you bring all this flour?

MANN: To show you it has become rancid.

LEICHHARDT: Then better throw away.

BUNCE: No, no. We can use it to thicken soups and stews.

LEICHHARDT: It only causes sickness.

MANN: There are only two hundred pounds left that are good.

They are further distracted from MANN *by a gunshot.*

LEICHHARDT: At last. Providence smiles on me.

BOEKING *comes running, still pulling up his trousers.*

BOEKING: Hely and Brown! Hely and Brown!

LEICHHARDT: Go and help them, quick. Did they bring the cattle?

BOEKING: I didn't see.

On the way BUNCE *stuffs the last of the sausage in his mouth.*

What are you eating? The blutwurst.

BUNCE: Sorry, none left.

LEICHHARDT: I must run, too.

MANN *still on the ground as he fell.*

MANN: Could you help me up first?

LEICHHARDT: I have never seen this.

MANN: Something to do with the fever. It has happened before, but
    not as badly as this.

LEICHHARDT: How very odd.

MANN: Usually it's only one arm or leg and I can free it myself.

LEICHHARDT *manages to sit* MANN *up but when he tries to lift
    him, he farts.*

LEICHHARDT: I can't lift. You must sit.

MANN: Before the others come. I have been weighing our stores,
    except for the sugar.

LEICHHARDT: Sugar I have taken charge of myself.

MANN: Yes, I know. And the tapioca. Why won't you let me weigh
    them out? It looks as though you distrust my management of
    stores.

LEICHHARDT: I have reasons. You are only second-in-command. I
    am first.

HELY *and* BROWN *come, supported by* BUNCE *and* BOEKING. *With rolled blankets on their back and guns over their shoulders they are a picture of misery and defeat.*

Thank God you are returned safely.

BUNCE: They didn't bring any cattle.

LEICHHARDT: Not a one?

BOEKING: They coming on foot. Without horses.

HELY: They ran off two nights ago. You can imagine it was indeed a nice situation, for two sick men to be left in a place they had never been before, no horses, no food, hardly able to walk a hundred yards and uncertain where the party was.

BROWN: This time we thought we done for, boss.

HELY: Until this morning when we realised we were three miles from the camp.

LEICHHARDT: What about the cattle?

HELY: There hasn't been a day go by when one or other of us hasn't been ill. At first Brown was too unwell to travel, then I was utterly unable to proceed. Brown was ill again and I became very ill with the most violent fever and ague, utterly unable to move. After that Brown was dreadfully ill, vomiting continually, and I succumbed to a sharp attack of terrible fever, burning fever. And when Brown finally recovered from being excessively ill I was entirely prostrated. It was then I decided to return as it was perfectly useless for two sick men to crawl on day after day after a mob of cattle which were already a long way off and every day going further.

MANN: Did you see any cattle?

HELY: Hardly a trace.

LEICHHARDT: Now my stomach is turned completely around. With the goats and sheep abandoned, we can go nowhere without cattle. I will pursue them myself tomorrow.

HELY: Brown and I haven't eaten in days. We are also entitled to the rations we missed out on.

LEICHHARDT: [*goes*] Mr Mann is in charge of stores.

MANN: Except sugar.

BUNCE: I'm afraid Mann is stuck again.

HELY: I demand justice. Brown and I have starved for five days—

MANN: Help me up and I'll see to it.

BUNCE: If you're in a hurry I think we might have to carry him.

   As they go.

HELY: You can't imagine how I've looked forward to those black puddings I saw you making when we left.

SCENE THIRTEEN

Holiday camp. Perhaps there is a tent or two off to one side or perhaps it is just a clearing. A bed roll or two.

EDVARDS *and* LAUMA *return from swimming. She has a towel wrapped round her and carries her sandals. He is wearing a shirt and carrying sandshoes and a towel. She is having difficulty walking over the stony ground.*

EDVARDS: Aah, soft city feet. You're not a peasant after all.

LAUMA: I never said I was.

EDVARDS: You said you could take this life in the wilds.

LAUMA: I can, and I will once my feet harden like your soul.

EDVARDS: Wait. Stop, OK. I can't bear to watch any more. You'll fall and break an ankle.

LAUMA: Are you going to carry me?

EDVARDS: I'd have a heart attack and when I dropped you, you'd have a cracked skull. Let me just put your shoes on.

LAUMA: My feet are wet and dirty.

EDVARDS: I will wipe them clean, OK.

   The way he does this is similar to the way he might inspect a horse's hoof. He uses his towel to wipe each foot in turn, putting the towel on the ground so she can stand on it to put on each sandal.

LAUMA: What are you doing? It tickles.

EDVARDS: How many years since I shod such a beauty?

LAUMA: Charming. Did you always kiss your horse's feet.

EDVARDS: That gives you away. Horses don't have feet.

LAUMA: But do witches have hooves?

EDVARDS: Not as pretty as these.

LAUMA: If you keep doing that I'll fall over.

EDVARDS: Not here, the ground's too rocky.

LAUMA: Is that all you ever think of?

EDVARDS: We'll never be as young again. I missed you. A week alone with Otto And Lydia can't have been fun.

LAUMA: I went, what do you call it, "snorkelling" on the Barrier Reef.

EDVARDS: I'll take you every day if you like.

LAUMA: I'm not trying to ensnare you.

EDVARDS: You don't have to try.

LAUMA: I'm not a witch.

EDVARDS: No of course not. I meant I already am ensnared. I'm trying to entice you. Entrap you. [*Embraces her wildly.*] "Wrap your arms around me / Wrap! / Every blood vessel steams and shouts" or words to that effect—

LAUMA: You forgot the first line, "Sacred is that moment that sweet suffering knows."

EDVARDS: To hell with the suffering and please let the devil quote his own scripture. "—shouts / Offer me, offer me your lips / Offer!" Offer me, offer, that's what it says.

LAUMA: [*kissing him*] Yes, all right, yes. And what about the rest?

EDVARDS: That's the bit I know. I'm a slow student, OK.

LAUMA: I wouldn't say that.

EDVARDS: Something about sin that isn't sin that makes us give in to sin. God let me sin like this to the end of my days. That last part I made up, OK.

LAUMA: OK. "Everything on earth contains this power / Protect it, and do not judge us / It flows through the night and through our flesh."

EDVARDS: Ah yes, flesh I remember that. "Flows over sorrow and over joy." Something something and again: "Wrap! Wrap your arms around me." And don't let go. Don't ever let me move one step away from you.

LAUMA: You know I can't promise you that.

EDVARDS: Why?

LAUMA: My travel permit won't let me stay.

EDVARDS: Paperwork. Ruth can fix that, OK?

LAUMA: Besides there's my family, my children and grand children.

EDVARDS: Of course, of course. I keep forgetting we're not young puppies. I know. We'll bring them all out, on the family reunion plan, set them free. OK. Otto can afford it no matter what Lydia says.

> ARMAND *enters, on his way through with some sketching equipment and a carry bag.*

ARMAND: Morning. Don't mind me.

EDVARDS: [*accent*] Hey photograph. Where is your camera?

ARMAND: A photograph of the happy couple.

EDVARDS: Tell us when to smile.

ARMAND: [*takes a photo of them*] You haven't stopped. Good swim was it? Or have you both got tight skin?

EDVARDS: It wasn't the fountain of youth, but it was the next best thing.

ARMAND: Might try it myself later.

EDVARDS: It only works if you go in with a partner.

ARMAND: I don't want to be any younger. It's taken me this long to get as smart as I am now.

LAUMA: There is an Indian saying that life without love is like a stunted tree growing in rocky soil.

ARMAND: I'm in the right landscape.

EDVARDS: You want me to translate.

LAUMA: I can see. Artists like to be unhappy in love. It helps their work.

ARMAND: Maybe I'm not an artist.

ILSE: [*enters*] I thought we were all going for a walk.

EDVARDS: I'm ready. I only have to put my shoes on.

LAUMA: I have to go and change. I won't be long.

EDVARDS: Don't run, don't run. Even if you take your time we'll still be waiting for Lydia.

> *He watches her go.*

ILSE: Poetry in motion.

ARMAND: Don't wait for me. I'm going to see if inspiration strikes. It hasn't yet. Maybe lightning will instead. [*Goes.*]

ILSE: Trees or rocks today?

EDVARDS: Rocks are easier. They don't rush about so much.

ARMAND: What is it Dad says, "A tree is a tree." Like a true Australian. At least I inherited something from him.

ILSE: Are you in love?

EDVARDS: We never speak the word.

ILSE: Nor did we. Do you say to her what you would say to me?

EDVARDS: No. It is never the same with another person. You know that.

ILSE: Why is it we never dare say aloud the most precious words?

EDVARDS: Because then we would have to live by them or with the knowledge we had betrayed ourselves. It is easier to betray another.

ILSE: One of us must have gone mad. How could we allow this? You—you're my joy, my happiness.

EDVARDS: [*going to her*] You shouldn't have come.

ILSE: [*kissing his hands*] It's worse when I don't know what you're up to.

EDVARDS: [*breaking away*] Someone will see us.

ILSE: I don't care. You're mine. I love you. See what you made me do. I've said it now. And I wasn't struck dead. I'll live to finish my house. If you don't want me to live in it that's all right. Yours is nicer anyway. What a beautiful day this is. It's not too hot for a good long walk. You'll probably need a hat. Let me do your shoes up. Please. I really can't bear to see you with her.

EDVARDS: Be sensible, be reasonable.

ILSE: I can do that. Put on a brave face. I can smile and joke with the best of them.

EDVARDS: We are such good friends.

ILSE: Is it that you want to hurt me?

EDVARDS: I hoped you'd understand.

ILSE: I can understand it if you do. I've hurt you. I don't know why. As you said, it was easier. I can be strong. I've been strong over the years. We both have. Don't look at me like that. I know I'm raving like a mad person. She is leaving in a day or two. Or however long it takes before none of us can stand each other's company. I don't mind so much, if you don't love her. This air, this sunshine. It really puts new life into old bones.

EDVARDS: [*going*] I'll see if Lauma's ready.

ILSE: You really ought to remember you're no spring chicken. I hope you're pacing yourself.

> KARL *enters with a folding chair, the racing form and a small transistor which he is already listening to with an earplug.*

Where are you going with that?

KARL: No one seems to have reserved this spot.

ILSE: We're all going for a walk.

KARL: What for?

ILSE: To have a look around, at the birds, the trees. The rocks.

KARL: I went for a walk yesterday. What's going to be different? A tree is a tree.

ILSE: Why isn't a horse a horse? You even back the same ones half the time.

KARL: In different races, and half the time they win. Now if you don't mind I want to get the scratchings.

ILSE: Did I tell you to come over here?

KARL: Otto and Lydia were fighting so much over there I couldn't hear.

ILSE: Why did we come if you're just going to sit around growing fat?

KARL: It was your idea. I didn't want to come and watch you make a fool of yourself.

ILSE: What do you mean?

KARL: Following Edvards and Lauma around all the time.

ILSE: We're all together, aren't we? We haven't been here before. Besides it was Edvards' idea and who knows when we'll see Otto and Lydia again?

KARL: I don't mind if it's another thirty years. Nothing is good enough for them.

ILSE: That's just Lydia.

KARL: They come up here in their fancy car boasting about everything they've got and where they've been and they're still not happy. If I had half—

ILSE: You would've had if you hadn't stuck it up a horse's backside or leaked it up against a wall.

KARL: If we've got nothing we should be ecstatic. But we have the sour demeanour of multi-millionaires. I'd much rather have the money. I really don't know why you wanted to come—

ILSE: You don't know or you can't say? Not while you're sober.

KARL: I can easily fix that.

Pause.

Now I've missed the scratchings for race three.

ILSE: You can't place a bet out here anyway.

KARL: No but I can still try to pick the winners, and listen to the races. You'll be doing what you want so you can allow me this one small pleasure. What harm can it do?

ILSE: At least you can't lose any money.

KARL: True enough. And it is only a small pleasure. You are my main one.

ILSE: Funny way of showing it.

KARL: Small pleasures are easier to manage. But I do still love you. Always have. Probably always will.

ILSE: What can be keeping them?

KARL: Can you believe that?

ILSE: What?

KARL: Randwick is rained out. Edvards and Lauma don't need a chaperone, Ilse.

ILSE: You want me to sit with you listening to horses?

KARL: You might bring me luck.

ILSE: I haven't for thirty years.

KARL: That's true.

OTTO: [*enters*] Lydia isn't coming.

ILSE: I don't know what's keeping Edvards and Lauma.

KARL: Go and look.

ILSE: Karl isn't coming either.

OTTO: She didn't sleep well.

KARL: I heard. Too hot, too many mosquitoes, you name it.

OTTO: I probably should stay with her.

KARL: Should've strangled her years ago.

ILSE: Leave her with Karl. He knows how to handle women.

> EDVARDS *and* LAUMA *enter.*

EDVARDS: If we're going we're going, OK.

OTTO: Hang on, Lydia's not ready. [*Calls.*] Lydia, we're going.

LYDIA: [*off*] Go then, go.

ILSE: Karl and Lydia aren't going.

OTTO: Lydia! We're not waiting.

LAUMA: We're going, Otto.

> *They go.*

OTTO: I'm not staying with her when she's in that mood. [*Stays.*]

KARL: Lydia's always in that mood.

> OTTO *goes after the* OTHERS. *No sooner is he out of sight than* LYDIA *hurries on.*

LYDIA: Oh, they've gone.

KARL: Yes.

LYDIA: They didn't wait.

KARL: No.

LYDIA: Did you see which way they went?

KARL: That way.

LYDIA: I can't see them.

KARL: I'm sure Otto's walking backwards keeping an eye out for you.

LYDIA: I'll strangle him.

KARL: Don't get lost now.

LYDIA: When he gets back. I didn't want to go anyway.

KARL: A tree is a tree.

LYDIA: At least you're here.

KARL: Mmmm.

LYDIA: What are we going to do left to ourselves?

KARL: Bored already?

LYDIA: Who knows how long they'll be?

KARL: Mmmm. Hours probably.

LYDIA: Is that what you're going to do the whole time?

KARL: I've got all the scratchings now. The races don't start for an hour or two. What did you have in mind?

LYDIA: If I had anything in mind do you think I wouldn't be doing it?

KARL: It's up to me then?

Pause.

No. Can't think of anything.

LYDIA: You could at least offer me a seat.

KARL: [*rising*] Would you like to sit down Lydia?

LYDIA: No I don't think so. What's happened to you Karl?

KARL: [*shrugs*] When someone asks that they're usually about to tell you.

LYDIA: You used to be so full of drive, so full of schemes.

KARL: I was a cheap hustler who always got himself into trouble. Now I keep out of trouble.

LYDIA: And so charming, in a rough sort of way.

KARL: That's a nice outfit you have on Lydia. Far too nice for bushwalking.

LYDIA: That's more how I remember you. No woman was safe alone with you.

KARL: You're quite safe now.

LYDIA: I remember one night I was looking for Otto you came up behind me, took hold of my breast and said, "You can't be happy with that weed."

KARL: I was much more instinctive in those days.

LYDIA: Why are we talking about that?

KARL: What else have we got to talk about?

LYDIA: Nothing.

KARL: Unless you follow the horses.

LYDIA: No I don't.

KARL: Nothing to talk about.

LYDIA: I read somewhere, when people make love they talk even less.

KARL: You mean our conversation would be even shorter? Not that I was suggesting—

LYDIA: No, nor was I.

Pause.

It could hardly be much shorter.

KARL: No, I suppose not.

LYDIA: I suppose if we were younger—

KARL: We'd have gone with the others.

LYDIA: And if fate had thrown us together—

KARL: And I was my old, well, younger instinctive self. I could kiss you, see if something stirs.

LYDIA: Why not?

> *They kiss. Lingeringly but without much passion.* ARMAND *enters. stops and watches.* KARL *and* LYDIA *break, look at each other and laugh.*

KARL: No.

LYDIA: Not for me either.

KARL: Sorry. Pretty silly activity when you think about it.

LYDIA: Yes. That's probably why it's best not to think about it.

KARL: We could try again.

LYDIA: No. I think I'll go lie down with a magazine.

KARL: I won't disturb you. We do get sillier as we get older.

LYDIA: [*going*] That's not all.

> As KARL *sits down he notices* ARMAND.

KARL: Jesus Christ! How long have you been standing there?

ARMAND: Not long. I'm sorry, I didn't think there was anyone left here.

KARL: It wasn't really how it seemed.

ARMAND: Nothing ever is. I couldn't imagine you and Lydia—

KARL: Neither could I. That's why I had to try it. I imagined it once, years ago. Not any more. Still it's not the sort of thing you do everyday. Made me feel, almost young again. [*Sits down with the racing form guide.*] Maybe today's my lucky day.

> ARMAND *puts down his sketching equipment.*

ARMAND: I might as well tell you now that you're here.

KARL: I've always been here. I sometimes wonder if you are. You appear to be with us and yet you aren't. You're always seeing something else. Through the lens of that damned camera. It's bad manners. [*Beat.*] You didn't take any photos of me and Lydia?

ARMAND: No. I didn't.

KARL: Too bad. Now it's her word against mine. I would have loved to have had one over her. Never mind.

ARMAND: I wanted to tell you I'm going back.

KARL: I don't think your mother's ready to go home yet. She's still climbing trees.

ARMAND: Back to London.

KARL: [*pause, accent*] That is shock.

ARMAND: I came back to try and see things differently, to try and... paint, but it's like I can't see at all. My hand and eye... well forget it, could belong to different bodies, on different continents, and drifting further and further apart. I'd settle for some childlike smear on the wall. I can barely make a mark. I'll probably go back to the same hospital in London.

KARL: [*accent*] But why? We could help set you up in practice. Mum would want to do that.

ARMAND: I could get a job here if I wanted it. I don't want to be here. It'd make me think... that I'd failed. At least I was doing something there. Working.

KARL: [*accent*] Well, if that's how it's to be. You be doing what you training for. I sure you good doctor. It's honourable profession. The painting, well, I think Mum be sorry about that. Can always paint in your spare time.

ARMAND: Yeah.

KARL: [*accent*] If must go so far for work, you must. I'm sure Mum understand. I better start saving so we can visit. Especially if grandchildrens coming. I should be placing bets today. I have that feeling. Lady luck is with me.

SCENE FOURTEEN

Explorers' camp.

BUNCE *comes cautiously.*

BUNCE: They've gone. Poor Brown didn't want to go.

HELY *and* BOEKING *half carrying* MANN *who has the scales.*

HELY: They won't find any cattle.

MANN: The Doctor keeps the sugar among his own packs.

BUNCE: [*finds it*] He left it behind.

      MANN *is perched on some stores, the scales taken from him.*

MANN: At the time we crossed the MacKenzie the sugar weighed fifty pounds, exclusive of the bag.

HELY: What does it weigh now?

BOEKING: Only twenty-seven pounds.

HELY: Twenty-seven pounds?

MANN: Only three pounds have been used for puddings over Easter.

HELY: Singlehandedly he has eaten twenty pounds in seven weeks!

BUNCE: This comes very hard.

BOEKING: He help himself when he likes.

HELY: He is a remarkably selfish man where eating is concerned.

BUNCE: It was distinctly understood we were all to share alike.

HELY: Boeking made thirty large black puddings but not one morsel was saved for me.

MANN: We all ate them.

HELY: At his insistence.

BOEKING: We didn't eat the sugar.

BUNCE: And he would not allow one spoonful of sugar at any time to be given to the invalids.

HELY: [*to* MANN] Open the bag so we can have our share.

BOEKING: Ja is only fair.

MANN: I cannot allow that.

HELY: You betrayed us once John Mann when we were resolved to go back.

MANN: We all compromised.

BUNCE: To go on while supplies lasted.

BOEKING: Half one bag of sugar will not last four thousand miles.

HELY: We have two years still to travel. If we're to have any sugar at all we'll have to help ourselves.

BOEKING: I say open the bag.

      HELY *and* BOEKING *open the bag and begin to eat sugar by the handful.* BUNCE *stands back.*

MANN: I am still second-in-command—

HELY: Then you should take us back.

MANN: —and in charge of stores.

> BOEKING *tries to feed* MANN *a mouthful.*

BOEKING: Then we make sure you get your share. Bunce?

HELY: Mr Bunce?

BUNCE: [*joining in*] Our flour will only last another month.

HELY: Then let's go on. It's only another four thousand miles.

BOEKING: Ja, is big shops on the way.

MANN: We'll all suffer for this.

HELY: What suffering have we not endured? What sickness? What privations? We can endure no more.

BOEKING: This will sweeten you.

HELY: We would be worse than madmen to go on.

> *A rumble of thunder. A flash of lightning and fast approaching rain.*

MANN: Cover the meat. We must cover the meat or it will be ruined.

BOEKING: Hurry, hurry or will be full of maggots.

> *A flurry of activity as the wind and rain come. Tents and tarpaulins are thrown over the frames and stores. Initially all except* MANN *help. They just throw a tarp over him where he sits.*

BUNCE: This expedition appears to be accompanied by nothing but misfortune. The moment the meat is almost dried rain comes and spoils it.

HELY: What are we doing? What are we doing?

BOEKING: We saving the meat.

HELY: What for?

BUNCE: You eat meat as well.

> *As the storm breaks over them* HELY *begins to uncover the meat and stores.*

HELY: Then we'll have to go on.

BOEKING: What you do now? Everything get wet.

HELY: That's the only one way to stop the madman.

BUNCE: Everything will be ruined. There'll be nothing left to eat.
MANN: Then we'll have to go back.

> BOEKING *and* HELY *wreck the camp, throwing everything about.* BUNCE *follows ineffectually in their wake.*

BUNCE: You are all madmen! Madmen.

> *Through the gloom and fury of the storm we also catch glimpses of* EDVARDS *and* LAUMA *running and sheltering from the rain.* ILSE *calling and looking for them.*

ILSE: Edvards! Come back.

> *Whenever she gets close they run away from her.*

ILSE: I won't play this game.
OTTO: Ilse, come on. Let's go back.
ILSE: Edvaaards!

> *She stops in frustration and defeat.* OTTO *leads her away.*

OTTO: I'm sure they'll be all right. Let's get out of here.

> *As they go,* EDVARDS *and* LAUMA *follow close behind.*

SCENE FIFTEEN

Holiday camp.

In disarray. The tents and bedding blown into the trees. The storm is abating. KARL, ARMAND *and* LYDIA *are sheltering under a collapsed tent. It rises and* ARMAND *looks out from under it.*

ARMAND: Otto! Mum! Over this way. We're over here.

> *A wet and bedraggled* OTTO *comes towards the camp, leading* ILSE. *The three under the tent make room for them.*

OTTO: Thank God, thank God! We made it Ilse. We made it.
ARMAND: You all right Mum?
ILSE: Just wet and cold.
OTTO: You thought we were lost but good old Otto pulled through.

ILSE: Pulled me through the middle of a storm. I couldn't get you to stop.

ARMAND: I'm afraid there's nothing to dry you with.

LYDIA: Stop shaking yourself like a dog. You're soaking wet.

OTTO: You might have noticed that it's raining Lydia.

LYDIA: I noticed. You might have noticed that there are now five of us in the same small tent.

OTTO: We might have been killed out there.

LYDIA: We might just as easily have been killed waiting for you to come back.

KARL: Will you two shut up? I'm listening to the last race.

OTTO: The what? What about Ilse?

KARL: She's back safe and sound no thanks to you.

OTTO: What do you mean?

KARL: Why couldn't you wait till the storm was over? She could have been struck by lightning or a tree could have fallen on her.

OTTO: Who are you to talk to me like that?

KARL: I'm the winner of 119,372 dollars, that's who. And I've got every last cent riding on the last race.

ILSE: What are you blathering about now?

KARL: I've picked clean winners all day. Armand has kept the tally so it's all above board. I started with one hundred dollars and built my stake race by race. Even the interference from the storm hasn't broken my run of luck. Sshh! [*Listens to his radio.*]

LYDIA: Where are Edvards and Lauma?

OTTO: We lost them.

LYDIA: How? What do you mean lost them?

ILSE: I think it would be fairer to say they lost us. Deliberately. They gave us the slip before the storm.

OTTO: I had a stone in my shoe and Ilse waited for me. We didn't see them again.

LYDIA: Aren't you going to look for them?

OTTO: Where? It's still raining.

LYDIA: You're already wet.

KARL: Sshhh! A little quiet if you please?

ILSE: Shush yourself.

ARMAND: Do you see what I see?

ILSE: Where?

LYDIA: What is it?

ARMAND: Storm gods by the look of it.

OTTO: Lauma and Edvards.

LYDIA: What happened to them?

ILSE: A tree must've fallen on them.

> LAUMA *and* EDVARDS *enter. They have covered themselves with leaves and vines, in their clothes and hair. Those in the tent edge closer to see, taking* KARL *with them.*

KARL: Where are you all going now?

ILSE: Can't you see who's back?

OTTO: Stop pulling, I'm getting wet.

ILSE: Worse than children. The older they get the stupider they get.

ARMAND: They're only having fun.

> EDVARDS *and* LAUMA *dance around in the rain laughing and singing "Perkonitis" and splashing those under the tent. In trying to get away, those under the tent trip each other up and they fall in a heap.* EDVARDS *and* LAUMA *help them up.* ILSE *just stands in the rain.*

> "Perkonitis"

> Perkonitis ducinaj
> Visu garu vasarin.
> Lai rib tautu istabina
> Jele sadu vakarin.

> Ko dosimi perkonam
> Par vasaras graudumin?
> Sieku rudzu, sieku miezu,
> Pusbirkava apenis.

LYDIA: I hope you're happy now we're all wet.

EDVARDS: The rain is warm.

OTTO: [*to* LAUMA] Where'd you get to? I was worried about you.

LAUMA: I was perfectly safe all the time.

ILSE: You ran away from us deliberately.

EDVARDS: The wood nymphs would have protected you. They followed you all the way back so you didn't come to harm.

ILSE: [*slaps him hard*] I'm not a child for you to play games with.

Pause.

EDVARDS: OK, I'm sorry.

LAUMA: So am I. I'm sorry, Otto. Ilse. We didn't mean any harm. We didn't think.

There is a strangled cry and much thrashing under the tent.

EDVARDS: What the hell is that?

ARMAND: It's Dad. He probably just lost his 120,000 dollars.

They help KARL *get himself untangled. He makes their task harder by struggling to free himself and shouting.*

KARL: I won! I won! I'm rich. Lydia I'm rich. Ilse, just think of it. Over half a million in one afternoon. Armand can work it out.

ILSE: Play money. Invisible play money. You're a fool.

KARL: I picked clean winners all afternoon. My luck is back after thirty years. We'll be rich in no time.

ILSE: What kind of luck is it that lets you pick winners when you can't get to lay a single bet?

KARL: You're right, it's rotten luck. But I didn't want to believe that.

LYDIA: Otto, I've just about had all I can stand of life in the wilds. I need a hot bath.

OTTO: I'll just go and run it, dear.

LAUMA: I have something to tell you, that might make you feel happier.

LYDIA: Don't tell me you're getting married?

EDVARDS: Not yet.

LAUMA: Otto, Lydia, I don't know how to say this, but you don't have to take me round on your holiday any more.

OTTO: Why?

EDVARDS: Lauma has decided to spend the rest of her time here with me.

OTTO: We haven't seen everything we planned yet.

EDVARDS: I'll show her round, OK. Relieve you to pursue your other obligations.

ILSE: I think it's time we all went home.

ARMAND: Look at the mess in this camp.

They begin to clean up. The sun even shines.

LAUMA: [*to* OTTO] I thought you'd be pleased.

OTTO: I am, for you. If that's what you want to do.

EDVARDS: What will you do?

OTTO: Lydia and I could continue the trip on our own, just the two of us. We've never really done that.

LYDIA: No. I couldn't bear it. I want to go home. Back to Sydney. The sooner the better.

OTTO: You know why I insisted we come up here, Lydia?

LYDIA: For Lauma. She's found better company. We're free to go.

OTTO: For us, you and me. The best years of our life, the most exciting time, was just after the war and our first years here, amongst friends. All the rest has been hard work, the daily grind, year in, year out, including living with you. Because we have a kind of sickness, us and our friends too. We had such dreams, such will to live life to the full, and look at us. Washed up after a storm. We have everything we could wish for in life, houses, cars, every gadget, except a sense of joy or wonder. We used to have that. But when we came to this country thirty years ago, we all had it. That was the biggest decision we ever made. The only real decision, and having made it we let life roll on. Now it's gone. We let it slip from our grasp. We all let it slip. And we all know this, deep in ourselves. Maybe Edvards and Lauma will rediscover it. Lydia and I went looking, in Latvia and now here. But we didn't find any joy or wonder because we're overcome by this disease, this inertia and worst of all I know I haven't the will to overcome it. I wish you better luck.

OTTO *goes and* LYDIA *follows.*

LYDIA: Otto, wait.

The OTHERS *go back to packing.*

KARL: I wasn't really lucky. I did cheat, I picked one or two winners and pretended that the others won. I wanted to show them I still had what it takes, but I probably never did. Who would have thought Otto would turn out to be such a philosopher? I suppose that's what money does for a man. Or a wife who doesn't love him.

ILSE: How does a man know if his wife loves him or not?

KARL: Look I'm not complaining.

ILSE: But how would you know? I need to know that.

KARL: I don't know.

ILSE: Then maybe I can still learn. If it's not too late.

SCENE SIXTEEN

BROWN *comes bringing* LEICHHARDT'*s coat. The cleaning up of the previous scene stops. The* WOMEN *help the* EXPLORERS *into their coats and with their swags.*

LEICHHARDT: With Brown I brought four bullocks, of the thirty-six. In the capture of these four cattle I saw the smile of Providence. With sixteen or eighteen I would continue to Swan River. With eight or ten I might explore further the reaches of the Burdekin and Isaac. If only these four are to be had I can still trace the MacKenzie to the coast. All plans were annihilated by arrival to the camp.

The EXPLORERS *join* LEICHHARDT. *The* WOMEN *clear the camp.*

MANN: It is a dreadful sight to see four or five persons lying down like a lot of pigs, groaning and moaning and not able to help themselves or each other.

BOEKING *just stands and looks.* LYDIA *helps the other* WOMEN.

BUNCE: I am anxious to proceed, but I feel myself called upon to prevent a sacrifice of human life to join them in returning. We have been out nine months and from sickness have made about three months progress. This day I add myself again to the number of invalids.

BOEKING: Really it is horrible to think of. We cannot do otherwise than return.

LEICHHARDT: This was the camp from which I had hoped to strike westwards. I saw no other course but to return to the Downs.

HELY: Heaven send we may get in safe and with good speed.

LEICHHARDT: One final irony. It was while searching for the mules and horses for our return. We had been gone a week.

BROWN: Look boss. Whole big mob of cattle. We go get him?

LEICHHARDT: I was tempted. It was the whole herd, less the four at the camp. No. I promised to return. And God was laughing in my ears.

    All except LEICHHARDT *and* MANN *go.*

At least now we travel with speed. In only seven days we have gone back one hundred and twenty miles. In nine months we barely made six hundred. No doubt the idea of returning home has a favourable influence on my companions.

    ILSE *comes with* ARMAND's *suitcase.*

MANN: Do not let us go back with nothing to show for our trouble. We could take a tour to the west, to the desert if possible, then south to the Darling River.

LEICHHARDT: You want to play leader? You have not the vision for it.

MANN: Where was your vision out on the plain?

    ILSE *brings clothes and* ARMAND *packs his suitcase.*

LEICHHARDT: That is where you must seek it. It does not reveal itself to the half-hearted discoverer. It is not to be bought in some catalogue. On my first journey I kept my eye on the horizon and the country's secrets were revealed to me and my spirit was lifted. This time, I allowed myself to be dragged down into the everyday, the mundane, the banal. I watched the ground under my feet for signs of hidden dangers. It was inevitable I should fall. Once down I could not raise my head again. But in my end is my beginning. This is my country to discover. It is my destiny and no one can turn me from it. Immediately on my return I will raise a new party and set out again for Swan River.

ARMAND*'s suitcase is packed.*

MANN: I would be willing to start with you again. But we'd have to put matters on a different footing.

ARMAND / MANN: If you really are set upon returning, then the sooner done the better.

SCENE SEVENTEEN

Airport terminal. TIM *enters to* ARMAND. *The usual airport terminal noises, garbled voices.*

TIM: Ruth got held up in some meeting. As usual. But she'll get here in time. As usual. Business as usual. Life goes on. Never a dull moment. Well unfortunately there are. Far too many of them. More than exciting ones. Waiting at airports is one. Of the dull ones. No reflection on the company. Do you feel like a drink?

ARMAND: No thanks.

TIM: You mind if I have one?

ARMAND: No go ahead.

TIM: Aren't you coming?

ARMAND: I'd rather not go to the bar.

TIM: Then I'd better not. You haven't checked your luggage in.

ARMAND: Plenty of time.

TIM: I suppose. Hey, I've been meaning to ask what you're doing about your Mercedes when it arrives?

ARMAND: I'm leaving it with Dad, till I can sell it.

TIM: That'll stir them up at the mill, a wog labourer driving round in a Merc.

ARMAND: He can enjoy it for a while. He deserves it.

TIM: Getting excited?

ARMAND: Scared I think.

TIM: They reckon that's another name for "excitement". I reckon excitement smells better. Not that I'm suggesting you have a bad odour.

Pause.

You seem pretty close.

ARMAND: Sorry?

TIM: To Ruth. Close to Ruth.

ARMAND: Not really.

TIM: She seemed to think so.

ARMAND: Oh.

TIM: You might've noticed we've been having one or two problems.

ARMAND: Yes I did.

TIM: Did she say anything to you?

ARMAND: Not much.

TIM: She thinks it's to do with my experience in Vietnam.

ARMAND: Does she?

TIM: Yeah. Wounded in the head. Only kidding. I didn't have an experience in Vietnam. I'm not saying I would've liked to, not like that. Luckily or otherwise I just didn't have one. But if I had, she'd have an excuse.

ARMAND: For what?

TIM: Spending all these years looking after me. I don't know what to do. I've tried having a nervous breakdown but it's just not in my nature. More in yours I reckon.

ARMAND: You reckon?

TIM: Shit, look at you! You're leaving a country you don't know if you like, going back to a woman you don't know if you love, to live in another country you don't know if you like, and to a job you know you hate. Seems to me this trip doesn't have a lot going for it.

ARMAND: Put like that it doesn't.

TIM: Let me put it another way. If you stay here you could still be in a country you didn't know if you liked, doing a job you knew you hated. That's mortal. We're all doing that. And you'd save yourself a few thousand bucks. The variable is the woman and I can't help you there. I need help myself. But I doubt if she can fix it so you get to love the country or the job, let alone the country and the job. And if you stayed and did what you thought you loved or even what you thought you had to do, who knows what could happen? You could make all the difference. Move the picture just a bit for all of us. We're all living outside the frame. Why don't I go find you a book.

> *He goes and the* TRAVELLERS *of Scene One appear. They are on board ship. We hear the steady throb of the engines, a makeshift band, crowd noise and seagulls. The women are together as are the men. The scene is played around* ARMAND.

LYDIA: Air! We're practically in the engine room. And those beds. This narrow and stacked one on top of the other like meat trays.

RUTH: It was a troop ship, Lydia, not a cruise liner.

ILSE: Women are already being seasick down there and we're still tied to the wharf.

LYDIA: It's because the air is so foul and hot. Is that to get us used to Australia by the time we get there?

ILSE: Don't make a fuss. It's the same for everyone.

LYDIA: No it isn't. They put us women on the bottom and the men on top.

RUTH: Now that's so you'll get used to Australia.

EDVARDS: The last few days have been unbearable. I never imagined I'd get to the top of the gangway without a hand clamping my shoulder, saying I couldn't go.

KARL: I'll always wonder if I made a mistake. I was making a good living here and maybe I could've gone to America.

OTTO: You'll never know. After three years of waiting, I'd go to Timbuctoo.

> *A loudspeaker announcement in German. Overlapping.*

ILSE: It's happening!

LYDIA: We're leaving.

EDVARDS: I can't believe it, OK?

RUTH: Getting away at last.

OTTO: Lydia, we're going.

KARL: What are those ropes? Seems to me we're still very much tied to the shore.

RUTH: Smell that fresh sea air, fresh and free.

KARL: I can only smell fear, and oil fumes.

OTTO: Go to the other side of the ship. It's open water.

ILSE: And jump in.

EDVARDS: This ship brought young men to Europe to be killed, and now it's taking back cripples to replace them.

LYDIA: There's nothing wrong with the rest of us.

KARL: What about that business with the passports? It didn't matter if you were a doctor or a baker, everyone on this ship is a labourer.

OTTO: That's the contract. Two years labour. They only need labourers.

KARL: Wouldn't you be just as good a labourer with book-keeper on your passport. Or carpenter on Edvards'.

ILSE: Or businessman?

RUTH: Is that what you told them?

ILSE: Poor Karl is in shock about not going to New York or Hollywood. He's having Australian nightmares instead of American dreams.

Another loudspeaker announcement in German. A blast on the ship's horn.

OTTO: They're dropping the ropes.

A cheer, off.

EDVARDS: No turning back, OK?

ILSE: I wonder if we'll ever come back home?

They join in singing with the band music. In English.

> "Blow Breeze" [*"Put Vejini"*]
>
> Blow breeze, set sail,
> Blow breeze, set sail,
> We are leaving our home
> For a new land.
> Blow breeze, set sail,
> Blow breeze, set sail,
> The past is the past.
> A new beginning.

TIM *returns empty handed. The* TRAVELLERS *disperse.*

TIM: Plenty I'd read, nothing you'd read. Here she comes.

RUTH: [*at a rush*] I thought I was going to miss you. I had to double park.

TIM: He hasn't checked his bag in yet. Give me your ticket. I'll do it for you.

ARMAND: I'm not going.

RUTH: What?

ARMAND: I'm not going.

RUTH: But you can't. Not again.

TIM: Jesus, why can't he?

RUTH: But why?

ARMAND: I don't know.

TIM: It's a nice sunny day outside. Maybe if it was overcast—

RUTH: Oh shut up Tim.

ARMAND: It doesn't feel right. That's all.

RUTH: What about Jessica? Won't she be waiting at the airport?

TIM: Not if she's bright. It'd be a good twenty-four hours before he'd get there.

ARMAND: I'll phone her. Say I'm not coming. Say I've changed my mind. Stop looking at me like that. I already feel like an idiot. I don't have a good reason. I just have to stay.

RUTH: Well if you're sure... Mum and Dad will be happy.

TIM: You'll be here for the house warming.

ARMAND: I have to watch the plane go.

TIM: Make sure you're not on it.

RUTH: Tim.

TIM: Well if you're watching it you can't be on it. Bit like sex really.

RUTH: Why don't we have a drink.

TIM: Good idea. A bar is the best place to miss a plane from.

RUTH: Lauma's staying as well. I managed to get a six week extension on her visa.

SCENE EIGHTEEN

LAUMA: Are you painting?

ARMAND: That's hard to say. Sorry. [*Accent.*] I forget. I trying. I don't know what there comes out.

LAUMA: I meant now. I didn't want to disturb you.

ARMAND: [*accent*] I'm now not working. Only with eyes like... playing with light.

LAUMA: That can be painting.

ARMAND: Yes.

LAUMA: Are you happy you didn't go?

ARMAND: No.

LAUMA: I thought so. Why not?

ARMAND: [*accent*] I don't know. I thought, no, I think... I can't remember words. There, people, for me waited.

LAUMA: Someone you loved?

ARMAND: [*accent*] Can it be love if can turn and walk away?

LAUMA: Sometimes, I'm sure.

ARMAND: Maybe.

LAUMA: Then why didn't you go? What held you here?

ARMAND: [*accent*] I don't know. It was like, for me, there was no choosing. I must stay.

   Long pause.

LAUMA: I wish you would tell me, what you can.

ARMAND: [*accent*] I'll need translator.

LAUMA: You're going well. Slowly, slowly.

ARMAND: [*accent*] Not so much for words... When from first I came home, it was to make some big painting... Nothing. I fail. What can do? Go. And when came time, I knew, if I go, that would be not right. I knew, I thought, I would not... come back. I thought, I am turning... from family... how they here struggled. I knew that there I must start anew and they have only just start here. And I must go further. I am their... record... It was in my mind to go look at Latvia this time, but I discovered that I am Australian, more even, than Latvian. I am here. I don't know... does that, mean... sense?

LAUMA: It does, it does. Thank you.

SCENE NINETEEN

The house block.

In the film version ILSE *would be in the kitchen making and baking pirags. Here* ILSE *and* RUTH *probably meet in the garden.*

RUTH: Hello Mum.

ILSE: [*accent*] I was not expecting till tomorrow.

RUTH: I came early. I thought you might still be making pirags.

ILSE: [*accent*] I just now finish. And start to water garden.

RUTH: Then I'm too late.

ILSE: [*accent*] Not for eating.

RUTH: I thought you might need a hand.

ILSE: [*accent*] Won't be many peoples. Will be only family, Edvards and Lauma.

RUTH: I've just been up to see them.

ILSE: We haven't seen much of Edvards since the house was finished. They tend to keep to themselves.

RUTH: Lauma is going back to Latvia.

Pause.

Edvards was very upset.

Pause.

I could've arranged for her to stay. But she decided to go back.

ILSE: I warned you not to stick your nose in.

ILSE: If she had gone before that six week extension—

RUTH: They asked me to arrange that. They wanted to be together.

ILSE: But not any more.

RUTH: They both still want to be.

ILSE: And Edvards is in pieces.

RUTH: She's leaving to sort out things with her family. She was worried what might happen to them if she didn't return and re-apply officially to the Soviets to come out again.

ILSE: Then what's all the fuss? Why doesn't he just go with her and be done with it?

RUTH: It takes so long to get an entry visa at the moment.

ILSE: It's surprising you hadn't thought of that.

RUTH: Why are you so against their being together?

ILSE: They won't be, will they?

RUTH: You're jealous of Lauma.

ILSE: Yes. If you must know. Yes. But not how you think. Edvards was my companion. I didn't easily find a place in this town because I didn't speak the language. I didn't find much welcome behind the frightened smiles as they tried to understand what I was saying. It was Edvards who listened, who I talked to, about any little thing, and some as big as the world. As they say in *Women's Weekly*, I poured my heart out to him, and he took good care of it. Lauma has turned him into a silly old man who thinks he is the first to discover a secret charm in a woman's soft pocket. When she goes who will have to pick up the pieces?

RUTH: Isn't that what friends are for?

ILSE: And mothers.

RUTH: You won't have to pick up after me.

ILSE: Won't you be gone? Don't look so surprised. Everyone else's life is an open book to you, and you think yours is closed?

RUTH: Armand told you.

ILSE: You certainly didn't.

RUTH: It's no secret. Tim and I aren't getting on.

ILSE: No better or worse than usual.

RUTH: I want more than that. I'm bored. Tim will do anything I want. He always has. No discussion, no debate, whatever I suggest. Any planning, organising, even earning the money, I do the lot. And he entertained me, he made me feel good about myself, but there has to be more. I married him, but he's not my companion.

ILSE: You have your job.

RUTH: They're lawyers, Mum. The last stronghold for men. They don't have to do anything they don't want to. They have women as servants and they think they're being entertaining if they make jokes about me being one of the boys in a skirt because I refuse to do their typing or get their coffee. I've been offered the job in Canberra.

ILSE: And you wouldn't take Tim.

RUTH: I haven't accepted. The truth is, if I left him, he would miss the family more than he would miss me.

ILSE: [*accent*] Listen darling, I can't tell you how to live, but I tell you one thing and I tell you true, maybe you don't like. [*No accent.*] You are my child, and I don't like to see you unhappy, but you can't talk to people the way you do.

RUTH: Like what?

ILSE: Like they're in the witness box. It will be a hard life and you could end up very lonely.

RUTH: Why didn't you leave, Dad? You must've had your chances.

ILSE: I didn't have to. I didn't marry for feelings. All that's different now is I don't have someone to talk to. Your father and I have been forced on each other. He can be an infuriating man to live with, but we manage.

ILSE *starts to go.*

Why don't you ask him about how a man knows if his wife loves him? [*Laughs as she leaves.*]

KARL *comes.*

KARL: [*to* RUTH] She makes me sweets all the time. Puddings and cakes. Thirty years we don't have sweets now I eat four, five times a week. I don't like sweets. But what can I do? She's making these special treats, to show she loves me, so I eat them. Otherwise she'd feel discouraged, or worse, she'd get upset. She can be a very difficult woman to live with. Edvards was a true friend. To use some racing parlance, he took a lot of the sting out of the ground. What do you make of this painting Armand gave us as a house warming gift? House-filling it certainly is.

SCENE TWENTY

House block. This is the evening of the house warming party which takes place in and outside the carport where some tables and chairs have been set up. ARMAND *ministers to a smoking barbeque.*

TIM *gets* RUTH *and* ARMAND *drinks.* ILSE *brings more food to put on the table.*

ILSE: [*laughs, accent*] You should see Dad. He stands there in middle of room looking at painting. Every time he walk past he shake his head.

TIM: There's a goodly amount to shake your head at too. Must be six foot by eight foot.

RUTH: Maybe you should have sold Mum a bigger house.

ILSE: [*accent*] Don't have to worry what to put on wall.

TIM: Don't need wall. Could have saved money. I sell next week.

ILSE: [*accent*] That my painting. You leave alone, I cut your fingers off. [*Goes.*]

RUTH: She would too.

TIM: I meant sell the wall, Mum.

RUTH: [*to* ARMAND] She really likes the painting.

ARMAND: I don't think "like" is quite the word.

RUTH: She's really proud of it then. We all are, even Tim.

TIM: And I'm a yobbo Philistine.

RUTH: He was the only one who picked it was us at the beach.

ARMAND: I never said it was.

RUTH: Aren't you proud of it?

TIM: It's all the dead fish and animals lying about that have me foxed.

ARMAND: God, I bet Dad wishes I'd caught the plane. I'd better go and see. Keep an eye on the meat would you Tim?

ARMAND *goes and* TIM *tends the barbeque.*

RUTH: You embarrassed him.

TIM: I only said what I saw, said the actress to the bishop.

RUTH: I'd prefer it if you weren't going to be barman all night.

TIM: OK, some of the time I'll be cook. Jesus, I've got it! The clever little devil.

RUTH: Who?

TIM: Armand. I understand the dead things now.

RUTH: And?

TIM: All will be revealed in good time.

RUTH: Do you think there is anything wrong with us?

TIM: Your family? Oh definitely.

RUTH: You and me. Our marriage.

TIM: You don't laugh at my jokes any more.

RUTH: I've heard them all, many times.

TIM: Familiarity breeds contempt. I understand.

RUTH: I'm trying, Tim. Tonight I'm really trying.

TIM: And you're so resigned to it. We were such good friends and lovers. We used to laugh a lot. Where did all the good times go? I'm proud you got your law degree but I don't actually want one.

RUTH: What do you want?

TIM: You Ruthie, the way you were, the way we used to be.

RUTH: I'm not like that any more. Nor are we. That's what I'm trying to tell you.

TIM: OK, OK. I'll grow up. I promise.

RUTH: I've spent half my life worrying about my parents staying together and my own marriage is falling apart and all I can do is watch it happen.

TIM: [pause, going to her] Loving someone is hard, Ruthie. Especially if they're like me. But we're intelligent people. If we can't work it out...

RUTH: I can't keep Lauma in Australia. She's leaving just when Edvards is head over heels in love with her. It isn't fair.

TIM: You're a regular little Cupid you are. Who have you got lined up for Armand?

RUTH: Mary's coming up next week and I had nothing to do with it.

KARL, EDVARDS *and* ARMAND *enter, closely followed by* ILSE *and* LAUMA, *bearing more food.*

KARL: [*accent*] Hey, Tim. We getting thirsty in there.

TIM: Every man for himself tonight. I'm the cook. Doctor's orders. What'd you think of the painting, Dad?

KARL: [*accent*] It's ah… all right. It's big.

ILSE: [*accent*] Big. What is big? Say what you think.

KARL: [*accent*] What you want me to say? I don't understand how anyone can paint that. It is like nightmares. I never seen anything like. Dead animals. Maybe at the beach after floods but not with peoples sitting around eating.

ARMAND: You understand it Dad. That's all it is.

KARL: [*accent*] Funny thing, it makes me hungry.

TIM: [*holding up a chop*] What is this Dad, but dead animal? Dead meat!

ILSE: [*accent*] Burnt meat. Watch what you do. [*To* KARL.] Dad. Karl, come on. Everything is ready.

KARL: [*accent*] Before eat, Ilse says I must make speech.

EDVARDS: What are you doing? It was my spanner that built the house so I'll make the speech and tell it how it was, OK.

RUTH: No, no, no. It's Mum's house. It only happened because of her. Mum makes the speech.

ILSE: What? Yes?

ARMAND: Yes, Mum.

ILSE: [*accent*] OK. How I start? Long time I thinking what Otto said, how we have sickness, thirty years ago was best time of our lives. I tell him when we visit next January how he are wrong. I do not think he would go again through that time. I give up nothing to have that life again. I don't want. Was too hard. I have more now. I have enough. Every day is still new decision to make just to live. Always must work at something. Our childrens has grown straight. They go their own way. They make us proud. Karl never want this house. He couldn't see point. He always think go back to Latvia. We all think, but we be buried here. And when that happen I sleep peaceful. Not be so foreign soil.

Some appropriate reactions from the gathering.

EDVARDS: I think the least Karl can do now is carry her over the threshold before he has too much to drink. OK?

KARL: What're you talking about? I can carry her round the house first.

ILSE: Oh no Karl. Really. No. You'll kill yourself and me as well.

> *But he won't take no for an answer.* ILSE *gets away with* KARL *in pursuit.* ARMAND, TIM *and* RUTH *rightly figure* ILSE *and* KARL *will need help.*

ARMAND: Come on Tim. We're going to have to save at least one of them.

> *They go, leaving* EDVARDS *and* LAUMA.

EDVARDS: You are going to leave me alone for so long.

LAUMA: Why talk about it now?

EDVARDS: Because it is all I can think about, OK. Till yesterday I thought you might stay. I'm barely sixty. I could live to be a hundred. We could have forty years, a lifetime together.

LAUMA: You can come to Latvia.

EDVARDS: No. I would have nothing there, except you. No money, no house, no life. [*Sings softly.*] "Father promised, mother forbade / The suitor pleaded in tears / The suitor pleaded in tears / Counting his small change." I will bring you back. Of that you can be certain.

LAUMA: I will be waiting.

EDVARDS: A little poetry for the occasion.

LAUMA: "I would like to turn back time / And go with you once more to the birch grove / I would like to turn back the sun / And once more pick the first red bilberry / And there, where a woodpecker pecks at a dry fir tree / I would drink the forest's quiet from your hands."

EDVARDS: Poetry feeds the soul but wastes the flesh.

> *The* OTHERS *return in a ragged group.*

RUTH: [*accent*] Look at this pair. They have no shame.

EDVARDS: We have no time, OK.

RUTH: [*accent*] You could stay here, Lauma. Apply for refugee status. You don't have to go back.

ILSE: Ruth, you never know when to leave well enough alone.

LAUMA: She could be my own daughter. She has my best interests at heart. Without her help I wouldn't have had this extra time. But it's time to go back. My children and their children are waiting. If I don't go who can say what might happen to them. And if I stay who's to say I would ever see them again. You understand.

ILSE: Yes. Those of us who will never go back. I wish you luck.

LAUMA: Thank you. I wish you luck, for your new life in this house. I won't forget you, any of you.

ILSE: You'd better come back or he will be a shell.

KARL: [*calls*] Can't all that crying wait till later. Lauma doesn't go for another week. This is supposed to be a house warming not a wake.

LAUMA: Take care of Edvards.

ILSE: I know, I know.

EDVARDS: [*accent*] Armand. I need doctor. I think my heart is breaking. What is the medicine?

TIM: What about a drink?

EDVARDS: [*accent*] OK. A drink will help.

SCENE TWENTY-ONE

A continuation of the last scene except that EDVARDS *steps out and becomes* LEICHHARDT.

LEICHHARDT: Why court danger and hardship? Why endure solitude? Why deprive oneself of home, marriage, fortune? I have ever been a prisoner of the unknown. "I would not hesitate again plunging into those dreary and inhospitable regions, to be the first to place my foot in the centre of this vast territory, and finally to raise the veil which surrounds its features, although they should whither the beholder." A sentiment of Sturt, another explorer.

BROWN: Like the last of the dinosaurs, eating his way across the plain. I was reading somewhere that some German scientist reckons that no particle of energy is ever destroyed, no new particle ever created. That means that dinosaurs' energy is still with us. And the explorers' energy. So what's new? That's what we always reckoned. That's how my uncle can be a wallaby and my grandmother an owl.

SCENE TWENTY-TWO

This is also a continuation of the previous two scenes. ILSE *and* KARL *step out as though cast into the near future.*

KARL: Are you happy with the house?

ILSE: I should be asking you?

KARL: To mow the lawn every week, to wash the roof and paint the walls every few years?

ILSE: We've always done that even when it wasn't ours.

KARL: I like it, I like it. As you say it is ours. Well, we have to pay it off. I suppose that makes us true Australians.

ILSE: I would like to go back, just once more, into a birch grove to listen to the whispers of our forbears, see my parents' graves. When I last saw them they were not as old as we are now. We did what we thought we had to. I'm sure they understand.

   EDVARDS *comes.*

EDVARDS: I have a letter from Lauma. Her family cried when they saw her. I suppose they thought the blacks would get her. Or that Australia and Afghanistan were the same place.

RUTH: It doesn't look hopeful Edvards. It's not that the Russians are keeping Lauma there, it's more that they aren't letting people out. They just say make an application and it gets lost in red tape. I'll keep trying.

EDVARDS: She sent me a poem. I won't bother you with it.

   He starts to go.

ILSE: Come to lunch on Sunday.

EDVARDS: Thanks all the same but not this Sunday.

ILSE: You know you're always welcome here. Any time.

KARL: I'll see you at the pub on Friday. Just for a few drinks, I can't be staying long.

ILSE: Armand is coming up this weekend.

EDVARDS: Then perhaps I will come to lunch.

KARL: [*looking at a painting*] What are they?

ILSE: Wood nymphs. Don't you remember?

KARL: What are they doing?

ILSE: It's obvious. She's reading a poem to him while he has his hand in whatever passes for wood nymphs' pants.

KARL: Are you allowed to paint pictures like this?

ARMAND: Only in my spare time.

EDVARDS: Is it for sale?

ARMAND: You can have it.

EDVARDS: I will buy it, OK. If for no other reason than Karl thinks this is your hobby. I will buy it anyway.

ARMAND: I sold my Mercedes. For twenty thousand dollars.

KARL: That's a good price.

ILSE: What would you know?

KARL: Not very much when I look at that picture. Meat hanging in trees…

ARMAND: Don't worry about it, Dad. I'm a doctor for you and a painter for me.

ILSE: No. You must paint for all of us, what we did, how we came with a vision for a better future, how we struggled, how we squabbled and lost our way because we didn't dare fail, how making it meant having things.

EDVARDS: You must paint more than us. Who are we? Figures in the landscape and then we are gone. You must paint the vision, look to the horizon…

KARL: One thing is certain. We'll never be as young again.

They begin to sing "Jauniba".

"Jauniba"

Mile dzel un mile glasta
Atver sirdi tai.
Nes ta tevi prieka brizos
Preti jaunibai.

Jauniba jauniba
Sartais vina trauks,
Dzer no ta, lidz rudens salnas
Novist dzives lauks.

Lai ko liktens plecos veltu
Tas mus nesaliec.
Cauri visiem dzives erkskiem
Izvedis mus preiks.

Jauniba jauniba
Sartais vina trauks,
Dzer no ta, lidz rudens salnas
Novist dzives lauks.

LEICHHARDT: History will always be redrawn to suit our own ends. Appearances are deceptive and words are riddled with lies. In the end, life is only sensation. You must know why you live, or else... nothing matters... everything is wild grass.

OTTO *and* LYDIA *join the* OTHERS *for the final chorus.*

END OF PLAY

MY FATHER'S FATHER

My Father's Father was first performed by the Melbourne Theatre Company at the The Fairfax, Victorian Arts Centre, on 1 March 1996 with the following cast:

KARL	Peter Adams
ILSE	Monica Maughan
ARMAND / GUNNARS	Paul English
EDVARDS / LEICHHARDT	John Dicks
MCQUAIDE / ALFRED / PORTER	Tom Considine
RUTH / ANITA	Genevieve Picot
LEONIDS / GILBERT / PETER	Mark Pegler
BROWN	Warren Owens
MARTA	Deidre Rubenstein
OLGA	Helen Tripp

Designed by Dale Ferguson
Lighting Design by Jamieson Lewis
Directed by Roger Hodgman

CHARACTERS

In Australia:

> KARL
> ILSE
> ARMAND, their son
> EDVARDS
> DOCTOR MCQUAIDE
> RUTH, EDVARDS' dead wife
> LEONIDS, RUTH's dead lover

The Explorers:

> LUDWIG LEICHHARDT (same actor as EDVARDS)
> JOHN GILBERT (same actor as LEONIDS)
> BROWN

In Latvia:

> MARTA, KARL's twin sister
> PETER, her son (same actor as LEONIDS/GILBERT)
> ANITA, KARL's cousin (same actor as RUTH)
> OLGA, ILSE's sister
> ALFRED, ILSE's brother (same actor as MCQUAIDE)
> PORTER (same actor as ALFRED/MCQUAIDE)
> GUNNARS (same actor as ARMAND)
> KARL'S PARENTS (same actors as ILSE and ARMAND)

The doubling of characters is intentional and integral to the structure and meaning of the play.

SETTING

The action of the play takes place in North Queensland locations in November 1992, in Latvian locations in May 1993; and in Australia in 1846.

AUTHOR'S NOTE

There are fairly rapid changes in time and location and it is important that the design should facilitate this movement and not hamper the flow of action from scene to scene with unnecessary blackouts or set devices.

The Latvian story, that is the scenes set in Latvia and North Queensland should be presented as part of a seamless whole. The Leichhardt story requires a different style of production to create the sense that it cuts across the Latvian story as if it were beamed in from Mars.

The play can be presented without the Leichhardt story. This involves two other minor adjustments. Cutting Brown from Scene Eighteen and replacing Scene Twenty-Five with an alternate scene included in the Appendix.

The style of speech is also important. When the Latvians talk amongst themselves they speak fluently and without accent. When they try to speak English their speech is accented. The reverse is true for Armand. When he tries to speak Latvian his speech is accented. In some scenes Armand is speaking in English and his parents reply in fluent (unaccented) Latvian.

Paul English (Armand) and Genevieve Picot (Ruth) in the 1996 Melbourne Theatre Company production (Photo: Jeff Busby)

Left to right: Tom Considine (Alfred), Monica Maughan (Ilse) and Helen Tripp (Olga) in the 1996 Melbourne Theatre Company production. (Photo: Jeff Busby)

PRELUDE

Out in the darkness we hear the slow, insistent tread of many feet accompanied by the rhythmic tinkling of tiny bells and the chorus-like chant, "Latvija".

A table cloth flutters into the light and settles. Once again it is thrown up and as it starts to fall, from under it, behind it come ghostly figures. Each of them wears, carries some national artefact.

The sound of their steps, the bells, the chant.

Into their midst a man comes sprawling: KARL's father, (ARMAND). The group disperses. The man starts to get up, slowly, warily. The bells ring insistently in the darkness. A shot. The man falls. Again the cloth flutters out and falls to cover the body.

KARL: Father!

The chant, "Latvija".
The group crosses again by the body. As they gather up the cloth, the body disappears.

PART ONE

SCENE ONE

Latvia, Riga Airport. May 1993. 3.00 pm.

Coming through the dispersing group are ARMAND, ILSE *and* KARL *with their luggage on a decrepit trolley. Throughout this scene and for the rest of the play,* ARMAND *takes photographs.*

KARL: Riga. End of the road. Only took forty-nine years to get back home.

ILSE: Looks worse than the war. Like the last sulphur bomb dropped only yesterday.

KARL: Don't think I'll kiss the ground. Might catch some disease.

ILSE: You can see the Russians have been here.

KARL: Sssh. There's plenty of them still around.

ILSE: I'm not going to kiss any backsides. I'm Australian.

ARMAND: Dad, see anyone you know?

ILSE: He probably wouldn't recognise them.

KARL: What are you talking about? Not recognise my own sister? My twin?

ILSE: If she looked like you I'd recognise her. You said she didn't.

KARL: I'll know her. But she won't be here yet. How was she going to know you'd get it into your head to take an earlier connection?

ILSE: Forty years you've been crying in your beer to get back to Latvia. Well you're here.

KARL: Two hours early.

ILSE: Does it make much difference which airport you sit in?

KARL: This has got to be one of the worst.

ILSE: Your first trip out of Australia and already you're the expert on airport architecture.

KARL: How much did he sting you for the trolley?

ARMAND: Two dollars.

KARL: Two dollars?! It only cost two dollars in Singapore but the wheels weren't falling off and you didn't have to push it yourself.

ILSE: [to KARL] What's two dollars to you? The price of a beer.

ARMAND: Beer was six dollars a glass in Singapore.

ILSE: [to KARL] What does it matter? If Edvards hadn't left you money in his will you wouldn't even be here.

KARL: You were too proud to take it. But who do you think paid for you?

ILSE: After forty-five years of marriage that's the least you owe me.

KARL: I used Edvards' money.

ILSE: I thought it was yours now.

KARL: It is.

ILSE: Then make the most of it instead of counting every cent like a beggar.

KARL: I'm paying for everything. What are you doing with your share?

ILSE: Never you mind. What's mine is mine.

KARL: And what's mine is yours as well?

ILSE: You wouldn't have got this far on your own.

KARL: A man can't win with you.

ILSE: You haven't done too badly.

ARMAND: Why don't you two sit at different ends of the building for a while?

ILSE: I've been sitting thirty-six hours.

Pause.

ARMAND: We could be waiting here a while. Mum's going to need somewhere to sit.

ILSE: When I can't stand I'll sit. Don't fuss.

ARMAND: [shrugs] OK.

KARL: Two hours isn't that long to wait. Nothing, after forty-nine years.

ILSE *starts to move off.*

Where are you going?

ILSE: I don't need you to wipe my bottom yet.

She goes.

KARL: I don't suppose she can really get lost here. Latvian is her mother-tongue.

ARMAND: She isn't very well you know.

KARL: She's a bit worked up, that's all. It's bound to be a bit of a shock. Even though she always said she didn't want to come back but deep in her heart... Fatherland and all that.

ARMAND: Fatherland. Mother-tongue. I suppose mothers teach us to talk and fathers get the land. It's your land again now.

KARL: It's half my sister's.

ARMAND: Let her have the lot. But you have to reclaim it first. For your father's sake. A way of remembering him.

KARL: Ah yes. Remembering, always remembering.

ARMAND: That's why we're here. They say if you want to know what a man's like, look at his father. Not that I'll see yours but at least I'll see where you lived, how you grew up.

KARL: I kept a couple of these little drinks from the plane. You want one?

ARMAND: No thanks.

KARL: [*drinks*] While Mum's not around.

ARMAND: What about you Dad?

KARL: What about me?

ARMAND: How do you feel? You know, coming home, are you excited?

KARL: No, Why?

ARMAND: Motherland, father-tongue.

KARL: I'm all right. Might as well drink the other one.

ARMAND: God knows how I'll go with my Latvian. No one will speak English. I'm going to sound like some idiot child.

KARL: It'll come back to you.

ARMAND: I never had it in the first place.

KARL: I'm tired of this waiting. In life it's always the waiting and it always seems so long. It's like I'm not here yet.

ILSE: [*returning*] Jesus Christ! Don't go to the toilets. Filthy. Urgh.

Dirty. And the stink. I've never seen anything like it. And this Russian woman with her hand out for money. No Latvian to speak of, [*accent*] so I tell her in clean English, "Clean shits first then ask for money."

A woman, MARTA, *has followed* ILSE *but stops at a discreet distance. She is joined by* PETER *carrying large bunches of flowers.*

KARL: What happened?

ILSE: I couldn't go, could I? I dried up. But she wouldn't let me leave till I gave her money so I left some Singapore rubbish.

ARMAND: Those people are looking at us.

ILSE: That woman was in the toilets, crying. I can tell you the smell brought tears to my eyes.

PETER: Do you think that's Uncle Karl?

MARTA: That woman spoke Latvian, and then she said something in a strange language. It could've been Australian.

PETER: I thought you'd know him.

MARTA: [*crying*] I haven't seen him since I was sixteen.

ILSE: Well they're not the KGB.

KARL: How can you tell?

ILSE: She's started crying again.

ARMAND: Don't you think she looks like Dad?

ILSE: When he's had a few drinks. Is that your sister?

KARL: How would I know? I haven't seen her since I was sixteen. She's sixty.

ILSE: How old do you think you are?

The two groups openly regard each other. KARL *and* MARTA *speak as one:*

MARTA: [*together*] Probably not. We're hours early.

KARL: [*together*] Don't think so. We're hours early.

KARL *and* MARTA *move towards each other, speaking as one:*

MARTA: [*together*] Karl! It is you. My God, my God.

KARL: [*together*] Marta!

They embrace and kiss.

From the moment I saw you I knew it was you.

MARTA: Oh Karl, oh Karl, oh my little brother, home at last, little Karly.

> *Throughout the following introductions* MARTA *keeps hugging and kissing* KARL, *giving him flowers and kissing him again, only letting go of him to meet* ILSE *and* ARMAND *whom she also enfolds in deep embraces after giving them flowers.*

You must be Ilse. Welcome sister.

ILSE: Hello Marta.

PETER: Aunt Ilse, welcome.

MARTA: Karl, this is my son, Peter.

PETER: Uncle Karl.

KARL: My son Armand, our second born.

ARMAND: [*accent*] Tante Marta. Good day.

MARTA: Little nephew. And you speak Latvian.

ARMAND: [*accent*] I have some little word. I more understand.

MARTA: My don't you look like your grandfather. Like our father, Karl, don't you think so? Peter?

PETER: I only saw him in photographs. Armand.

ARMAND: [*accent*] Good day.

MARTA: Oh yes. The spitting image. The same nose, and brow. Oh no, here I go again. I'm going to cry. Karl. Give me your hand. Big little brother an old man already.

KARL: I'm no older than you.

MARTA: Don't say that, you naughty boy.

PETER: You must be tired.

ARMAND: [*accent*] Was not much bad. For Mum was tireding, a bit.

ILSE: It is a long, long way. It seems from another time.

MARTA: Yes, yes. It is, it is. Why are we standing here? A couple of hours in a car and we can be at table. I've prepared a feast for a king.

ILSE: Thank you but I can't go anywhere yet. My relatives are expecting me.

MARTA: Forgive me. Of course they will be. And we can invite them as well.

PETER: Isn't it likely they'll have prepared a table?

MARTA: My little Karly is coming with me. I'm not going to let him go.

Suddenly OLGA *rushes on and hugs* ILSE. ALFRED *follows.*

OLGA: Oh. Oh. Oh. You're here. Oh. You're here.

ILSE: Yes I'm here. Don't cry.

OLGA: But you're here. You're already here.

ILSE: I'm here. I'm early. Don't cry.

OLGA: What if it's not you. Say my name.

ILSE: Olga.

OLGA: It really is you and you really are here. [*Laughing.*] For a moment there I was afraid I might've grabbed the wrong woman.

ALFRED: Are you going to let me welcome our sister?

The WOMEN *include him in a three-way hug.*

ILSE: Alfred.

ALFRED: Little sister.

OLGA: I knew it was you from your photograph.

ILSE: We arrived early.

ALFRED: Forty years too late.

OLGA: All these years we've been waiting. I would've known you even without the photograph.

ALFRED: Is this your family?

MARTA: Some of us are Karl's family.

Another round of greetings. And flowers.

ALFRED: You're the only man here around my age. You must be Karl. I'm Alfred. Welcome.

KARL: This is my sister, Marta, and my nephew, Peter.

ILSE: [*to* OLGA, *overlaps* ALFRED] My son, Armand.

ARMAND: [*accent*] Tauntie Olga. Gib dies.

OLGA: You're very welcome. And you speak Latvian.

MARTA: He understands more than he speaks.

ALFRED: Aha, the doctor.

OLGA: He's a painter now, Alfred. The first painter in the family.

KARL: He was the first doctor too.

ALFRED: I'm your Uncle Alfred. What do you think, Olga? In ten years or so when Armand loses some hair and a few teeth, he'll be the spitting image of our father.

ARMAND: [*accent*] Must be I have same look from nose.

ALFRED: The likeness is uncanny.

MARTA: I really think he looks more like Karl's father.

ILSE: I have to sit down now.

ARMAND: Sit on this suitcase. [*Accent.*] Better now we move. Mumma bit has to put down head.

OLGA: It's not that far to my place.

MARTA: [*to* OLGA] Just as you arrived I was saying we must get our guests to the table. They've had a long journey and are tired and hungry. I've everything prepared. And you are most welcome to join us as well.

OLGA: Oh... I... um. Well, you see...

MARTA: Is there some problem?

OLGA: It's just that... How distressing.

ALFRED: Out with it woman. Olga has prepared a table as well. She's gone to a lot of trouble.

MARTA: Of course you would have.

PETER: What did I tell you?

ALFRED: Let the guests choose.

ILSE: I don't care. Let me know when you've made a decision.

MARTA: We'll just have to fight over them, won't we?

SCENE TWO

North Queensland. EDVARDS' *house. November 1992. Sunset.*

A table cloth flutters into the light and settles on a table. ILSE *smooths out the cloth, ensuring that it hangs evenly all round. She puts a table runner of Latvian design down the centre of the table along with matching place mats. She then goes on with setting the table. Several of the bowls and table decorations are of Latvian design.* ARMAND *helps her, bringing chairs.*

ARMAND: How many ghosts is Edvards expecting?

ILSE: He keeps talking about Ruth.

ARMAND: Jesus. She's been dead over forty years.

ILSE: Dead is dead. Time doesn't come into it. They were married. Maybe it is forever no matter what.

ARMAND: Ironic isn't it? Ruth drowned all those years ago and Edvards is going to die by suffocation because of the mesothelioma.

ILSE: He thinks they'll be together again, as if she'd never run off with Leonids.

ARMAND: Didn't he drown with her? What if he turns up?

ILSE: Edvards will have to make his peace with them. Or not.

ARMAND: I suppose there's a bunch of ghosts coming from Latvia?

ILSE: They can't come here. They don't belong. Spirit belongs to place.

ARMAND: You mean you cooked all that food for two ghosts?

ILSE: Stop saying, "ghost". It's spirit, soul.

ARMAND: We'll have to give them a hand.

ILSE: No one's to sit at the table or eat anything.

ARMAND: Keep your hair on. Is that why we have to put sand round the table? You can see if anyone sneaks in for a feed.

ILSE: It's how barns used to be decorated for feast days, in olden times. Clean sand on the floor and pine needles.

ARMAND: How come it's the only Latvian custom I've missed out on?

ILSE: It's from way before my time. Edvards found it in a book. We do have a kind of all-souls day.

ARMAND: You've never observed that.

ILSE: It's a day to remember loved ones and tend their graves. I don't have dead in Australia.

ARMAND: You'll have to go to Latvia then, to make your peace.

ILSE: God willing. This is what Edvards wanted.

ARMAND: It's good you and Edvards are getting on again. You haven't for years.

ILSE: Time doesn't come into it any more.

ARMAND: No.

ILSE: That's why you've come up here twice in two weeks. It's more than I've seen you in the past few years.

ARMAND: Edvards asked me to give him something. To help him die. Some pills, or an injection.

ILSE: But you don't work as a doctor any more.

ARMAND: Occasionally as a locum.

    Pause.

It happens more often than people think. Giving someone larger and larger doses of morphine, till they slip away, peacefully.

ILSE: Quietly.

ARMAND: Edvards wouldn't be able to scream even if he wanted to. He won't have the breath.

ILSE: Have you ever before?

ARMAND: No. I've been asked and it's difficult, not to, especially when you know how cruelly someone will die.

ILSE: What if I was to ask you?

ARMAND: What? Not to?

ILSE: Suppose in a few years, if I was in pain, and I said I'd lived long enough?

ARMAND: You wouldn't ask me.

ILSE: When you were small you wished for Dad and me, and Edvards, to live forever.

ARMAND: It doesn't happen.

ILSE: Now you have to wait for us to die to free you from the pain of waiting.

ARMAND: But I'll be here. When your parents died it was twelve thousands miles away. You only found out months afterwards. You hadn't seen them in thirty years and never will again.

    RUTH's *ghost comes. He doesn't see her. Maybe* ILSE *does.*

ILSE: [*shivers*] UWRRR. How cold your hand is.

ARMAND: What? Who're you talking to?

ILSE: Felt like a cold hand on the back of my neck.

ARMAND: Someone walked over your grave. I'll come and visit you more often.

ILSE: You're not burying me yet.

EDVARDS *comes slowly with two roses. Sees* RUTH *coming towards him.*

EDVARDS: Ruth.

RUTH: From your own garden?

EDVARDS: [*overlapping*] From my own garden.

RUTH: You used to steal them when you courted me.

EDVARDS: I grew these. I knew you'd come tonight.

ILSE: Does Edvards want something?

ARMAND: Talking to himself. It's contagious.

RUTH: Stolen flowers smell sweeter.

ILSE: Edvards?

>   RUTH *goes.*

EDVARDS: [*to* RUTH] I should've known she'd drive you from the house like a hobgoblin.

RUTH: I'll come back tonight.

EDVARDS: When she's gone.

ARMAND: I don't know what to do. About Edvards.

ILSE: You never know how much someone wants to die.

ARMAND: [*going*] I'd better get his oxygen.

ILSE: Who were you talking to?

EDVARDS: A Martian wanted to have sex with me.

ILSE: What rubbish are you talking now?

EDVARDS: Something I read in *Post* magazine.

ILSE: Pictures of half naked girls.

>   *She brings him a chair, helps him to sit.*

EDVARDS: If I can't look I might as well be dead.

ILSE: If you did more than look you would be dead.

>   EDVARDS *presents* ILSE *with the flowers.*

EDVARDS: From my own garden.

ILSE: Aren't they beautiful?

>   ARMAND *brings a small oxygen cylinder, administers it with a mask. During the rest of the scene* EDVARDS *uses the mask to breathe whenever he runs out of breath.* KARL *comes with a couple of dusty bottles.*

KARL: My God Edvards, how long have you had this horse-kick hidden under your bed?

ILSE: Don't think you're going to start schloorping.

EDVARDS: It must be tasted before it goes on the table.

KARL: Mum, you having one?

EDVARDS: Ilse too, OK? The best mulberry syrup.

ILSE: With the worst proof spirits. No thank you.

KARL: For friendship's sake.

ILSE: Are you deaf? I said no. One drunk in the family is enough.

ARMAND: Take it easy. No one's getting drunk.

EDVARDS: [*toasts*] We'll never be as young again.

> *The* MEN *toss back their drinks.*

KARL: Whooo! Horse-kick all right.

EDVARDS: One good thing deserves another.

> KARL *refills* EDVARDS' *glass.*

ILSE: You know he's not supposed to drink. Don't encourage him.

KARL: Encourage him? I can't keep up with him.

ARMAND: One or two won't hurt him.

EDVARDS: Doctor's orders. The worst it can do is kill me, OK?

ARMAND: No more for me. I don't think it improved with age.

KARL: [*toasts*] Two of a good thing makes it better.

> KARL *and* EDVARDS *down their drinks.*

EDVARDS: I'm getting the taste now. Let's have another.

KARL: [*to* ILSE] What am I supposed to do?

ILSE: You've often said the only way to die is with a bottle in your hand. He's your friend. If that's how he wants to go you're the best man to help him on his way.

EDVARDS: You don't have to make the whole journey with me. But I'm sure we'll meet up down there.

ARMAND: Come on, Dad. We have to get the leaves before it gets dark.

KARL: How crazy can you get? Food we're not allowed to eat, booze we're not allowed to drink but we are allowed to fill the house with sand and leaves. Bloody crazy.

EDVARDS: That's the form, OK? Take that bottle with you. It'll help.

ILSE *takes the bottle.*

ILSE: Don't think you're going to empty that on your own.

KARL: What the hell has gotten into you? You're as bloody crazy as he is.

KARL *and* ARMAND *go.*

EDVARDS: Is that what you think? I've gone crazy?

ILSE: I think you're a trouble maker. Why do you always have to lead him by the nose?

EDVARDS: The devil loves to fan the flame. Karl has always been such a boy. Isn't that what appealed to you?

ILSE: Who can remember? It's too long ago.

EDVARDS: I can. I remember you from forty years ago. I still remember you in other ways too, other times.

ILSE: Maybe we've known each other too many years.

EDVARDS: We won't for much longer, OK?

ILSE: Forgive me. I didn't mean it like that.

EDVARDS: It's a fact. I've never cared for life that much. Even before Ruth died. Later when you and I were lovers. Probably why you wouldn't move in with me. I know how much you've always wanted to live. My hour has almost come and I only have one last request.

ILSE: What?

EDVARDS: Raise your skirts for me.

ILSE: Have you gone mad?

EDVARDS: No madder than before.

ILSE: Well neither have I.

EDVARDS: I just want to look. OK?

ILSE: At what? An old woman's baggy pants.

EDVARDS: The secret they contain.

ILSE: It'd frighten you to death.

EDVARDS: OK. All the more reason to risk it.

ILSE: Not for me. You said you could remember.

EDVARDS: Your essence, your spirit. Is it vanity that stops you?

ILSE: I'm blushing with shame. You should be ashamed for asking.

EDVARDS: I'd be more ashamed if I hadn't. When I remember Ruth, [RUTH *appears.*] she's always as young as when she died, like her photographs. When I look in the mirror... OK?

ILSE: After forty years in a swamp her body's going to look worse than yours or mine.

EDVARDS: Inside this old carcass I'm as young as I ever was. But then I'd never have dared to ask you.

ILSE: The older we get the sillier we get.

EDVARDS: Why be sensible at our age? Who are you saving your dignity for? Karl hasn't the imagination to ask you. To me you are still as young as when you dared to kiss my damaged cheek after I returned from the dead. That's who I'm appealing to.

ILSE: You'll talk yourself to death.

> ILSE *reaches under her skirts and removes her pants and discreetly raises the hem.*

EDVARDS: I've lived long enough, almost.

ILSE: Do you have any regrets?

EDVARDS: The light could be better.

ILSE: If you can't be serious—

EDVARDS: I am serious, OK? I can barely see.

ILSE: Lucky for me.

EDVARDS: It is truly the eighth wonder how we come into the world.

ILSE: And the ninth is how quickly a woman can lose her senses.

EDVARDS: I should have remarried. [RUTH *goes.*] Too long I lived an empty life. Without marriage life has no centre. I have no children. My only connection with this land will be my bones. You should have left Karl and married me.

ILSE: I'd had my children by then.

EDVARDS: But I wouldn't have grown tired of you.

ILSE: I might have. Of you.

EDVARDS: That hasn't made you leave Karl.

ILSE: Someone's coming. Hurry, hurry.

EDVARDS: I can't run anywhere.

ILSE: My pants! Where are my pants? [*Going.*] Why did I listen to you?

EDVARDS: For a moment I was the devil gazing on the gates of paradise.

SCENE THREE

Central Australia. In the desert. 1846. Sunset.

BROWN *comes. He has a bag of sand and pours a ring of sand round the table and round* LEICHHARDT.

BROWN: Dr Leichhardt?

LEICHHARDT: Brown? Is that you?

BROWN: If I was bad blackfella, Dr Leichhardt, you already be dead like them others.

LEICHHARDT: Is not one left alive?

BROWN: Bad blackfella kill all men. Lucky we gone from camp or we be dead too.

LEICHHARDT: Did you bury them?

BROWN: Can' go. Bad blackfella watchin' alla time. I can' do nothin'. I try to find you somethin' eat, somethin' drink. Can' get nothin'.

LEICHHARDT: Providence has deserted me. Blinded, without supplies, to suffer thus. How am I spared? What do you do?

BROWN: I makin' ring roun' here, makin' it with sand.

LEICHHARDT: Is that some blackfella magic?

BROWN: Bugger if I know. I tryin' to trick them blackfella. Maybe him think this strong whitefella magic, better stay away.

LEICHHARDT: A circle of white sand and the sacred oak with the sacred spring at its base is mentioned in the ancient Norse sagas. Is there a tree nearby?

BROWN: Only one small tree.

LEICHHARDT: An omen. The last tree before the desert. Carve the tree. "L 1846".

BROWN: That might be good trick. I see you chop him plenny time on tree. I make him here with sand.

LEICHHARDT: And "DIG."

BROWN: Dig? Won' get no water here.

LEICHHARDT: [*scratches blindly in the sand*] "D-I-G" on tree.

BROWN: I know that tree. You dig hole in him, get water out. Not roun' here.

LEICHHARDT: No, no. Chop those marks with the axe on the tree. I can't see to do it. Then bury my journal underneath.

BROWN: You want bury that bad story?

LEICHHARDT: My journal must be found. Five of my party met their death in native attack. Their story must be told.

BROWN: Better we go back to Jimbour Down. Won' have to bury no book, tell 'em straight out.

LEICHHARDT: My last journey ended in abject failure, I give my word to God, I will cross this continent from east to west or die in the attempt.

BROWN: I got a bad feelin' 'bout that God, Dr Leichhardt. He don' like how we goin'. Better for blackfella too when he don' go where he don' know. When we go home, Brown know real good how to find tucker, where find water.

LEICHHARDT: Home is where one is loved, one's deepest wounds and hurts tended, one's troubled soul comforted. But I would be a laughing stock. To go home for the last time, I must go on.

BROWN: If you die people say Brown no good. Horses already bugger up, can' go no more. Pretty soon we be walkin'.

LEICHHARDT: In the sagas, to dream of horses was to die by hanging.

BROWN: Quicker die from spear or empty belly.

LEICHHARDT: Sacrifice the horses.

BROWN: Eh?

LEICHHARDT: We can drink the blood, eat their livers.

BROWN: You wait here. I get him. I reckon this magic mus' be workin'. Them blackfella stayin' away.

LEICHHARDT: Give me the axe. Take me to the tree.

BROWN: You don' have to worry. That tree not big enough for hangin'.

SCENE FOUR

MARTA*'s place. An old barn. May 1993. Early evening.*

MARTA *puts bowls and platters of food on the table.* PETER *is spreading the sand evenly with a broom.*

PETER: Your little Karl doesn't look so little. Looks very well fed. Fattened up even.

MARTA: It doesn't mean he's rich.

PETER: I didn't say anything about his money.

MARTA: I know how you think.

PETER: I learned from you. They say an apple never falls far from the tree.

MARTA: As far as I'm concerned Karl doesn't have to put his hand in his pocket, I'd give him my last mouthful. What do you think they eat in Australia?

PETER: Ko-arle bear.

MARTA: I hope this will be good enough.

PETER: Why? Is he rich then?

MARTA: I really don't know. Or care.

PETER: Has he come to reclaim your father's farm for himself? Or Armand?

MARTA: Peter! How could you?

PETER: You hadn't heard anything from him for forty years.

MARTA: It was only twenty years.

PETER: Nuhuh. That's when Aunt Ilse stopped writing. Uncle Karl never wrote.

MARTA: I'm not much of a letter writer either. He's like me. The same blood, the same heart.

PETER: In that case he has come to claim your father's land.

MARTA: How can you say that?

PETER: Latvia's free, as soon as the new government says we can claim title to property confiscated by the Russians, he's back.

MARTA: Karl isn't like that. And he can't take it with him.

PETER: Latvia's full of absentee landlords.

MARTA: Now you sound like my cousin Anita.

PETER: She's got her land.

MARTA: I wanted to wait till Karl was here. It's only common courtesy and there's papers for him to sign before the land can come to me.

PETER: Why's he out there talking to Aunt Anita?

MARTA: [*close to tears*] I don't want to hear any more. You'll ruin everything. Latvia is Karl's true home. He's come back to see me. You know how long I've waited.

PETER: I'm sorry. I was teasing. Don't cry, they're coming. I'm sorry mama.

MARTA: I only want the land for you. I'll talk to Karl. He'll understand. You'll see.

PETER: I know. Come on, cheer up. I bet you Aunt Anita says she didn't bring much.

MARTA: In her case it'll be true.

> ANITA *enters with* KARL *and* ARMAND *who have armfuls of pine needles.* KARL *also has a couple of bottles of duty free booze.*

ANITA: Marta, I'm afraid I haven't brought much. My, what a spread. Your cooking has always put mine to shame.

MARTA: I'm sure you have other gifts, cousin.

ANITA: I've never been a terribly good housewife.

PETER: Perhaps that's why you've never caught yourself a husband.

ANITA: I've never found that much use for one.

PETER: Now that you're a lady farmer—

ANITA: It's much easier on a woman to hire a man for work than it is for her to be some man's wife.

PETER: I suppose that's why my wife threw me out.

MARTA: Peter take those pine needles from your Uncle Karl.

> PETER *does so. Starts to scatter them around.* ARMAND *follows suit.*

KARL: I have a couple of bottles of liqueur for the table.

MARTA: Oh aren't they pretty? They must've cost a fortune.

KARL: Not really. Not at duty free prices.

MARTA: Thank you little brother.

ANITA: I wouldn't have recognised Karl.

MARTA: You weren't born when he left for the war.

ANITA: I keep forgetting you're twins and both much older.

> MARTA *takes the pine needles from* PETER.

MARTA: I'll finish that. Get your Uncle and cousin a drink.

PETER: That means she wants one Uncle Karl.

MARTA: Ooooh you...

> *She hits him with the pine needles.*

PETER: You don't have to have one.

MARTA: Save Karly's bottles for later.

ARMAND: [*accent*] Right is, what I doin'?

MARTA: Perfect.

ANITA: When I first saw Armand I would've sworn I was looking at my Uncle Antons.

MARTA: Our father died before you were born as well, God rest his soul. You never saw him.

ANITA: I've seen photographs. It's a good likeness.

ARMAND: [*accent*] Same nose, same line.

> ILSE *enters.*

[*accent*] I thought you went little bit sleep?

MARTA: Yes you should've, Ilse, till we're ready.

ANITA: I'm afraid I woke her when I arrived.

ILSE: Sleep wouldn't come. It's like I'm dreaming and I'm still awake.

ARMAND: [*offering her a chair, accent*] Better sit down.

ILSE: [*sitting*] I'll be all right. My clock has been turned inside out. It's time to get up in Australia.

> PETER *offers drinks.*

PETER: Not too early for you then Uncle Karl?

KARL: For me, never.

PETER: What about you, Aunt Ilse? It'll help you sleep later.

ILSE: I can't. Thank you but it just doesn't agree with me. Upsets my stomach.

ANITA: No thanks, not for me either.

MARTA: Anita! How could you not? When your cousin has come so
    far?

ANITA: Just this one. He's come for you, not me.

MARTA: I should hope so. My brother, Karly, from across the world.
    It's true what they say about twins. Our hearts belong together.
    I've only been half alive since you left. Didn't you feel that too?

KARL: [*shrugs, laughs*] Well...

MARTA: You naughty boy. No wonder you never wrote.

KARL: I often thought of you, of Latvia. I honestly couldn't believe
    I'd be back.

PETER: All the more reason to write, you'd think.

    Pause.

KARL: I'll make it up to you, you'll see.

MARTA: I never gave up hope.

KARL: It's already morning at home. So here's to the new day in a
    new Latvia.

    They down their drinks.

PETER: Another, Uncle Karl?

ILSE: You can't just keep drinking. Wait till we eat.

PETER: It's such a long journey. I'm sure Uncle Karl has developed a
    little thirst.

KARL: I could drink another one.

ARMAND: [*refuses a refill, accent*] No thongs.

MARTA: Smell these Karly. When's the last time you smelled fresh
    pine needles?

KARL: Last week. The week before that. We've millions of acres of
    pine trees.

MARTA: Oh you've got everything over there.

ANITA: I've had my one thanks.

PETER: Mama?

MARTA: Why not. Then I have to bring the rest of the food.

ANITA: I love how you've set up the table. It's like we're taking part
    in some ancient ritual.

MARTA: God knows it's like Karl has come back to us from the dead.

ARMAND: [*accent*] Is there not so bad, in Australie.

PETER: Another nail in the coffin.

KARL, PETER *and* MARTA *down their drinks.*

MARTA: Now if you'll excuse me.

ANITA: I'll lend a hand. [*Going.*] Don't you just love Armand's accent?

PETER: Just help yourself Uncle Karl. [*Goes.*]

ILSE: He can wait like everybody else.

ARMAND: My Latvian's pretty crook.

ILSE: You'll be fine. You'll soon pick it up.

KARL: [*to* ILSE] Don't count my drinks. All right?

ILSE: It would be all right if you behaved like a normal human being. [*Getting up.*] Don't think you're going to spend all your time in Latvia getting drunk.

KARL: Don't you worry about that.

ILSE: I don't want everyone pitying me for marrying such a fool.

ARMAND: It's too late to worry about that. Forty-five years too late.

ILSE: Alfred and Olga must've got lost. Perhaps they're annoyed we decided to come here first.

ARMAND: I'll come out to the road with you?

ILSE: It's not that far.

ILSE *goes.* KARL *pours himself another drink.*

ARMAND: Dad, don't get pissed before dinner. Mum's got enough to cope with at the moment.

KARL: No, no. I'll be all right.

ARMAND: You'll be pissed.

KARL: What would you know?

ARMAND: That much I do know. What I don't know is where Anita fits in, and I've never known much about your sister, [*Accent.*] your dween.

KARL: Anita is my cousin, daughter of my father's brother, Uncle Ilmaris.

ARMAND: I know even less about your mother. And you only talked about your father when you were pissed. How he'd been shot by the Russians. I know bugger all really.

KARL: What was there to say?

ARMAND: I don't know. That's what I'm saying. Maybe you don't know. Maybe too many brain cells have gone.

KARL: What are you talking about?

ARMAND: At home, in Australia, you're like a fucking ghost, floating along in a beery haze in a strange land. Edvards said, in Latvia I'd see who you were but it wouldn't surprise me to find out that you were never really here.

KARL: You're too clever for me.

ARMAND: Have another drink. I'm sure you'll be able to tell me all about it when you're pissed.

SCENE FIVE

North Queensland. Edvards' house. November 1992. Early evening.
KARL *pours himself a drink.*

KARL: I reckon I've earned this.

EDVARDS: I didn't ask for pine needles.

ARMAND: I thought, traditionally, it'd be pine.

EDVARDS: I've lived my years with eucalypt. Gum leaves.

KARL: Count yourself lucky to get these. I'm too old for climbing fences. You must've been drunk when you dreamed up this idea.

EDVARDS: Stone cold sober.

KARL: Ah well, that's the problem.

        ILSE *comes with the last of the food.*

ILSE: It's an Australian pine. Casuarina torulosa. It will have to do.

ARMAND: I was trying to please you. I'm sorry, OK?

EDVARDS: OK, OK. Whatever your mother said. Baffled by science, OK?

KARL: A tree is a tree.

ILSE: To you. [*To* EDVARDS.] Don't you get in a sulk.

KARL: After all this can someone explain to me why we can't sit down and enjoy our labours?

EDVARDS: In the morning, OK? That's the form. Then someone must break the bread, drink from every bottle. Tonight, I sit alone as host to the banquet.

ILSE: You should go to bed too to save your strength.

ARMAND: I can stay with Edvards.

ILSE: Why don't we all stay, for a while? It's early yet.

KARL: And do what if we're not allowed to eat or drink?

ILSE: Keep Edvards company.

EDVARDS: I wait alone, OK? Like every night. What can happen? Sometime I will die. I hope so every night. If you want what's best for me shoot me. Promise me that you can stay.

KARL: I'd rather come back in the morning.

EDVARDS: One drink, OK, before you go. Ilse too, for old times' sake. Armand, if you would?

ILSE: I'd rather drink it tomorrow.

EDVARDS: There's always tomorrow. Even at the gates of paradise.

KARL: I don't think you'll be going there.

EDVARDS: I've gazed at the gates many times. [*Taking a glass from* ARMAND.] This stuff will scare the devil. Before we drink I want to tell you about my will.

ILSE: It's really none of our business.

KARL: Why talk about that and tempt fate?

EDVARDS: You'll be able to do your cursing to my face, not over my bones, OK.

ILSE: If that's how it is, maybe you shouldn't tell us.

KARL: We should drink first, while we're still friends. To friendship.

EDVARDS: And to life. It's been priceless.

   They drain their glasses.

OK. Armand is named executor. The house and everything in it he shares with his sister, sold up and split fifty-fifty.

ARMAND: Thank you.

EDVARDS: [*to* KARL *and* ILSE] What's in the bank is yours. On the condition you use a little of it to go back to Latvia.

ILSE: No. Thanks, but no. We don't need it.

KARL: What d'you mean we don't need it?

ILSE: What I said. It's time to go home.

KARL: No! You don't talk for me.

ILSE: You don't need more money to piss against the wall. And you don't need to buy more hay for three-legged race horses.

EDVARDS: Go back to Latvia. You should.

ILSE: Why didn't you?

EDVARDS: I had nothing to go back to.

ILSE: What about that mopsy, Lauma? You could've gone back to her anytime in the last ten years.

> KARL *pours himself another drink.*

ARMAND: Mum you're being silly.

EDVARDS: I waited too long. Now it's too late. If I was well enough I'd risk it, OK?

ILSE: You think because you're dying you can tell us how to live.

KARL: He can tell me.

EDVARDS: You both have family there, Karl can reclaim his father's land. You've dreamed of going back just like the rest of us, OK? Latvia is free. Now you've no reason not to go.

KARL: I'd go back tomorrow.

ILSE: Always tomorrow. What's stopping you today? Go tonight. The sooner the better.

KARL: I don't understand you. We've been talking about going back for months.

ILSE: All your life in your case, as long as you've had a few drinks.

KARL: Yeah, yeah.

ARMAND: Take it easy. No one says you have to go. No one says you have to take the money.

ILSE: [*accent*] I don't want. I don't take.

KARL: I'm happy to have it.

EDVARDS: I'm not dead yet, OK.

KARL: No, well, afterwards of course.

EDVARDS: To get the money, you have to use some of it to go to Latvia.

ILSE: If ever I go back, it will be on my own money. I won't be sent like a parcel.

EDVARDS: That's up to you. Don't leave it too late. The sorrow of that I do know.

KARL: Does the will say we have to go together?

EDVARDS: Fifty-fifty for each one.

ARMAND: Leave it now, Dad. Edvards is tired.

KARL: I'll be back in the morning.

EDVARDS: [*to* ILSE] I didn't mean it how you think.

ILSE: You always have to stir things round.

EDVARDS: I don't have much time. I'm doing what I can. What I have to.

ILSE: You won't have to live with it.

EDVARDS: I'm sorry you feel like that. OK.

ILSE: I'll say goodnight. That's all.

EDVARDS: Goodnight. I meant what I said. It has been priceless.

    ILSE *goes.*

KARL: She'll come round. I don't have to tell you what she's like.

EDVARDS: Maybe one day someone will tell you.

KARL: There's plenty I don't understand, but not a lot I don't know.

ARMAND: Just go. Take Mum home. I'll stay with Edvards for a little while.

KARL: If you want to see ghosts you'll have to drink a lot more. I've never got past the pink elephants stage myself.

ARMAND: Goodnight Dad.

KARL: [*going*] Goodnight, goodnight.

EDVARDS: OK, goodnight.

ARMAND: Dad will keep drinking when he gets home. He was just getting the taste for it. Poor Mum.

EDVARDS: She didn't have to stay with him, OK?

ARMAND: Did you love her?

EDVARDS: Not enough.

    Pause.

ARMAND: I've often wondered, you know, why Dad hit you that time? Knocked you down?

EDVARDS: Were we drunk?

ARMAND: Yeah, very.

EDVARDS: That's why then.

ARMAND: No. I was only fourteen or fifteen—

EDVARDS: At least twenty years ago, OK?

ARMAND: It was late at night, early in the morning. We were all asleep. You and Dad were up drinking and talking.

EDVARDS: Like so many drunken nights I can't remember.

ARMAND: This one was different. It's the only time I know that Dad hit anyone. Knocked you off the chair. Kicked you. He was yelling, "I show you, I show you."

EDVARDS: Who knows what drunks fight about, OK? Some imagined slight. Take your pick.

ARMAND: A few times, I could've hit him.

EDVARDS: What would it take?

ARMAND: I don't know. Maybe he'd have to hit me first.

EDVARDS: Could you strike back?

ARMAND: Why didn't you?

EDVARDS: It's not something you learn from a book, OK, or that you can make up your mind about. The body does it, or not. Only the body knows how many blows are too many. Flesh and bones, sinew, are the greatest teachers. Any pinprick, any slap, any broken bone or sickness will teach you more than any brain or book or love, OK? How little it takes to go one more day. How little food, how little air. Love it can do without altogether. The flesh can keep going long after the mind has given up.

ARMAND: I brought the morphine for you.

EDVARDS: Then it's best for you not to be here.

ARMAND: I couldn't let you inject it.

EDVARDS: I'll drink it in a glass of beer. I'll get rid of everything beforehand. Doctor McQuaide will sign the papers.

ARMAND: You'd be alone.

EDVARDS: I'll wait till the sun's coming up. The same sun will shine on you, OK? On Ilse, and Karl. The same sun shone on me and Ruth when we were married, shone on my mother, brother, father, his father before that... quite a dawn chorus.

ARMAND: I could fix it, you know, for you to go to hospital, fix it for you to get the morphine.

EDVARDS: Did I say I was sick? I picked a lousy way to die. OK. Now the body says rest, OK? To be ready for my guests.

ARMAND: I'll sit with you a little while. Dad will be talking to himself for hours yet.

SCENE SIX

North Queensland. KARL's *and* ILSE's *house. Patio. November 1992. Same night as previous scene, some time later.*

KARL *is sitting, drinking beer. He is drunk, talking to himself, in accented English.*

KARL: She say she won't go back to Latvia. Why? I always want to go but she say no. Always say no. Why? Edvards giving us the money she say she don't want. Why not? He can't use, soon be dead. He can't go back to Latvia. We can go. Edvards can go before, I don't know, he has the money, nothing to worry about, Lauma waiting, but no, he doesn't go. Why not? I have the money I be going. Before I can't go. Just can't. Make too much trouble for everyone. What I can do? Now anyone can go, no more Russians, not like before. I always want to go. See my father's grave, my mother's grave, get my land back. I can buy even, no problem. I want to see before I die. Not like Edvards. He can't go. Always show how clever he is, how much money, now too late for him. That's how clever. We can go. I always want to go. Always Ilse say no. She want to go I can take her. But no, always no. Why? This time I say, no. No darling, we take the money, we go. Why not? Tell me that. You don't go that's OK with me. I can go. I go. By myself. No worries. I show you. I show you.

SCENE SEVEN

North Queensland. KARL's *and* ILSE's *house. Drunken night. 1965. 1.30 am.*

An earlier time that ARMAND *remembers/dreams while at* EDVARDS' *place in 1992. Light on* ARMAND. *From the darkness:*

KARL: [*accent*] I show you. I show you.

> KARL *hits* EDVARDS *in the face sending him sprawling.*

[*accent*] You want me show, get up.

> ILSE, ARMAND *come from the darkness.* EDVARDS *tries to crawl away.* KARL *kicks him.*

[*accent*] See how I show you again.

ILSE: What the hell? Karl!

ARMAND: Dad! Stop it! Dad!

ILSE: What do you think you're doing? Armand do something! Stop him.

ARMAND: It's not blood.

ILSE: Karl. Edvards. For God's sake stop.

KARL: [*accent*] I show him.

> ILSE *gets* KARL *away from* EDVARDS. ARMAND *watches.* KARL *sits at the table.*

ILSE: You show nothing. Sit down and shut up. Drunken brawling. What do you think this is?

ARMAND: It isn't blood.

> EDVARDS *begins to crawl away.* ILSE *tries to get him up.*

ILSE: I thought you'd know better. Get up. It's time you went home.

ARMAND: It's horse-kick, with plum syrup.

ILSE: Edvards, get up. You ought to be ashamed. Never again.

> ILSE *sees* EDVARDS *out.* ARMAND *picks up the chair, tidies up the bottle and glasses.*

ARMAND: No more. You've had enough. Go to bed. Let's have some peace.

KARL: Don't you take my glass.

ARMAND *doesn't take* KARL*'s glass.*

ARMAND: Why were you hitting him?

KARL: You wouldn't understand.

ARMAND: Don't start crying. Here have another drink.

KARL: You're a good boy. Your father's son.

ARMAND: Not that shit again. Why aren't you dead?

KARL: What?

ARMAND: Why aren't you dead? Years ago you said the Russians would come and kill you like they killed your father.

KARL: It's true. They can come any time.

ARMAND: You haven't got a tractor.

KARL: [*accent*] What I need tractor?

ARMAND: That's what you said. They killed him for his tractor and his land. Took him behind the barn and shot him.

KARL: He wasn't the only one.

ARMAND: You've only got chooks and a bicycle.

KARL: [*accent*] What you talking chooks?

ARMAND: We haven't got a barn so the Russians will have to take you down the backyard behind the chook-shed, under the mango tree. "Prepare to die Latvian land-owning pig." [*Falls to his knees.*] "No! I only rent flat. I don't own tractor or barn. All I have is bicycle and chooks. Good layers. Take bicycle, take chooks and ten shilling I keep from pay to place a bet."

KARL: [*accent*] You think I am coward?

ARMAND: Why haven't the Russians come for you? They could find you at the top pub any Saturday. We're all waiting. "Latvian scum must be searched out and shot."

The tinkle of bells, the chant, "Latvija". A shot rings out and ARMAND *falls. "Latvija".*

KARL: [*accent*] I show you Russians.

KARL *rushes at* ARMAND *who rolls away.* KARL *slips in the spilled booze and crashes to the floor.* ILSE *comes.*

ILSE: What's the yelling about now? What happened?

ARMAND: It's not blood. It's the horse-kick. He slipped and fell.

ILSE: Come on, get up. Go to bed.

ARMAND: Why don't you just leave him there?

ILSE: So when he gets up he starts drinking and carrying on again?

ARMAND: Sometimes I could just kill him.

ILSE: Armand!

ARMAND: It wouldn't take much. Push him down the stairs when he comes home pissed.

ILSE: I don't want to hear you talk like that. How can you even think it?

ARMAND: We'd be better off without him.

ILSE: He's your father. The only one you've got.

ARMAND: I won't easily forget.

ILSE: That's the last time I want to hear that talk.

ARMAND: One thing I promise you, I won't be like him.

ILSE: Karl, come on. You can't sleep here.

 Between them they get KARL *to his feet.*

ARMAND: Dad get up. Time to go to bed.

KARL: OK. One more for the road.

SCENE EIGHT

Latvia. MARTA*'s place. Continued from Scene Four.*

MARTA *is still bringing food to the table.* KARL *is pouring one of the liqueurs he brought. As the scene progresses the talk becomes more raucous and excited until people talk over the top of each other and are shouting to be heard.* ARMAND *takes photographs.*

Without being overly prescriptive I've indicated (\ ) where the next speaker starts overlapping.

KARL: I think we should all drink a toast before dinner. Kick off the celebration.

ANITA: Armand what do you think of your Latvia?

ARMAND: [*accent*] What I can say? I no much seeing.

PETER: It's more or less what you saw driving here.

ALFRED: Surely you formed some impressions.

MARTA: Karl and Ilse must've told you about it as you were growing up.

OLGA: How does your soul respond, your heart, to your fatherland?

ARMAND: [*accent*] Terrible greenness. Light green.

Pause.

ALFRED: What did you teach the boy?

ILSE: What could he know from what we told him?

KARL: Painters only think about the colours.

ARMAND: [*accent*] I know how is look, from books, from kinema.

PETER: Kino.

ARMAND: [*accent*] Yes, kino, how looks this greenness, these trees from Europe.

OLGA: You must feel you've finally come home then?

ARMAND: [*accent*] No. I am Australian. My heart, there belonging. That land, that sky, different greens. That is my fatherland.

Pause.

KARL: I feel like I've finally come home. I remember Latvia like I never left.

ALFRED: I suppose it's important where you're born.

ARMAND: [*accent*] I don't have Latvian words. I don't mean to say wrong. What I know after small time here, is here is family, long time lost family. Hearts welcome, same noses.

ANITA: Terrible green but the same noses.

KARL: We should drink to that.

PETER: Uncle Karl you've done the hard work. I'll pass them round.

ALFRED: What about you sissy? Have you come home?

ILSE: I cry for my Latvia. My heart broke when I saw what had happened to her. Rusting machines round every corner and as for those mountains of rotting stable manure—

ALFRED: It is early spring, sissy. It will be spread on the fields.

ILSE: Forgive my plain speaking but the countryside looks like one big shit heap. We didn't used to live like that.

OLGA: That's right.

MARTA: She's speaking the truth.

ILSE: All the farms were well kept with gardens, neat fences, the roadside verges were mowed. Latvia was a garden.

KARL: Can we drink to the end of shit heaps then?

ALFRED: We can't drink to that.

OLGA: Why not? They're Russian.

ALFRED: The Russians still practically outnumber us in our own country. We don't want them here but they won't go home.

PETER: Cunning devils know they won't starve here.

ALFRED: They're insects. Parasites.

ANITA: It's not so long ago we were Russians \ too and there was no Latvia.

MARTA: We were never Russians.

PETER: We were Soviets, Latvian Soviets. Now we're free, and there's still Russians here. Let them clear out.

KARL: Let's \ drink to that.

ILSE: I don't mean to criticise, but how could you let the country go to waste like that?

MARTA: That's easy for you to say. \ You weren't here.

ILSE: Our lives weren't as easy as you think. We started with nothing. To put clothes on our backs we had to work hard.

ALFRED: But at least your clothes are good quality. The Russians impoverished us. It was their plan.

OLGA: We worked hard. \ We wanted to get ahead.

ALFRED: But all our good work, all our best produce, best manufactures—

PETER: Best you name it.

ALFRED: —all loaded into trains, kilometres long, leaving the country in a straight line for Moscow. And coming back the other way, wagon-load after wagon-load of garbage. \ Bent, broken timber.

OLGA: Plastic shoes, dirty, \ thin fabrics.

MARTA: Stinking, polluted, \ stale food.

ANITA: At times we couldn't get food or soap.

PETER: The vodka was poisonous. \ It killed people.

ALFRED: But always cheap enough to enslave you.

KARL: We still haven't drunk that toast.

ANITA: We still can't get medicines. \ [*To* ARMAND.] Can you believe that?

PETER: The Russians trained us to expect nothing. Even how not to work because there was no reward for effort. Work or not \ you received the same wage.

ILSE: You'll all have to work \ now.

ANITA: Now some of us have to learn how to work.

MARTA: At the end of the day you had to queue to buy low quality goods.

ILSE: No one is going to give you anything \ for nothing.

OLGA: We are working, Ilse. We've never stopped working. \ We just couldn't get ahead by working.

ALFRED: We've got a whole new breed of insects sucking on our blood. Don't want to work and now they expect unemployment benefit.

ILSE: Oh they're everywhere. We have millions of them.

OLGA: Take ours and you'll have another million.

ALFRED: Young people refuse to work the land any more.

KARL: We're never going to have this toast. We might as well have one.

  PETER *and* KARL *down their drinks.*

ARMAND: [*accent*] What happens to whom owning land?

ANITA: The original landowners can reclaim their property so long as they can prove title.

KARL: How can we do that? \ Who's got those papers?

OLGA: You'd be surprised what people have kept hidden \ all these years.

ANITA: All the original records still exist.

PETER: One thing the Russians were good at was bureaucracy. They kept everything, just in case there came a day when they wanted to give it to someone in the neck.

ARMAND: [*accent*] What happen to people living there?

ALFRED: They have to find somewhere else to live.

ANITA: Our biggest problem is absentee landowners.

PETER: Are you saying that people like Uncle Karl shouldn't be able to reclaim \ what is rightfully theirs?

MARTA: What was wrenched from them by force?

ANITA: I'm just saying that if people—

MARTA: Latvians, \ not people.

ANITA: These Latvians, outsiders, come back and reclaim family properties, often evicting other Latvians—

ALFRED: More often evicting insects, vermin.

PETER: Let's drink to the extermination of insects.

ANITA: —who've looked after the place for years. Then after lording it over us for a summer they go home, leaving the house empty, the land lying fallow and growing weeds. \ It's no good for the country.

PETER: But it's only your outsiders who have the money to put in crops, \ make the improvements, buy machinery.

ILSE: There should be some law that they have to live here.

OLGA: Otherwise the whole country will end up a shit heap.

ALFRED: Olga!

OLGA: Ooops.

ALFRED: What's got into you?

KARL: It wasn't the liqueur that's for sure.

MARTA: Let's forget all this tonight. We have guests and we sound like a bunch of moaners.

OLGA: Yes, we can rebuild Latvia tomorrow.

ILSE: You won't do it in a day and may God give you strength but I won't see it in my time.

ALFRED: Who knows? Our eyes never thought to see this day though our hearts always longed for it to happen.

MARTA: Now it's time to come to table. Karly where are you going? You're over here next to me. And bring that bottle with you.

ALFRED: Let's drink to the long awaited return of loved ones.

ANITA: The new Latvia.

> *They down their drinks.* KARL *starts "Zilais Lakatins": a song which bridges into the next scene.*

KARL: [*singing*]
> Bij vasara toreiz tik zaiga

　　　Un ziedeja plavas un sils.
MARTA & KARL: [*singing*]
　　　Tu preti man naci tik maiga
　　　Tev galva bij lakatins zils.

ALL: [*singing*]
　　　Atmina lakatins zilais
　　　Mati ka saulstaru riets.
　　　Biji man viena, nakts tu vai diena
　　　Milas viskrasnakais zieds.

SCENE NINE

Latvia. MARTA*'s place. May 1993. Later the same night.*

MARTA *with* KARL, *heads bowed together. Both of them have had rather too much to drink.* MARTA *is very indulgent of* KARL *who sings the last of the song.*

MARTA: Must be time you went to bed now, Karly.
KARL: Why?
MARTA: Everyone else is 'sleep.
KARL: I can't sleep. Completely wide awake.
MARTA: Poor Karly's body's all mixed up.
KARL: Why? Nothing wrong with me. I can go all night.
MARTA: Doing what?
KARL: What d'you think?
MARTA: I don't know. You said it.
KARL: That too.
MARTA: With Ilse? I don't think so.
KARL: No, maybe not. Only one thing left to do then.
MARTA: Don't you think you've had enough?
KARL: I can drink all night, darling. You want to dance?
MARTA: No Karly. I'm tired.

KARL: I can dance holes in my shoes and still walk home like we used to.

MARTA: Oh Karly you don't walk.

KARL: Why should I walk? I have a car, a brand new car, beautiful car. Cost me thirty thousand dollars.

MARTA: That is expensive.

KARL: I wanted the best. Windows that go up and down when you press a button. Air conditioning, automatic, power steering. When you come to Australia I'll take you everywhere.

MARTA: I don't think I'll be coming to Australia.

KARL: Why?

MARTA: I can't afford it. I can just get through the month on my pension.

KARL: I've got plenty of money darling.

MARTA: If you're paying that's a different story.

KARL: [*accent*] I pay for everything. I can afford, no worries. Air fare, hotel in Singapore—

MARTA: I don't understand what you're saying.

KARL: Why?

MARTA: You're speaking English.

KARL: Oh well. I'll pay for you. Buy you new dresses, shoes, perfumes...

MARTA: What will Ilse say?

KARL: Why?

MARTA: I'm sure she has some say in how you spend your money.

KARL: [*accent*] No way. She has hers money. I have my. That's how she want.

MARTA: You're speaking English again.

KARL: Listen darling, I'm bringing you to Australia for our golden wedding anniversary.

MARTA: When will that be?

KARL: 1998.

MARTA: I have to wait five years? None of us will be alive.

KARL: [*accent*] OK. Any time you like. You always welcome in my house. If she don't like she can go.

ARMAND *comes to the edge of the light.*

MARTA: I hope you don't mind my saying this, but why did you
marry such an old woman? You could've married someone
younger, someone prettier.

KARL: She wasn't so old when I married her.

MARTA: But she's old now. And I don't think she's very well.

KARL: She's strong as a horse. Bury us all. You don't know her.

MARTA: I know what I see. You'll be taking care of her just when
she should be taking care of you. You're still a young man.

KARL: She's just tired from the journey.

MARTA: You must be tired too, Karly.

KARL: Why?

MARTA: Don't drink any more.

KARL: Why not?

MARTA: You'll be sick tomorrow.

KARL: Never in my life, never have I been sick from drinking. Never.

MARTA: Never?

KARL: No. Never.

MARTA: Dad used to get terribly sick.

KARL: I could drink him under the table when I was sixteen.

MARTA: He couldn't drink at all at the end.

KARL: [accent] Drink all day all night no problem.

MARTA: Make that the last one, then we'll go to sleep.

KARL: [accent] I can't sleep. I just can't. If I can't I can't and that's
it.

MARTA: You're a funny boy Karly when you speak English.

KARL: Explain to me why I should go to sleep when I simply cannot
sleep.

MARTA: You don't have to but I have to. Summer nights are short.
The sky's already lightening. Anita will be back after breakfast.

KARL: What for?

MARTA: You said you wanted to see the land this morning, visit
Dad's grave. She offered to drive us. I don't have a car.

KARL: I'll buy you a car. Whatever you want. While I'm here I'll
take care of everything.

MARTA: Are you that rich?

KARL: When I claim Dad's land, I'll buy you a tractor.

MARTA: I can't drive a tractor.

KARL: Peter can do it.

MARTA: Dad would've wanted you to have the land.

KARL: That's my land, but darling, I can't put it in my pocket. I'll sign it all over to you.

MARTA: What about Armand?

KARL: Couldn't tell the back end of a cow from a straw broom. What would he do with a farm? I said, I'm giving you the land, and that's that and good luck.

MARTA: Oh thank you Karly. Peter's had some bad luck lately. He lost his job and his wife threw him out. He has nothing. This will give him a new start.

KARL: I'll fix it. He's my only nephew. Fix the land, the tractor, everything. Don't worry, I can afford it. I could buy him ten times the land.

MARTA: Oh Karly, I knew everything would be all right once you came home.

KARL: What is family for?

MARTA: Thank you, thank you.

> *She kisses him and kisses him.* KARL *notices* ARMAND.

KARL: [*accent*] What you look?

ARMAND: No one can sleep with you talking so much.

KARL: [*accent*] Why? I not stop anyone sleeping.

ARMAND: Marta needs to sleep. Mum's awake.

KARL: [*accent*] I can't sleep. They want to sleep let them sleep.

ARMAND: You lie down and shut up they will.

KARL: [*accent*] Don't tell me shut up!

ARMAND: Someone has to.

MARTA: Don't get upset Karl.

KARL: [*accent*] Don't look! Go 'way! I said don't look!! You think I don't know how you think? Where's the camera? Sneaking round like the dead. Go!

MARTA: Karl, don't yell. You're upsetting yourself for nothing.

KARL: [*accent*] I said go! Go! Stop looking! You not my father.

MARTA: He's overtired. I'll make sure he gets some rest. [*To* KARL.] Come on little brother. I have to lay down.

ARMAND *goes while* KARL *is distracted by* MARTA.

KARL: Gone. Like a ghost. He could make very good money as a doctor but no, thinks he's an artist, wastes his time painting pictures no one can understand.

MARTA: Come on Karly. Time to move.

KARL: Have a drink first.

MARTA: No Karly. You've had enough.

KARL: [*accent*] Never. Sometimes too much but never enough.

MARTA: You're talking English again. Bring your glass with you. Come and put your head next to mine the way you used to. You can talk and I can sleep. You need to rest.

SCENE TEN

Latvia. A railway station. May 1944. Night.

ILSE's *dream. Raining. Softly, the bells and* "Latvija". ILSE *comes through the rain and steam. A* PORTER.

PORTER: You've come again tonight, miss.

ILSE: You said I should. Last night when I missed the train.

PORTER: The weather doesn't look promising.

ILSE: Do you think the rain will ever stop?

PORTER: It's mothers' tears. For sons gone to war and daughters not come home.

ILSE: I'm trying to get home.

PORTER: This rain has played havoc with the train timetables.

ILSE: I have news that will stop my mother crying. I'm engaged to be married. My mother and sister are waiting for me.

PORTER: Where?

ILSE: Jelgava.

PORTER: You just missed the Jelgava train.

ILSE: I can't have. It's not supposed to leave for another hour.

PORTER: Sorry miss. We had to send it away early or it wouldn't get through. What with all this rain and the Russian front advancing towards Jelgava.

ILSE: When's the next train?

PORTER: In half an hour.

ILSE: There's another train to Jelgava?

PORTER: No miss, the next train leaves for the coast. Jelgava is no longer safe.

ILSE: That makes it more important to get home.

PORTER: The next Jelgava train is not scheduled till tomorrow night.

ILSE: That's what you said last night.

PORTER: There was a Jelgava train tonight. You just missed it.

ILSE: It didn't run to schedule.

PORTER: There's a war on.

ILSE: My mother and sister are waiting. Night after night in the rain.

PORTER: If I could stop the rain the trains would always run on time.

ILSE: My mother's crying, my brother's gone to war and I'm trying to get home.

PORTER: It's best to be early, miss.

ILSE: Night after night I arrive early and night after night the train leaves earlier.

PORTER: Come back tomorrow night.

ILSE: No. I'll wait here.

PORTER: I haven't got a waiting room.

ILSE: I'll wait in the rain.

PORTER: You'll catch your death.

ILSE: I'm not leaving till I catch the train.

PORTER: What if the train doesn't come?

ILSE: You said there's one tomorrow night.

PORTER: Scheduled.

ILSE: If I wait here it can't leave before I can catch it.

PORTER: It won't leave at all if Jelgava is behind Russian lines.

ILSE: You mean I'll never get home?

PORTER: It's not for me to tell you that.

ILSE: My mother. How will she know?

PORTER: Either the train won't arrive, or if it does you won't be on it.

ILSE: Should I come back tomorrow night?

PORTER: You can't catch a train from a hotel room.

ILSE: But you said there mightn't be a train to Jelgava.

PORTER: A train schedule is not a reliable guide to the future. The next train leaves for the coast in twenty-seven minutes.

ILSE: I don't want to go to the coast. I want to go home. I have good news.

PORTER: The trains may never run on time again.

He goes.

ILSE: My mother will never stop crying.

Swallowed up in the fog and rain. The tinkle of bells. "Latvija".

SCENE ELEVEN

Central Australia. 1846. A few days after Scene Three.

The sound of chopping. LEICHHARDT *crawling blindly towards the sound, dragging his gear behind him. The ghost of* JOHN GILBERT *enters.*

GILBERT: Dr Leichhardt, ah, I find you alone.

LEICHHARDT: Brown!

GILBERT: He can't hear you. He's carving your inspirational message into yet another tree. L— what is it now? Still 1846? I've so lost track of time.

LEICHHARDT: John Gilbert.

GILBERT: Yes Dr Leichhardt. You remember me.

LEICHHARDT: I would not forget—

GILBERT: The blemish on your otherwise successful first journey.

LEICHHARDT: —the circumstances of your untimely death.

GILBERT: Now you have five more untimely deaths on your conscience.

LEICHHARDT: Is that why you come to bedevil me?

GILBERT: You took my journal.

LEICHHARDT: I sent it to your employer, John Gould, in London, along with your bird specimens.

GILBERT: It is lost then. If Gould has the bird skins my journal will remain unread, forgotten. Now who will remember me?

LEICHHARDT: You will always be remembered from my account of my first journey.

GILBERT: I wrote against you, of your incompetence, your arrogance and blind stupidity.

LEICHHARDT: So I was told and did not read it.

GILBERT: I wrote to warn them and now five more lie dead as a result of your leadership.

LEICHHARDT: I have left an account of their deaths in my journal buried under a marked tree.

GILBERT: Take me back to Sydney with you.

LEICHHARDT: But I am going to Swan River.

GILBERT: Is this the great desert you are meant to be skirting? That ancient sea?

LEICHHARDT: I am blind. Brown is leading me.

GILBERT: Did you expect so many trees to be on her shores?

LEICHHARDT: Trees?

GILBERT: Is the sun on your back each morning and where does each day end?

LEICHHARDT: I am betrayed. [*Calls.*] Brown! Brown!

> BROWN *comes carrying a hatchet. He has* LEICHHARDT's *journal bundled up, slung across his shoulders with twine. He cannot see* GILBERT.

BROWN: Where you crawlin' now, Dr Leichhardt, like big goanna? I leave you sittin' on a rock in the sun.

LEICHHARDT: You were chopping a tree.

BROWN: Yeah. Choppin' marks how you show me. "L". I make some sign for Brown too.

LEICHHARDT: Yesterday you said there was only one tree where you buried my journal.

> BROWN *drags* LEICHHARDT *into the shade.*

GILBERT: He still has your journal with him, hung round his neck.

Don't you feel it?

BROWN: Plenny tree here. You rest inna shade, sun too hot. I bring you something eat.

LEICHHARDT: If we are going west, how is it suddenly there are plenny tree where there was only one before?

BROWN *leaves the hatchet, brings food from the table.*

BROWN: Here is waterhole. Plenny tucker, plenny water. We stay couple days, rest up till you walk again. Eat now.

GILBERT: No. Don't.

LEICHHARDT: What is it?

BROWN: Bird egg. I show you.

LEICHHARDT: Like you show me the way to Swan River?

BROWN: I takin' you blackfella way. Goin' where is waterhole, plenny tucker.

LEICHHARDT: I know which way is west by the sun on my back each morning. You think I don't know where you are leading me? You mean to take me back.

BROWN: Eat now. Make you strong. Then you see Brown goin' right. Here, put in your hand.

GILBERT: Let him eat from your hand then you'll be able to take the journal.

LEICHHARDT: You eat. Then I'll know it's good.

BROWN: I can eat.

BROWN *guides* LEICHHARDT's *hand to his mouth. As he begins to eat,* LEICHHARDT *stuffs the food in* BROWN's *mouth and grabs at the string holding the journal.*

LEICHHARDT: My journal.

BROWN *struggles to get free.* LEICHHARDT *strikes him with the hatchet. The binding breaks on the journal.*

LEICHHARDT: My journal.

BROWN *struggles to get free.* LEICHHARDT *strikes him with the hatchet. The binding breaks on the journal.*

GILBERT: Oh no. You don't have to...

BROWN: Oh! You not goin' drink my blood, eat my liver. I try to save you. You break my bones. You kill Brown.

Charlie Fisher and Harry Brown. A sketch by C. Rodius from *Leichhardt's 'Journal of an overland expedition'*. (Mitchell Library, State Library of NSW)

Leichhardt's party's camp at Dried Beef Creek, November 1844. From C.P. Hodgson's *'Australia from Port Macquarie'* (Mitchell Library, State Library of NSW)

LEICHHARDT *strikes him again.* BROWN *stumbles away.*

LEICHHARDT: Give me my journal.

BROWN: This country take Brown, take your story, too.

   BROWN *goes, scattering pages.*

LEICHHARDT: My journal! Stop him! Stop him!

GILBERT: I can be your eyes now.

LEICHHARDT: I don't trust you. With the sun on my back I can walk away from each morning, walk to the west into the hottest fire. The red of day, the black of night.

GILBERT: You are going to your death.

LEICHHARDT: That is all our destinies.

SCENE TWELVE

North Queensland. EDVARDS' *house. November 1992. Early morning.*

EDVARDS *sitting, waiting. A sound that could be snoring, a soft moaning as* EDVARDS *struggles to breathe.* RUTH *comes into the light. He doesn't look at her.*

RUTH: Edvards.

EDVARDS: Ah Ruthie. So you've come back.

RUTH: I said I would.

EDVARDS: I've been waiting for you, OK?

RUTH: I walked until it grew too windy. It looks like rain. Does it hurt, Edvards?

EDVARDS: Every cell bursting for breath. I wish I could die. How cold your hand is.

   Snatches her hand away.

RUTH: Why won't you look at me?

EDVARDS: You might be some temptress come to steal my soul.

RUTH: Look at me.

EDVARDS: Turn around first.

RUTH: Why are you like this?

EDVARDS: Demons and witches have no back. Show me your back.

RUTH: You wish to torture me.

EDVARDS: My wife, her lover, [LEONIDS *enters*.] OK, leave me again and again. Should I have no feelings? Twist my lips in a smile, bless and forgive?

RUTH: I've been dead a long time.

> RUTH *turns and starts to go to* LEONIDS.

EDVARDS: Come back! Come back, OK?

RUTH: [*stays*] What did you see?

EDVARDS: I remembered when you left with Leonids you didn't even look back.

RUTH: I didn't dare.

EDVARDS: Did Leonids come with you?

RUTH: [*looking at* LEONIDS] No.

> EDVARDS *knows he's there.*

EDVARDS: I don't remember what he looked like.

> LEONIDS *lets go* RUTH's *hand, steps into the shadows.* RUTH *turns back to the table.*

RUTH: I don't remember any of these things.

EDVARDS: We brought nothing from Latvia. Ourselves. They're things I bought, OK? For you. Things we might've bought together. Take something. Some keepsake.

RUTH: To remember you by? You won't even look at me.

EDVARDS: You're still as I remember you, as beautiful, as graceful as a girl. I have grown uglier by the year.

RUTH: If it's pity you want—

EDVARDS: That's all you had left for me.

RUTH: Compassion.

EDVARDS: They are the same.

RUTH: I was in love with Leonids. I loved him.

> LEONIDS *appears.*

EDVARDS: At least you could have satisfied my vanity.

RUTH: Inside that old carcass aren't you as young as you ever were?

EDVARDS: OK. Doesn't mean we don't get sillier as we get older. Make yourself at home, OK. Ilse prepared the banquet.

She comes back to him with the flowers from the table.

RUTH: From my own garden.

EDVARDS: I actually grew those.

RUTH: I stole them.

EDVARDS: I used to steal them when I courted you. Take them.

RUTH: For you. I have to go.

EDVARDS: I'm so tired. Let me put my head in your lap.

She lets him.

Life becomes a habit and man forgets what heaven is. How could I ever forget this?

RUTH: Hush!

EDVARDS: Ruthie, you know what it's like to die without air, OK? You drowned in a flooded river.

RUTH: I can't help you.

EDVARDS: Is drowning a peaceful death?

RUTH: It's only when your lungs fill with water you surrender.

EDVARDS: I'm going to die like a fish on the riverbank.

RUTH: Go to sleep.

EDVARDS: Promise me you'll take me with you.

RUTH *sings the lullaby, "Aija zuzu".*

RUTH: Aija, zuzu, laca berni
                   Pekainami kajinami.

Repeat.

EDVARDS: My mother used to sing that to me. They say men call for their mothers when they die.

RUTH: It wasn't your name I called at the end.

EDVARDS: It was Leonids, OK.

LEONIDS *comes for* RUTH.

RUTH: He's waiting. We're still together.

EDVARDS: Forever, OK. In memory, OK.

LEONIDS: It'll be dawn soon.

RUTH: He's asleep.

LEONIDS: I can't stay.

RUTH: A little while longer.

LEONIDS: It won't be the same as before. When he's buried you won't be lying beside him. You drowned with me. Our bones were never found, never laid to rest.

RUTH: Who will remember us when he's gone?

LEONIDS: When we're forgotten we'll find peace.

> RUTH *gently lowers* EDVARDS' *head. She removes his oxygen mask. She takes a long draught for herself. As they go, she hesitates and looks back. He stirs.*

EDVARDS: [*as though in a dream*] Can't touch her. Can't stop her. Can only watch her go.

> *He can't get up, struggles for breath.*

Ruth! Leonids! Wait! Take me with you. You can't desert me again. Come back! Come back!

> ARMAND *comes. Gets* EDVARDS *to take oxygen.*

ARMAND: Edvards? What the hell... ? It's all right, Just hang on. Come on now, breathe. Take a little oxygen. That's right. Just breathe.

EDVARDS: [*accent*] You see, how end will be, OK.

ARMAND: Don't talk. You wouldn't be so bad if you hadn't sat up all night. You'd be more comfortable in bed.

EDVARDS: [*accent*] How comfortable is hell, OK? [*He rips the mask off.*] A sick animal finds its place to die. I can watch the sun come up from here.

ARMAND: I can't give you the morphine.

EDVARDS: [*accent*] Won't be like drowning. Will be heart failure.

ARMAND: I thought I'd be able to. I'm sorry. Jesus Christ, Edvards...

EDVARDS: [*accent*] When He comes be too late. Call Doctor McQuaide. I already talk with him.

ARMAND: [*going*] Don't move.

EDVARDS: [*accent*] Let phone ring long time. He's drug addict.

> *The first rays of dawn. The first birds sing. Figures in the shadows. Birdsong becomes human voices, chattering.*

So that's the future. OK. The longest journey.

END OF PART ONE

PART TWO

SCENE THIRTEEN

Latvia. A railway station. May 1944. Night.
ILSE's *dream. Raining. Softly, the bells and "Latvija".* ILSE *comes through the rain and steam. A* PORTER *approaches.*

PORTER: You've come again tonight, miss.
ILSE: You said I should. Last night when I missed the train.
PORTER: The weather doesn't look promising.
ILSE: Do you think the rain will ever stop?
PORTER: It's mothers' tears. For sons gone to war and daughters not come home.
ILSE: I'm trying to get home.
GUNNARS & PORTER: This rain has played havoc with the train timetables.
ILSE: I have news that will stop my mother crying. I'm engaged to be married. My mother and sister are waiting for me.
GUNNARS & PORTER: Where?
ILSE: Jelgava.
GUNNARS: The Jelgava train has been cancelled until further notice.
ILSE: Gunnars!? Oh thank God. Oh Gunnars. Night after night I've been waiting here in the rain—it seems an eternity since I saw you.
GUNNARS & PORTER: Sshhh.
GUNNARS: Someone might be watching.
ILSE: But what are you—?
GUNNARS: I came to warn you. It's no longer safe for you to go home.

ILSE: My mother and sister will be waiting. I want to tell them about our engagement.

GUNNARS: The Russians have taken Jelgava.

ILSE: You mean I'll never get home?

GUNNARS & PORTER: I'm not supposed to tell you that.

ILSE: That's what the porter said on the other nights.

GUNNARS: They don't want to cause panic, but with the Russians advancing it'd be better for you to leave Latvia.

ILSE: Leave Latvia? What'll happen to my mother and sister?

GUNNARS: They'll be all right. You'll be more help to them once you're somewhere safe.

GUNNARS & PORTER: The last train for the coast leaves in twenty-seven minutes.

ILSE: We'd better hurry. The trains always leave early.

GUNNARS: I can't come with you. I've been called up.

ILSE: But we're supposed to get married.

GUNNARS: We'll have to postpone the wedding till the war is over. You'd best give me the ring. People are cutting fingers off for gold, breaking teeth. What's in the case?

ILSE: A change of clothes. Some keepsakes.

    The PORTER *takes her case.*

GUNNARS: I'll keep them safe for you.

ILSE: Gunnars, you can't leave me with nothing.

GUNNARS: You may have to run for your life.

ILSE: Was it you, here, on the other nights?

GUNNARS & PORTER: This platform is closed.

GUNNARS: You'd better go or you'll miss your train.

ILSE: Gunnars.

    Steam train whistle.

GUNNARS & PORTER: That train is leaving for the front.

GUNNARS: I have to report for duty.

ILSE: What platform do I leave from?

GUNNARS: The porter will tell you.

ILSE: What about my mother and sister?

GUNNARS: Write to them, but only when you're somewhere safe.

ILSE: But I'm leaving Latvia with nothing.

GUNNARS: I'll come for you when the war is over. I'll find you.

>*And he's gone.*

PORTER: I'll find you.

ILSE: Is the rain really mothers' tears? What if sons don't return from the war and daughters don't come home? My mother will never stop crying.

SCENE FOURTEEN

Latvia. Cemetery for KARL's *father. May 1993. Mid-morning.*

In Latvia cemeteries are forests and gardens, the dead being buried amongst tall pines.

MARTA *carries flowers.*

MARTA: Do you know where you are?

KARL: You said. The cemetery where Dad's buried.

MARTA: But do you remember it?

KARL: I wasn't here when he died.

MARTA: We used to come here all the time to tend our grandparents' graves, and the great grandparents'.

KARL: Maybe. Like in a fog.

PETER: Uncle Karl's whole world is in a fog this morning.

ILSE: There has to be a fog when your eyes are floating in booze.

ANITA: His clock is mixed up, that's all. He probably wants to go to sleep now.

ILSE: Nothing doing. Then he'll keep us all awake for another night with his chirruping.

MARTA: This is where the old people lie, side by side, still in the same bed.

ILSE: No peace even in death. Although they do tie their mouths shut when they're dead.

ANITA: Karl isn't saying much this morning.

ARMAND: [*accent*] Is beautiful how you have graves between trees.

We have only grass, a few flower shrubs, roses.

MARTA: I've let the old people go a bit.

ANITA: I come out here from time to time.

MARTA: It's not easy to get out here so often without a car.

ANITA: They are my grandparents too.

MARTA: I mostly tend to our father. Here he sleeps.

PETER: I'll find you a rake. [*Goes.*]

MARTA: We'll need fresh water for the flowers too.

ARMAND: [*accent*] "Antons Lacis. 1901 to 1944." Only forty-three years.

KARL: Our father.

ARMAND: Edvards would've liked to have been buried like this, under trees. But he would've wanted gum trees.

> MARTA *hands* KARL *the flowers.*

MARTA: Hold these. I'll get some of these weeds out.

ILSE: These mosquitoes!

ANITA: One disadvantage of having the graves in the forest.

ARMAND: [*accent*] You want me to find somewhere where you can sit down, Mum?

ILSE: Best to keep moving or I'll lose so much blood you'll have to bury me here.

ANITA: Aren't you feeling well?

ILSE: I'll be all right. Karl drinks, I get the hangover. It's the perfect marriage.

MARTA: Mum always came out here, on the bus twice a month for thirty-five years. Even in her last days when she was bent double.

KARL: Didn't she want to be buried with Dad?

MARTA: She only had me to come and visit her so she wanted to be buried close to where I live. I had to promise I'd visit her every fortnight. I should have brought something to trim these hedges. They look so untidy.

PETER: [*brings the rake*] I'll have to go down to the stream for water. None of the taps seem to be running.

MARTA: Take some jars off one of the other graves.

ARMAND: [*accent*] I come along help you.

> ARMAND *and* PETER *go.* ANITA *moves away.*

MARTA: Anita never comes out here. Never. Mum would've told Dad she wouldn't be lying here. She used to sit and talk and tell him everything. Even what vegetables she was growing. She wouldn't have known him after thirty-five years. I have to look at photographs to remember what he looked like.

KARL: I was only seventeen when I last saw him.

MARTA: How old do you think I was? He was dead within two months of your leaving.

KARL: Two years in the ground before I knew.

MARTA: Because you didn't write for two years.

KARL: It was the war.

MARTA: Other sons wrote home. Other brothers. Even during the war.

KARL: I didn't think he'd die so young. I got good and drunk.

MARTA: Mum came out here and told him you went to Australia. "Why does Karl have to go so far? Why can't he stay somewhere close, so he can come home?" He never gave her answer.

KARL: I got good and drunk when she died as well.

ILSE: If they were the only times that might mean something, who died last night?

KARL: We could move him.

MARTA: What?

KARL: Move our father. Next to mother in town.

ILSE: Karl. Think before you open your mouth.

MARTA: Disturb his peace after fifty years?

KARL: Mum and Dad would be together. At least she'd have someone to talk to. You could visit both at once.

MARTA: This is where he lived. This is where he died. His parents are buried here.

KARL: Move them too. I'll pay for it, and new headstones with both names, whatever it costs.

ANITA: You're not moving my grandparents. I won't let you.

MARTA: It's not too much for me to come out here. I might need a photograph to remember what he looked like. But I've never forgotten him. I was there at the end.

> MARTA *goes as* ARMAND *and* PETER *return.* ANITA *follows* MARTA.

KARL: Marta! Think! How could I be here?

ILSE: You always get your brightest ideas when your brain is numbed.

KARL: I was trying to make things easier for her.

ILSE: It's your father you were talking about, not stray bones.

> ILSE *goes after* MARTA.

KARL: I wish my brain was numb.

PETER: I think there's some beer in the car.

KARL: [*producing a flask*] Trying to cure a hangover with beer is like trying to get warm by pissing in your trousers.

ARMAND: [*accent*] But you never have hangover.

KARL: Never. Here's to the departed. This he understands. I didn't mean to upset anyone.

> *Drinks and passes the flask to* PETER.

PETER: Just between us, Uncle Karl, Mum feels guilty about grandad being out here while grandma is in town. She always gets upset.

> PETER *takes a swig. During the following, rakes over the grave, takes the flowers from* KARL, *puts them in the jars.*

KARL: What are you looking at now?

ARMAND: I'm trying to imagine what your father was like. How much you're like him, how much I'm like you.

KARL: I don't look like him. You do so they all reckon. I don't know. I'm more from my mother's side.

> *Pause.*

ARMAND: Did he like to drink?

KARL: Not that much.

ARMAND: Yeah but you think you don't drink that much.

KARL: I drink more than he did. He liked to have a vodka at the end of the day. He'd just sit with it, not saying much, Mum did all the talking. I don't know how much he listened. It was like he was waiting for something. When he was a young man, in his apprenticeship, young and strong, he lifted something heavy and he said he felt something snap inside him. This crack and he knew immediately something had gone wrong. He said he knew his life had turned. He was never well from that time. He was still young when Marta wrote, "We lost Dad after ten hours."

ARMAND: Forty-nine years ago and you still haven't asked?

KARL: Not today. You saw how she gets.

> PETER *gives* KARL *some flowers to put on the grave.*

PETER: Uncle Karl—

KARL: I never had a photograph. And I've never forgotten him.

ARMAND: [*accent*] Yeah. But how much you have to drink to have memories?

> ARMAND *takes a photograph of* KARL *putting flowers in one of the jars on the grave.*

SCENE FIFTEEN

North Queensland. EDVARDS' *house. November 1992. Dawn.*

EDVARDS *sits at the table.* MCQUAIDE *is preparing a syringe.*

ARMAND: I couldn't get him to go to bed.

MCQUAIDE: He wants to sit, let him sit.

EDVARDS: [*accent*] Is morning already, OK?

ARMAND: If you'd gone to bed you wouldn't have had that attack.

EDVARDS: [*accent*] Attack coming sooner or later what difference? I must sit at table and wait.

MCQUAIDE: Looks like you're expecting a party.

EDVARDS: [*accent*] Already started. You special guest Doctor McQuaide.

> MCQUAIDE *is ready, puts the syringe aside, sits down.*

MCQUAIDE: Yeah? I'm honoured. You seem fairly comfortable now Eddy.

EDVARDS: [*accent*] I ready.

MCQUAIDE: Doesn't have to be today, not if you're expecting guests.

EDVARDS: [*accent*] Already come, already go.

MCQUAIDE: Didn't eat much.

EDVARDS: I thought my brother would have come.

ARMAND: Mum said those spirits couldn't come from Latvia. They belong to that place.

MCQUAIDE: Could do it tomorrow or the next day.

EDVARDS: [*accent*] I see sun come up. What be different tomorrow?

ARMAND: You sure this is what you want, Edvards?

EDVARDS: [*accent*] I sure, OK? Better than drowning.

ARMAND: Do you want me to phone Mum and Dad?

EDVARDS: No, OK?

ARMAND: I thought you might want—

EDVARDS: I go alone, OK? We all die alone.

ARMAND: I can't let you do this. I can't let someone… kill you and— I'm looking on. I trained as a doctor.

EDVARDS: [*accent*] Watch as painter, OK? Better still take photo. Just before I go, just after. That could make good painting— what you call it? Dipstick.

ARMAND: Diptych.

EDVARDS: I shot my own brother during the war.

ARMAND: Jesus, Edvards! I didn't know that.

EDVARDS: [*accent*] My brother fight for Russians. I fight for Germans. I see him fall, OK?

MCQUAIDE: You think it was your bullet that killed him?

EDVARDS: [*accent*] Doesn't matter who pulls trigger when brother fights brother on mother's soil. We were so close his eye meets my eye. Do you know what look was on his face? Apology, OK? To me, his murderer.

ARMAND: Perhaps he was forgiving you.

EDVARDS: Yes, because he knew I would cross into enemy lines to bury him. Just as I knew he'd get himself shot rather than fire on his brother.

ARMAND: You can't blame yourself for that.

EDVARDS: [*accent*] I blame God. He plays with our lives. My brother lies in Latvian soil where I bury him. I am machine gun by my army and I am bury in Australia. That God's joke.

ARMAND: If you'd like to be buried there. We can take you back. You can afford it.

EDVARDS: My blood has already soaked the ground there. And I've suffered here too long for my spirit to leave. [*Accent.*] Let bones sleep here. Now is my apology, OK? Go if is easier, but now is my time.

ARMAND: I'll stay.

EDVARDS: OK.

MCQUAIDE: This first one is just a muscle relaxant, just puts you to sleep.

EDVARDS: [*accent*] For long time, OK?

MCQUAIDE: A very long time. When you're asleep I'll give you the second one.

EDVARDS: [*accent*] For never wake up.

MCQUAIDE: For never wake up. Unless Armand asks me not to. Then I won't. I can't.

EDVARDS: [*accent*] He knows, OK, my life in his hand.

EDVARDS *gives* ARMAND *his hand to hold.* MCQUAIDE *administers the injection.*

MCQUAIDE: OK.

EDVARDS: [*accent*] Will I dreaming?

MCQUAIDE: They say you don't. But who knows?

EDVARDS: [*accent*] No one comes back to tell.

MCQUAIDE: Should be very peaceful.

EDVARDS: Good. [*To* ARMAND.] Don't cry, OK? What's there to cry about?

ARMAND: Why not? I won't see you again and I'll miss you.

EDVARDS: [*accent*] Miracle is happening.

ARMAND: What miracle?

EDVARDS: [*accent*] Sun comes up.

ARMAND: Oh. Yes.

EDVARDS: [*accent*] What "Oh yes"? If sun don't come up or if moon comes up in place then you think it was miracle.

ARMAND: Probably.

EDVARDS: But the sun comes up, OK, day after day. It shines on all our miserable lives, and I have lived to see it again. That is a miracle.

MCQUAIDE: I'll leave you to get some sleep now, my friend. Till next time.

EDVARDS: [*accent*] I'll have beer waiting.

MCQUAIDE: Look forward to it. It's been a privilege to know you.

EDVARDS: [*accent*] And thank you. Now eat something. Plenty to drink on table.

ARMAND: There's beer in the fridge.

MCQUAIDE: I'll get it. [*Goes.*]

EDVARDS: You want to take bones to Latvia, take your own.

ARMAND: What do you mean?

EDVARDS: Go to Latvia. With your father, OK? Someone has to go with him and Ilse is just as likely not to.

ARMAND: You've been a second father to me. At times more like my father than my father.

EDVARDS: There you'll see who he is. What we were. [*Accent.*] And don't forget. Dipstick.

SCENE SIXTEEN

Australia. The past and present converge, the time ghosts inhabit.

LEICHHARDT: The loveliness of morning, just before and after sunrise. The air so clear and transparent. The promised land lies always to the east. Walk to the west and you walk into the hottest fire. With the sun on my back, I walked away from each morning. I saw where each day ended.

BROWN: What story you makin' up now? I show you proper way for go. But you murder me then go wrong way and die.

LEICHHARDT: At night I fell on a soil as unyielding as stone. When I lifted my head, my skin was scorched to the ground. My eyes saw nothing. The red of day, the black of night. Blinded. The horses fell down and died.

BROWN: I kill them! You tell Brown.

LEICHHARDT: Their tongues bloated so large they choked.

BROWN: I whack 'im with axe same way you whack Brown. I kill 'im for liver for you to eat, blood for you to drink.

LEICHHARDT: My body dried out and my mouth filled with sand. Before a man dies, his breath whistles round his ribs as if he were already a skeleton hung in an exotic garden. A wind chime. I have heard my own bones sing.

BROWN: I have heard me own bones breakin' when some madman start choppin' me with an axe. I didn' do no whistlin'. I was screamin' bloody murder.

LEICHHARDT: You stole my journal.

BROWN: I was savin' that book so no one don' have to sing no story how Brown bad blackfella let you die.

LEICHHARDT: You deserted me.

BROWN: What you reckon? Someone want to squeeze your liver drink your blood, you run.

GILBERT: You deserted me in such a wilderness.

BROWN: Now you singin' some new story you singin' up some other spirit.

LEICHHARDT: Mr Gilbert comes to haunt my dreams. He died of an unfortunate accident on my first journey.

GILBERT: You shot me. And left me to rot in a burnt clearing.

LEICHHARDT: I lit a fire over your grave so the natives would not see the earth had been disturbed.

GILBERT: I was scoured out by a flood.

LEICHHARDT: Fire and flood! That is the singular character of this remarkable country, extremes so often meet.

GILBERT: Some natives found me after the flood receded. Not having had so tame a spirit in their clutches before, they opened me up, as I would have liked, to learn my innermost secrets.

BROWN: Lucky they didn' use no axe.

GILBERT: How disappointed they were to learn the viney-viney was like them. They washed my organs in aromatic leaves—

BROWN: If Dr Leichhardt be there he eat 'em.

GILBERT: They laid me to rest in the branches of a tree. Light and airy and warm. A kind of heaven. But the birds gave me no peace and my bones were carried off by wild pigs.

LEICHHARDT: As if it were the bones that matter. Whatever you thought or knew or remembered would have become just so much dust along with your precious bones, were it not for me.

GILBERT: Had you not murdered me?

LEICHHARDT: Had I not taken you into my exploring party.

GILBERT: I might have lived longer.

LEICHHARDT: To increase still further the fame of John Gould for bird paintings by his forgotten wife, inspired from bird skins killed and collected by whom knows who? You might as readily collect marbles or river stones.

GILBERT: Or mountain ranges, or rivers?

LEICHHARDT: Two of which I named for your remembrance.

GILBERT: Out of guilt for killing me and leaving me to rot in an unmarked grave.

LEICHHARDT: I carved a tree with your name.

GILBERT: Which was burned in a bushfire. Only after one hundred years had passed did anyone come looking for my grave. Yet when you wade into some inland sea and disappear with seven men and seventy-seven animals without leaving so much as a foot print or some scrap of moleskins, the search for your bones continues for one hundred years.

LEICHHARDT: Like you, my bones were never found. Never laid to rest. My last journal is lost forever. At least your diary was discovered—

GILBERT: Unread for a hundred years.

LEICHHARDT: Amongst the papers of John Gould. And ruined my reputation.

GILBERT: If anything your fame has grown. That someone so inept, so irresponsible, so foreign, could manage to achieve so much by following the blind urges of an unruly brain.

LEICHHARDT: I was following my destiny.

GILBERT: Into that sea of flames that you made mine. You were all but forgotten until my diary resurrected you as visionary, mad genius.

LEICHHARDT: Object of derision.

GILBERT: Subject of a novel and an opera.

LEICHHARDT: Not I. Some Johann Ulrich Voss.

GILBERT: They're singing you up in Sydney, your failure is your making, your reputation is restored to truly nearest God.

LEICHHARDT: Providence was ever my protector. Come, I will lead you back to Sydney.

GILBERT: Is there a tree on your horizon?

LEICHHARDT: Now that you mention it, ja there is.

GILBERT: It's one of yours.

They go in different directions. BROWN *remains.*

BROWN: Who is singin' Brown? Where is Brown Mountain? Where is Brown River? Brown know which way to go, no one listen. No tree grow where Brown was fall by axe.

BROWN *goes in yet another direction.*

SCENE SEVENTEEN

Latvia, the land. May 1993. Mid-morning.

A lone oak tree, apparently dead except for one lower branch. MARTA *on* KARL's *arm, leading him. He has his eyes shut.*

EDVARDS *has remained sitting at the table. Through the scene he lowers his head to his arms, sleeps.*

MARTA: Oops. Careful now.

KARL: How much further?

MARTA: No Karl, keep your eyes shut until I tell you.

KARL: I'll break a leg.

MARTA: You can open your eyes now.

KARL: This is it? Our land? Really?

ILSE: It could be the fog still hasn't lifted.

MARTA: It's hard to tell without the house and barn.

KARL: One old oak that's nearly dead.

PETER: It has one green branch.

KARL: We carved our names in it.

MARTA: Not that one. There used to be another one over there.

ILSE: So where was the house? There has to be a hearthstone or something.

KARL: If I used to climb that tree the house would've been here.

MARTA: There was a fire and what was left was pushed into the ditch to make bigger cow paddocks for the commune.

KARL: That house down near those trees is familiar.

MARTA: Uncle's house.

PETER: Anita's house now.

KARL: That close?

PETER: Half a kilometre or so.

KARL: It used to seem so far.

ARMAND: [accent] What happen to lake, about which you talked?

KARL: That was... ? It's only a ditch.

MARTA: Filled in.

ARMAND: [accent] How big lake can be if can fill up with half house?

KARL: We used to trap freshwater crays. We had a boat. I'd row, Marta would pull up the pots. When we had a box full I'd take them to the station on my bike and send them to the markets in Riga. We made good money during the war.

MARTA: There used to be a... pond.

KARL: Everything seems so small, so close. Everything used to be so big. Every time I climbed that oak tree it was an adventure.

ILSE: It would be now too.

KARL: I couldn't say now, how much land we had.

PETER: Five hectares, wasn't it Mum?

ILSE: Is that all? My father farmed more than that as a peasant.

MARTA: We weren't farmers. Uncle was the farmer, Dad was the local mechanic. He owned a combine harvester. How much land there was altogether... well, the brothers had an arrangement.

ARMAND: [accent] Dad all the time dream he is land baron, Russians running in back of him.

KARL: Five hectares around the house. There was more land than that.

PETER: Anita, you must have some idea what land there was. You've claimed your father's share.

ANITA: I let a lawyer friend handle my claim. There were some seventy hectares in my father's name, but as for boundaries or arrangements or anything like that... best thing is to go to the claims office, check out the titles.

KARL: I can't see it. I just can't see it. Where was the barn exactly, where the house?

ILSE *goes to* KARL.

In my dreams I could always see them and now even the dreams are gone.

ILSE: When houses go, everything is lost, all the life that was ever lived in them.

KARL: All gone. Maybe Edvards was right not to come back.

SCENE EIGHTEEN

North Queensland. EDVARDS' *house. November 1992. Just after sunrise.*

EDVARDS *is at the table,* ARMAND *sitting by him, still holding his hand.* MCQUAIDE *is sitting at the table.* RUTH *and* LEONIDS *are there.*

EDVARDS *now stands watching this scene.*

MCQUAIDE: He's in a deep sleep now.

ARMAND: Yes.

EDVARDS: So you came back again. Tell me I'm dreaming.

RUTH: You're dreaming.

EDVARDS: Then I'm only remembering you.

RUTH: And Leonids as well.

EDVARDS: Forever, OK? In memory.

LEONIDS: I was your friend. I betrayed you.

EDVARDS: I've forgiven you, OK? Long ago. Forgotten you.

LEONIDS: If you had forgotten me I'd be gone. I yearn to find some peace, to moulder in the darker reaches of this world's memory, to become just so much dust or smoke drifting in the air. Yet you keep dragging me into the light. If I loved wrongly I cannot now

make amends. When you go I'll go with you down the same
secret road but then you'll never know I'm there. Then I'll be
forgotten.

EDVARDS: [*to* RUTH] I can't think of you without thinking of him,
OK? You come to torture me.

RUTH: Best not think of me at all.

EDVARDS: Why can't I dream of Latvia when we first married?

RUTH: Who's left there to remember us?

EDVARDS: No one.

LEONIDS: And next to no one here.

MCQUAIDE: Give him the second shot?

ARMAND: It's what he wanted.

MCQUAIDE: Best not put it off.

ARMAND: Do it.

    MCQUAIDE *administers the second injection.*

EDVARDS: I'm thinking, I'm dreaming, OK, I'm remembering
everything I want to forget.

RUTH: I still dream of Latvia every night and every day.

EDVARDS: Do you think of me at all? Am I in that dream?

RUTH: I'm here.

    RUTH *and* LEONIDS *sing* "Dzimtene". BROWN *comes and sings
as well.*

RUTH, LEONIDS & BROWN: [*singing*]
> Par dzimteni dziesma
> Man serigi skan
> Par dzimteni dzivot,
> Kur velets nav man.
>
> Es svesuma klistu
> Ar ilgosanos
> Vai dzimtenes krastus
> Reiz ieraudzit bus.
>
> Although life is fine in
> Those far foreign lands
> I dream of my homeland
> All day and all night.

Kur zvaignites rakstits
Mans bernibas stasts
Nav aizmirstams maminas
Milotais glasts.

EDVARDS: It's said we die alone, OK? It must be said as a joke. This is hell. To die alone would be a luxury.

BROWN: My Latvia is here. My people came and lived here. We were born here. We died here. We look to our own. There's nowhere to go. Right here is where I die. Right here is where I go on living.

RUTH *removes the oxygen mask, breathes from it.*

RUTH: I can't catch my breath.

LEONIDS: We'll soon be at peace.

RUTH *and* LEONIDS *go, separately.*

MCQUAIDE: He's stopped breathing.

RUTH: Leonids.

MCQUAIDE: The heart will keep beating for a minute or so.

ARMAND: His pulse is fainter.

ARMAND *takes a photograph.*

EDVARDS: Before we are born we are an idea, OK? After life we are an idea, some memory. Perhaps life is nothing more than a series of ideas. Mine weren't so bad.

ARMAND *takes a photograph of* EDVARDS.

ARMAND: I can't feel it.

SCENE NINETEEN

North Queensland. KARL *and* ILSE*'s place. Her dream. Early morning.*

EDVARDS *comes with the flowers he'd picked the previous evening. The tinkling of a bell.*

ILSE: Karl. There's someone at the door.

EDVARDS: Ilse.

The tinkle of the bell.

ILSE: Karl, answer the door. Oh for God's sake...

*The tinkle of the bell. A square of light spills across the stage.
ILSE comes into it. EDVARDS in the darkness.*

Who is it?

EDVARDS: It's Edvards. I brought some flowers for you.

ILSE has the urge to take the flowers, but resists it.

ILSE: No I don't want them.

EDVARDS: From my own garden.

ILSE: I said I don't want them.

The bell more urgent.

EDVARDS: I grew them especially for you.

ILSE: I can't take them. Go away.

EDVARDS: At least take a look at them.

ILSE: No. Just go. Please.

Now a pounding on the door.

EDVARDS: It's dark out here. Let me come in. How can you close the
door on a friend?

ILSE: I'm sorry.

EDVARDS: I don't mean you any harm.

ILSE: Nor I you.

EDVARDS: Then take the flowers.

ILSE: Leave me alone.

EDVARDS: You don't have to touch them. I'll put them in a vase.
They are so beautiful they'll make you weep. All you have to do
is let me in.

As though the door was being shaken.

ILSE: Oh no. He's going to get in. Karl!

EDVARDS: Just look at them Ilse. They'll soften your heart. You'll
see I mean no harm. Ilse. Open the door. It's Edvards. It's dark.
Let me in. If only for friendship's sake.

*ILSE drags a bed from the light out into the open. EDVARDS
continues as though she were still indoors.*

ILSE: I'll sleep out here on the road. He won't come out here. Karl will be here soon. Then I'll be safe.

EDVARDS: Ilse. I have flowers for you.

ILSE: Karl! Karl!

> *As* KARL *comes on the light changes to morning.* ARMAND *carries* EDVARDS *and lies him on the bed.* ARMAND *sits with him.*

KARL: What? What is it? Who's cut your throat?

ILSE: Go to Edvards' place.

KARL: It's still too early. He's probably still asleep. What's the big hurry?

ILSE: Edvards is dead. You better go up.

KARL: What? Did Armand phone?

ILSE: No.

KARL: Well how do you know? Who told you?

ILSE: Last night when you were drunk, he was your friend and you were spending his money. This morning you can't even move.

KARL: Why?

ILSE: Why are you standing? Just go. [*She goes.*]

KARL: I'm going, I'm going.

SCENE TWENTY

North Queensland. EDVARDS' *house. A few minutes later.*

KARL *is there.* MCQUAIDE *sits at the table, in the early morning sunshine, drinking a beer.*

MCQUAIDE: Nice morning, don't you think.

KARL: [*accent*] Good day. Doctor McQuaide.

MCQUAIDE: For this time of year.

KARL: [*accent*] I was not expecting...

MCQUAIDE: Me either. Not sitting here enjoying a beer. It is a bit early but the situation calls for it. Edvards died this morning.

KARL: Edvards?

MCQUAIDE: Not that long ago. In his sleep.

KARL: Edvards?

MCQUAIDE: Peacefully. I'm sorry. An inadequate summary of someone's passing but in this case it's true enough. Can I get you a beer or something? I'm having another.

KARL: Armand?

MCQUAIDE: Sitting with Edvards.

KARL: [*accent*] I can go in?

MCQUAIDE: Most certainly.

> KARL *goes.* MCQUAIDE *get himself a beer.* ARMAND *comes out.*

We always say he went peacefully, she went peacefully. Why is it we never say someone went in a fit of bad language shredding his bed linen? I, for one, will not go peacefully into that long night. I've signed the death certificate.

ARMAND: Heart failure.

MCQUAIDE: It would've been.

ARMAND: This way or the other.

MCQUAIDE: You don't approve? Condone?

ARMAND: Heart failure is my condition too.

MCQUAIDE: Not many of us can kill those we love. Probably just as well. Beer?

ARMAND: Something stronger.

MCQUAIDE: Yes, why not?

> ARMAND *pours them a shot glass of horse-kick.*

There's quite a spread here. Didn't the guests turn up?

ARMAND: I think they did.

MCQUAIDE: Didn't eat much.

ARMAND: Help yourself. Sanctify the feast.

MCQUAIDE: Aah no thanks. Still a bit early to eat. His own brew?

ARMAND: Horse-kick.

MCQUAIDE: Cheers. An appropriate sentiment for Edvards.

ARMAND: Yes.

> *They drink.* MCQUAIDE *has a beer chaser.*

MCQUAIDE: Your mother told me you don't practise much any more.

ARMAND: Medicine, no.

MCQUAIDE: Painting pays does it?

ARMAND: Not as much. Enough.

MCQUAIDE: I've never seen that before. The photographing. At births, yes. Never at a death. I think you caught him.

> KARL *comes back.*

KARL: [*accent*] That not Edvards.

ARMAND: Dad?

KARL: [*accent*] I cannot stay there.

ARMAND: Come and sit down.

KARL: [*accent*] Is easy, you forget. Very quickly. Who person is. Who was. But that not Edvards.

ARMAND: No. That's OK.

KARL: [*accent*] Doesn't even look like. If you take photograph maybe does.

MCQUAIDE: It can be quite a shock. Never get used to it.

KARL: [*accent*] All this table he asks Ilse to make for last night. He knew. Two doctors here. And still gone. He knew.

MCQUAIDE: Let me get you a drink.

KARL: Now is time to eat something. Edvards said.

ARMAND: That's what he said. In the morning.

KARL: Drink first.

MCQUAIDE: There you go. Well, I'll be off, unless there's something else I can do?

ARMAND: We'll be all right. Thanks. It wasn't the oath that stopped me.

MCQUAIDE: No. Or you would've stopped me. Leave the certificate for Jonesy when he picks up the body.

> MCQUAIDE *goes.*

KARL: He knew all right.

ARMAND: Yeah he knew.

> *Pause.*

KARL: My father knew.

ARMAND: What?

KARL: That I wouldn't see him again. When he kissed me. I still remember the prickle of his stubble, how wet his mouth was. And he just looked at me and looked at me, as if he wanted to hold me in his mind.

Pause.

We'd been drinking. It was my seventeenth birthday and I had my call-up papers from the Russians. I had to report in two days.

The tinkle of the bells. "Latvija". Again we are cast into the world of memory, working across time. KARL's *place in Latvia in 1944.*

MARTA *is there.*

Marta and I were dancing.

KARL *and* MARTA *start to dance.*

MARTA: Karl, you're drunk.

KARL: Why not? Tomorrow I might be dead.

ILSE *is there. Becomes* KARL's MOTHER. ARMAND *becomes his* FATHER.

MOTHER: That's always been your excuse. Tomorrow any one of us might be dead.

MARTA: Don't talk like that Karly.

FATHER: There's a knock at the door.

The knocking is like the stamping of many heavy feet. Tinkle of the bells. "Latvija".

MOTHER: It's the Germans. A soldier. He says he's come for Karl. They're calling him up tonight. Oh my son.

KARL: Tonight?

MARTA: Tell them to come tomorrow.

MOTHER: They're pulling out tonight.

KARL: I can't go with them. I'm supposed to report to the Russians in two days.

FATHER: The Germans are at the door.

MOTHER: Can't we hide him?

FATHER: They know he's here.

KARL: I'll have to go with them. Or they'll shoot me.

MOTHER: I'll pack you some things.

KARL: This is only my second best suit. They'll give me a uniform. But what about you when the Russians come? If they find out I went with the Germans they'll shoot you.

MOTHER: We'll have nothing they want. We'll manage.

The stamping, louder. The bells softer. "Latvija".

FATHER: Better not keep them waiting. Come on mother. We all must drink. Wish your son well.

They all drink. Rushed farewells.

MARTA: Oh Karly, be careful.

She goes.

KARL: [*to* MARTA] At least I'll be killing Russians. Goodbye mother.

MOTHER: Son, my son. Don't forget where your home is. Come back safely. We'll be waiting, don't worry about us.

She goes.

FATHER: Remember us.

FATHER looks at KARL. Kisses him on the mouth. The tinkle of the bells. "Latvija".

You'd better go now. Write before you come back, find out how things are.

KARL and ARMAND back at EDVARDS' place.

KARL: We'd been drinking. It was my seventeenth birthday. He scared me, you know, looking at me like that. It made me fear for my own life. I was going off to the war.

ARMAND: Maybe he thought if he scared you enough you'd stay alive.

KARL: He knew he wouldn't see me again. He was trying to tell me. Two months later he was dead.

ARMAND: Did you hate him?

KARL: Why?

ARMAND: I hated you. You scared me. When you'd get drunk and cry in your beer and tell us how the Russians had shot your father and were coming to shoot you.

KARL: It was the drink talking.

ARMAND: I was only a kid. I didn't understand that.

KARL: I was wrong to do that, to say those things.

ARMAND: Do you remember the last time you said anything about your father being shot? It was the night you and Edvards had that fight. You were hitting him, he wouldn't fight back.

KARL: He was my friend. My closest friend. And he's dead. Why talk about this now?

ARMAND: I wanted him to be my father. I didn't want to be like you. I wanted to be like him. But that night I realised, for better or worse I had you. And I still don't know who you are. You don't say much when you're sober and I don't listen when you're drunk. I probably haven't been the son you wanted me to be. But it's not too late. We could go to Latvia together, if you'd like.

KARL: I can go now. I have Edvards' money. We have to take your mother. She knew Edvards was dead. She sent me up here. We'd better go and tell her.

ARMAND: You go. I'll stay till they collect Edvards' body. Tell Mum I'll bring some flowers. She'll want to tie a wreath.

SCENE TWENTY-ONE

Latvia. OLGA's *house. May 1993.*

ILSE *is making a wreath, tying fresh flowers and greenery to fresh canes.* OLGA *passes,* ILSE *ties.*

OLGA: I never learned how to do that.

ILSE: I learned at mother's knee. Watching the way she used to tie them depending on the flowers people would bring, not by what they could afford to pay. She had quite a reputation. I tie them in Australia, when someone I know well dies.

> ARMAND *breaks bread at the table and goes back to sit with* EDVARDS.

And for the Red Cross on Anzac Day. It's their remembrance day. Armand used to help when they were children. He and his sister would get up early and go round the neighbourhood begging the best flowers.

ARMAND *takes the flowers from* EDVARDS' *hand.*

They'd take so much pride in my wreath lasting so much longer than the usual crepe paper ones. One heavy dew and they're soggy. Mine would be left a week longer on its own after all the others were cleared away.

OLGA: She stopped tying them, you know? When our poor brother, Imants, died in the war. If she couldn't lay a wreath for her own son she said she couldn't see the point.

ILSE: I'd sit exactly the way she'd sit, turn it this way and that, look at the flowers, look at the greenery, to make the best arrangement.

OLGA: Never tied another. Not even when Dad died. A bunch of flowers in a jar would have to do him, she said.

ILSE: This was one way I found to remember her. Father I remember as lord and master. I was always six when he was around. Even when I was twenty-three.

OLGA: Mum never thought you'd died in the war. Even when we hadn't heard anything for four years.

ILSE: I thought you all might have.

OLGA: We were all here, except Imants, and you, in exactly the same place.

ILSE: I waited till I was somewhere safe. It sounds lunatic, I know, but when you're so far away, all sorts of rumours fly about, you fear all sorts of things.

OLGA: Sometimes when it rained, Mum would stand in the doorway, or at the window if it was cold and watch the road. "My girl is crying," she'd say, "I can hear her."

ILSE: The rain was in my dreams too. I thought it was mother's tears.

OLGA: The sun came out. We got on with our lives. We had to.

ILSE: My rain didn't stop when I wrote. As luck would have it I'd gone to the wettest place in Australia.

OLGA: You should've seen father when he got your first letter. He ran home. He ran from house to house, to Alfred's, to neighbours, anyone that knew you. He ran and ran all afternoon. "If anyone knew the family at this address, and knows where they are now, please send this letter on." That's what you wrote on the envelope. I still have it. It came to me when they'd both died. I have all your letters and cards, every photograph, every little gift, every little handkerchief. When the winter nights are long I take them out and re-read every word, in order. Those hard early years when you started with nothing, having the children, learning the language, Karl's drinking, I know your whole history off by heart from the beginning. Every little heartbreak, every happiness. [*Silence.*] Until you stopped writing twenty years ago. [*Silence.*] You must have had reasons, mother said. She was certain you weren't dead. I didn't have her faith. Especially when you kept your silence when we wrote and told you Mum had died. And last Easter when you wrote to say you were coming to Latvia, I ran and ran like father did, over to Alfred's place.

    ALFRED *is there.*

ALFRED: Well little sister, I'm waiting till you come to my place.

ILSE: Didn't we arrange it for the day after tomorrow?

ALFRED: And of course you'll stay the night.

ILSE: I thought we were coming back here.

ALFRED: Then you'll have stayed here three nights and not one at my place.

OLGA: [*to* ILSE] It's up to you.

ALFRED: You'd have your own room. I'd fire up the boiler for baths.

ILSE: I'm sure I'd be very comfortable but we'll be with you the whole day. We're only coming back here to sleep before Anita takes us back to Marta's.

ALFRED: You must sleep at my place. You're not really being my guests unless you sleep under my roof.

OLGA: Now you're being silly Alfred.

ALFRED: Silly now is it?

OLGA: How can you say that when Ilse's come all this way—?

ALFRED: Then why can't she grace me with her presence?

OLGA: Ilse can do what she wants.

ALFRED: Naturally you had nothing to do with it. Butter wouldn't melt in your mouth. Tell me why my little apartment isn't good enough for Ilse and her family to stay in?

OLGA: We both agreed they'd be more comfortable here.

ALFRED: You've always got that little bit more, more this, better that, a better house, more money, a bit more land to keep a few pigs, poultry, the milking cow—

OLGA: But I've always given—

ALFRED: Naturally, given. To show you have enough to spare. How well you're doing. The lady of the manor, sharing with the peasant.

ILSE: Alfred! Don't say any more.

   Silence.

ALFRED: Sorry little sister. Sorry. I apologise.

ILSE: We'll all be together tomorrow and tomorrow night and then we'll be with you all the next day.

ALFRED: Sorry little sister, if it's too much to ask that you sleep under my roof, you're not proper guests at all.

ILSE: I'm not meaning to slight you in any way, my brother, I've found the travelling hard and I need to sleep in the same bed for more than one or two nights. I'm an old woman who's not all that well, who's tired of packing and moving on, tired of eating, tired of changing beds, tired of not hurting feelings, tired of being the perfect guest so I'm staying put and that's that.

ALFRED: I'll come back tomorrow when we go to the graveside.

OLGA: Alfred. Don't go like that.

SCENE TWENTY-TWO

North Queensland. KARL *and* ILSE's *patio. 1992. Morning.*

ILSE *continues making the wreath.*

KARL: My best friend is dead.

ILSE: His bones are not even in the ground and already you're counting his money.

KARL: Edvards left it to both of us. Fifty-fifty.

ILSE: I don't want my share. Not one cent.

KARL: Why?

ILSE: I just don't and that's an end to it.

KARL: I know how close Edvards was to you.

ILSE: What do you know, or think you know?

>   *Pause.*

KARL: I know, that I came to tell you that he'd just died and you already had the wreath half made.

ILSE: He was my friend too. More than a friend.

KARL: That's why Edvards is giving us the money.

ILSE: He owes me nothing.

KARL: He doesn't owe me either but I'm taking it.

ILSE: What for? You don't need it.

KARL: It's mine, to do with what I like. I'll buy a new car.

ILSE: You can't wash the one you've got.

KARL: I'll go to Latvia.

ILSE: Oh yes, go to Latvia. You could've gone to Latvia a long time before this.

KARL: You wouldn't go.

ILSE: Did you need me along to wipe your bottom?

KARL: Armand's coming with me.

ILSE: I knew you'd never go on your own. You'd have someone to look after you.

KARL: I can afford to go first class.

ILSE: The only reason you couldn't afford it before was because every spare dollar you pushed up the backside of some crippled racehorse.

KARL: I can even afford to do that.

ILSE: It won't be long before you lose it all.

KARL: I've never had this much money before in my life. I had to work hard just to make ends meet.

ILSE: Edvards worked for it, not you.

KARL: Sometimes you get lucky in life. You don't spit on it. I deserve this break and I'm making the most of it. The least you could do is accept what he gave us.

ILSE: No, not on his terms. That's not giving, that's buying.

KARL: So if he'd given it to you, no conditions, you'd have taken it?

ILSE: I don't need it. I'd give it to the children.

KARL: What the hell for? I've done enough for those bastards.

ILSE: Bastards now are they?

KARL: They both earn more than I do. Why the hell should I give it to them?

ILSE: It's enough for me that they're my children.

KARL: They're not missing out. Edvards left them the house.

ILSE: What are you missing out on?

KARL: From now on, nothing. What's mine is mine. If there's anything left when I'm gone, they're welcome to that.

ILSE: If I don't take my share it'll probably go to them anyway.

KARL: You can do what you like.

ILSE: I do. I have enough to live on, everything I need, everything I want.

    ARMAND *comes with some flowers.*

ARMAND: Mum I thought you might need more flowers.

    ILSE *takes the flowers.*

ILSE: Aren't they beautiful?

ARMAND: They're from Edvards' place.

ILSE: Take them away.

ARMAND: Why? What's wrong?

ILSE: I have enough from my own garden.

ARMAND: I'll put them in a vase.

ILSE: No. I don't want them in the house.

    ILSE *has finished the wreath.*

SCENE TWENTY-THREE

Latvia. ILSE's *mother's graveside. The day after Scene Twenty-One.*
OLGA *helps* ILSE *into a coat.*

OLGA: Here Ilse, put on this coat. It looks like it might rain. Alfred will hold the wreath.

ILSE: Looks like I'm the only one who feels cold.

ALFRED: We don't want you coming down with anything.

KARL: If I keep my boiler stoked I don't feel the cold.

>ALFRED *returns the wreath to* ILSE.

ALFRED: It's a fine piece of work. Mum will like that.

ILSE: Their grave is beautifully kept.

OLGA: Alfred does most of it.

ALFRED: I came out here yesterday so you'd see it at its best.

ILSE: Thank you little brother. Where should I put it?

ALFRED: Wherever you like.

>As ILSE *places the wreath on the graveside* ARMAND *takes photographs. She stands there in silence for a few moments. She falters.*

ARMAND: Mum.

ILSE: Alfred. Olga. You come here too.

OLGA: This is your time.

ILSE: All the children together.

>OLGA *and* ALFRED *join* ILSE, *on either side of her.* ILSE *takes their hands.* ARMAND *takes photographs.*

I didn't know what to say.

OLGA: Don't worry. They understand.

ALFRED: Tell them why you ran, little sister?

ILSE: What?

ALFRED: Why did you run?

OLGA: Alfred. This is not the time.

ALFRED: What better time? What better place? That was the unanswered question.

ILSE: What can I say? There's nothing that... that doesn't taste like gravel in my mouth.

ALFRED: I hope you'll forgive me, little sister, but I won't let you run this time.

OLGA: Let go Alfred. That's between Ilse and...

ALFRED: When you've gone I'll have to come back and answer for you. That you were afraid for yourself, everyone was. We're all alive. We worked, we raised families, buried our dead in the usual way. Life's been a bit harder than it need be but that's the Russian way.

ILSE: I know the Russian way, to take a man from his work, not give him time to pack, not kiss his wife or children goodbye. To leave them crying in terror, not giving any reasons why. I've seen them.

ALFRED: We've all seen them. But what would they want with you? We were only peasants, lucky to finish primary school. They needed us to do the work.

ILSE: I was afraid and I hated them. I ran for my life. Of that I'm not ashamed. Tomorrow I would run again. As far, for as long, as my strength would allow.

ALFRED: You didn't have to live with Mum's heartbreak.

ILSE: Ohh! Ohh! Is that harder than to live without it? I had to live with my own heart-ache. Knowing what pain I caused her. Knowing I would never see her again, see father again, never bask in her love though I knew she loved me and always would. I didn't get to sit at her feet again, my head on her knee, her hand on me, her love around me. I didn't get to hear her voice again, to hear her call my name, to listen to her laugh, to see her cry. I'm sorry mama that I made you cry. But I always remembered you, always remembered I was, I am still your daughter. And I loved you. I always loved you.

   Pause.

KARL: That's all there is to say, Ilse.

ILSE: I love you. Mama. Father. I love you.

OLGA: That's all there is to say.

ALFRED: They'll sleep better now.

SCENE TWENTY-FOUR

Latvia. MARTA*'s place. A few days later.*
ANITA *comes to* MARTA *with a basket.* KARL, ILSE, ARMAND.

ANITA: I'm sorry we're late. Karl and Ilse wanted to stop at the markets on the way back to do some shopping. Then of course Karl had to stay and have a drink in the market.

> MARTA *looks in the basket.*

MARTA: Pig food.

KARL: What?

MARTA: Third rate pig food.

KARL: It's all fresh. Cheeses, sprats, sausage—

MARTA: I wouldn't feed it to pigs.

ILSE: It's the same as we've been eating here.

MARTA: That's the kind of hostess I am. I feed my guests pig food.

ILSE: I didn't say that.

MARTA: That's how you think though. You come here with your Australian dollars and American cheques and when you reach into your pocket you cover it with your other hand in case a bit of change should escape.

ILSE: Marta! How can you... ? We wanted to live the way you do.

MARTA: We don't want to live the way we do. We want to live better.

KARL: This isn't the cheapest stuff, you know?

MARTA: Just the worst.

> KARL *puts the shopping on the table.*

KARL: What's wrong with it?

MARTA: What's wrong with it? Where's your nose? It stinks. God only knows what it's made from. Half those stallholders are thieves and murderers.

ILSE: We went to the same ones you go to.

MARTA: But I know them. They wouldn't dare give me this rubbish.

KARL: Anita was with us.

MARTA: Oh yes, Anita. I won't have it on my table. Let Anita have it. [*Throws the food at her.*] Take it, take it all, take the sausage, the cheese, these poisonous, spray painted fish. You've taken everything else.

> ANITA *catches some things, ducks others.* KARL *retrieves some, and* ARMAND.

ANITA: Marta! Don't.

KARL: What the hell's got into you?

MARTA: Didn't Anita tell you? What did you talk about as she drove you round all week?

KARL: I truly don't know what you're talking about.

MARTA: I bet you got on famously. You're peas in a pod you two. Did you promise her a tractor too?

ANITA: He didn't promise me anything.

MARTA: What about the things you promised me, Karl? New dresses and perfumes and trips to Australia. \ All lies as well?

ILSE: [*overlapping*] He'll promise you anything when he's drunk. If you believed him \ you're a fool.

KARL: I've had enough. [*To* MARTA.] My God you're a sour old sow. [*Tosses food at her.*] You want to feed this to the pigs, go ahead. I don't care. You want money? Take it. [*Throws money.*] What do you want? Dollars? Roubles? Take it. Do what you like with it. How much do you want?

> *Now it's* ILSE's *turn to retrieve the food.*

ILSE: Like children. One's as bad as the other.

MARTA: [*throwing the money back*] I don't want your money. You say you're rich and lord it round the place how you're going to do this and you're going to do that and you do nothing.

KARL: What haven't I done?

> PETER *is there.*

MARTA: You've done nothing for Peter. He's your only nephew. You could give him a hand up in the world. He doesn't have a father to help him or guide him but you can't even get him a piddling piece of land \ so he can at least feed himself.

PETER: [*to* MARTA] Mum, stop. You're going about this the wrong way.

KARL: Peter was going to the titles office. I said I'd sign it over.

MARTA: You've already signed it over to her. \ Enough was never enough for her family.

PETER: You'll give yourself a heart attack. Uncle Karl \ probably doesn't know.

KARL: I haven't signed anything. I haven't seen anything. I don't know what you're talking about.

MARTA: Ask Anita. She's the clever one. She's the one with the lawyer.

ANITA: I only claimed what was mine by right, in my father's name.

MARTA: And what about the rest?

ANITA: \ What rest?

KARL: What the hell is going on here?

PETER: Let's all settle down first. Come on Mum. Uncle Karl will probably need a drink first.

KARL: I need two.

PETER: We could all use a drink. It's my own drop Uncle Karl.

ILSE: What kind of circus will we have when you're all drunk?

ANITA: Not for me either thank you.

MARTA: Then you tell him.

ANITA: What have I to tell?

KARL: Let's drink first.

They drink. PETER *pours another round.*

MARTA: You tell him Peter. My heart will break.

PETER: You'll need this, Uncle Karl. Maybe you should sit down.

ILSE: For God's sake, keep pouring that into him, he'll fall down. It must run in the family.

ARMAND: Mum.

PETER: There's no separate title, Uncle Karl.

KARL: What do you mean?

PETER: You don't own any land. You never owned it.

MARTA *begins to cry.*

ARMAND: [*accent*] I don't understand.

MARTA: Anita understands. How you could stand there the day...
you even drove us to the land...

ANITA: I'm sorry. But the farm where you lived was under my
father's name.

MARTA: My mother did not sell it to him.

PETER: Because she never owned it.

KARL: There must be some mistake. You know we lived there. My
father built a house, two barns. I lived there all my life.

ANITA: There's only ever been one title. It's always been in our
name. A brother built on a brother's land.

KARL: But to build there and live there for years and years.

MARTA: My father would've had some agreement.

ANITA: Perhaps it was to be signed over but the war came and your
father died... nothing was written down. There is no separate title.

KARL: I lived there all my life. It was to be mine when I came back
from the war.

ARMAND: You lived here only seventeen years. You're sixty-six.
You lived most of your life in Australia.

ILSE: All your life you've been coming back here.

KARL: My father left me nothing. He had nothing to give.

ILSE: What have you got to give your children?

MARTA: Why didn't mother tell me?

KARL: There was nothing to tell.

PETER: It wasn't your land. That's why she moved into town when
your father died.

ARMAND: [*accent*] One thing that I want to know. Dad doesn't
himself know, how his father die.

KARL: Give me that bottle.

ARMAND: [*accent*] Aunt Marta?

MARTA: We found him in the barn, near the combine. Blood was
coming from his mouth. We couldn't get the doctor to him in
time. And there was no way to stop the bleeding.

ARMAND: [*accent*] Was he shot?

MARTA: Shot? He had a ruptured ulcer in his stomach. In ten hours
he was dead.

KARL *rushes to the back of the space. He throws up.* EDVARDS' *ghost is there in his burial suit. Only* KARL *sees him.*

EDVARDS: OK. So this is what you've got to show me.

ILSE: This is the man who's never been sick from drinking.

MARTA: Oh Karly. My poor little Karly.

ILSE: No more poor little Karly. He's old enough to know better.

EDVARDS: I waited all these years for you to show me. OK. You were a boy when you left, master of nothing. But how long can a man sit and wait for nothing? Doing nothing with his life, crying to go home. Where is home, OK? A grown man with a family and you still expected your father to provide for you some kingdom even after he's dead. Where is it? What've you got to show me? Come on, show me. Show me.

KARL *takes a bottle from the table.*

ILSE: Karl, what are you doing to yourself? Aren't you ashamed at all?

KARL: Why? [*He goes.*]

ILSE: If you keep drinking like that I'll be taking you home in a box.

MARTA: There was blood.

ARMAND: [*accent*] That's not blood. Horse-kick. Let him go Mum. He'll be all right. I'll keep an eye on him. You get some rest.

They go. MARTA *starts to pick up the money.* ANITA *puts the food she's been holding on the table. Goes.*

ANITA: I'll leave these on the table.

MARTA: This isn't how I thought it'd be.

PETER: Mother, mother, good gentle mother, don't cry. Let me help you. Don't cry. The land's gone now, long ago. We never had it. But you're alive and I'm alive and you'll see, things will get better. We can still grow things, we'll breathe again. I'll make good, I promise, I promise.

MARTA: It's Karly I'm crying for. It was his whole life.

SCENE TWENTY-FIVE

Australia/Latvia, the warped time/space of ghosts. Darkish.
LEICHHARDT, GILBERT *and* BROWN *are at the opera, a performance of 'Voss'.*

LEICHHARDT: Is this how I am remember? This opera 'Voss'? It makes me want to vomit! Should I now come with my head under my arm perhaps, as in some music hall trick.

GILBERT: Your beheading—

LEICHHARDT: It was not mine head which was cut off. It was Voss.

GILBERT: Yes, and how like you in so many ways, brains baked in the sun till you thought you were God traipsing through the promised land.

BROWN: What story is this? I'm not that Jacky. Shit I'm not even Brown. But I'm decked out like Bennelong going to the opera.

LEICHHARDT: If I am Voss then you must be satisfied to be Palfreyman.

GILBERT: But I wasn't on your third journey. I died on the first.

LEICHHARDT: Nevertheless, you are Palfreyman, the naturalist, collector of birds.

GILBERT: I was certainly the first one to die. But I did not walk arms outstretched so, into a native attack. I said we needed a guard on the camp.

LEICHHARDT: Your Voss sends Palfreyman forth, unarmed.

GILBERT: I did not play Jesus to your God. I was not speared in the side but shot by you.

LEICHHARDT: It is not history.

GILBERT: No it's art, an opera. And your beheading—

LEICHHARDT: Not mine, but Voss. And why must it be so gruesome?

BROWN: What they were singing was, "Man is God with his head cut off."

GILBERT: Prophets were often beheaded in the Bible to show they were not God but mortal.

BROWN: I wouldn't use a knife like Jacky did. Too much like hard work. I'd use an axe.

GILBERT: It is what's known as artistic licence. Voss's beheading proved he was mortal.

LEICHHARDT: Man is nearest God when he learns he is not God, as did your prophets.

GILBERT: You are no prophet.

LEICHHARDT: But you said I am Voss.

GILBERT: A work of art.

LEICHHARDT: An opera based on a novel inspired by your discovered diary and my disappearance.

BROWN: I'm getting nowhere with you blokes. And I don't need these clothes. Give 'em back to Bennelong.

> *The clothes fly up.* KARL *comes sprawling into their midst. He starts to rise slowly. The tinkle of the bells. The soft chant of "Latvija". What sounds like a shot.* KARL *falls and lies still.* LEICHHARDT *checks the body.*

GILBERT: What happened? Was he shot?

LEICHHARDT: I didn't kill him.

BROWN: The blow from an axe rings like a thunder clap in your head.

GILBERT: Is he dead?

LEICHHARDT: He can't be dead. I must bleed him. Give me a knife.

GILBERT: No!

BROWN: No! And don't give him an axe.

> ARMAND *comes to* KARL.

ARMAND: Dad?

KARL: Am I dead?

ARMAND: No.

LEICHHARDT: He's only drunk.

ARMAND: Don't drink any more.

GILBERT: This is not the opera.

LEICHHARDT: No, is only dreaming.

The tinkle of the bells and "Latvija".

BROWN: Their land is singing them like that opera was singing you. That Jacky danced bloody good but he didn't do any singing. Only whitefellas were singing and maybe that's why you're still here. I could probably sing you to the land, do a bit of a dance, give us all a bit of peace. But I reckon the only dance you blokes are interested in is the foxtrot. I've got my own history to worry about. And the land.

[*Goes.*]

LEICHHARDT: I am shaken to my stomach. I never held my father.

GILBERT: I never held mine.

LEICHHARDT: I am lost.

GILBERT: The true explorer is often lost, not knowing how to get where he's going.

LEICHHARDT: I cannot, will not believe I shot you.

GILBERT *takes* LEICHHARDT *on his back.* ARMAND *helps his father up.*

GILBERT: I am your Palfreyman.

ARMAND: Come on Dad.

LEICHHARDT: You do not have to carry me.

GILBERT: A palfrey is a saddle horse, a beast of burden. You are my burden, your history, and now your Voss.

ARMAND *and* KARL *go, the* EXPLORERS *follow them.*

LEICHHARDT: I followed my destiny. You followed yours. What I meant before, it is not history you were shot. It is not so written. Your end couldn't be in your own diary. And in my journal you were speared.

GILBERT: Seven men went to God following you into history.

SCENE TWENTY-SIX

Latvia, the morning of departure, and North Queensland.

A chorus of "Zilais Lakatins" while the scene changes.

The Latvians are at the table, eating and drinking. In theatrical terms it completes the ritual that began with the laying of the table in Scene Two. These fragments are like a series of snapshots.

[A]

ARMAND *takes a group photograph.*

MARTA: You should bring your family for a visit.

ARMAND: [*accent*] They're Australian. They don't speak any Latvian.

ALFRED: It's your duty to teach them.

PETER: Even if the old people don't come, bring your family.

MARTA: Family is always welcome.

ALFRED: It's your duty to bring your family.

PETER: Blood is thicker than vodka.

KARL: It's not too early to have one. It's our last morning.

    They drink.

[B]

OLGA: A man came asking for you. After the war.

ILSE: Gunnars?

OLGA: I don't remember his name.

ILSE: So he survived as well.

OLGA: We hadn't heard from you. We had nothing to tell him.

ILSE: He was my fiancé.

OLGA: He only called the once.

ILSE: I've never told Karl.

[C]

ALFRED: It didn't work out for you with the land.

PETER: I'm one of your insects, worms, grubs, parasites sucking the blood of the nation.

ALFRED: Some people don't want to work. And why should they if the government is prepared to pay them not to? I can see you're not one of them.

PETER: What in particular are their distinguishing characteristics? I'll have to learn them.

[D]

ARMAND: I killed someone.

ANITA: I'm sorry, I don't speak English.

ARMAND: It sounds melodramatic, I know. And strictly speaking I didn't. I didn't try to stop it happening. I couldn't do it myself but I watched. Is that worse?

ANITA: I'm taking English classes next winter. It is the international language, especially for doing business.

[E]

MCQUAIDE*'s surgery.* ILSE, ARMAND.

ILSE: [*accent*] Doctor McQuaide, I want you tell me true. How long do I got?

MCQUAIDE: No one is prepared to say these days. If I say three months and you live three years I'm a liar.

ILSE: [*accent*] Then you be good liar.

MCQUAIDE: They can't say till they operate. With chemo-therapy... maybe longer.

ILSE: [*accent*] Maybe shorter.

MCQUAIDE: Maybe.

EDVARDS *appears to* ILSE.

EDVARDS: Ilse, I wondered if you could make some new curtains for my house. I have all the window measurements. And money for the fabric.

ILSE: [*accent*] What if I say, Doctor McQuaide, I like maybe go overseas.

MCQUAIDE: You can do what you like.

ILSE: [*accent*] Before last hours come.

MCQUAIDE: Sooner the better.

ILSE: [*accent*] Before operation?

MCQUAIDE: The surgeon will want to take a look as soon as possible.

ILSE: [*accent*] Then can lose a strength?

MCQUAIDE: It's possible.

EDVARDS: There's no rush, Ilse. I'd just like to brighten up the place, OK?

ILSE: [*accent*] Then better go when still can.

MCQUAIDE: Go back home.

ILSE: [*accent*] Is how we thinks. In our heart. See where we born one more time.

[F]

OLGA: I'm not criticising, but why did you stop writing twenty years ago? We couldn't understand your silence.

ILSE: It was in our Latvian papers that the Russians were checking up on citizens who had contacts with emigrés.

  PETER *passes through filling glasses and goes.*

PETER: Not Russians. Soviet Latvians.

MARTA: They were. They were reading our letters.

ILSE: They said it could go badly for relatives over here.

OLGA: That sort of thing did happen. You missed out on a promotion, or a particular apartment.

MARTA: Or they interrogated the children at school.

PETER: Not the Russians. Latvian Soviets.

ILSE: I didn't want to cause you any trouble.

OLGA: But we kept writing. What did you think?

ILSE: That I wouldn't be the one to bring some calamity down on your heads. That's all.

[G]

PETER: What will you do, just as a matter of interest with the land?

ANITA: A Danish consortium are interested in leasing it with other parcels of surrounding land, for intensive dairying.

PETER: A capitalist commune.

ANITA: They'll farm it, efficiently, profitably. It's what this country needs, an injection of foreign investment and know-how.

PETER: And you'll live in Riga.

ANITA: I have other business interests.

PETER: So you'll be an absentee landlord.

[H]

KARL: Peter will be all right. Then what will you do with yourself? You really should take a lover, Marta.

MARTA: Oh Karly, what are you saying?

KARL: Fine woman like you going to waste. There must be some poor devil out there you could make happy.

MARTA: You really are a wicked boy.

[I]

PETER: I could understand if you'd wanted the land.

ARMAND: [*accent*] I never wanted land.

MARTA: Doctors are almost the worst paid profession here.

KARL: They're amongst the best in Australia. Very well paid. Not like artists.

MARTA: We've still got the witch doctor system.

PETER: Take along a sausage, a loaf of bread, the usual bottle of vodka and hope the doctor hasn't started on the last one.

[J]

OLGA: Would you ever think of coming back to live here?

ILSE: No. Never.

ALFRED: That's very definite, little sister.

ILSE: Stop calling me little sister. I'm your big sister. Olga is your little sister.

ALFRED: Sorry, but I've grown into big brother to both of you.

ILSE: I can't start again. It's too hard. Too late.

OLGA: It will be hard. Not so much for us old ones. We don't have that much time left. But for the young ones.

ILSE: I don't have the strength. Not in my body. Not in my will.

[K]

ARMAND: You don't have to go to Latvia, Mum. You could stay here for treatment.

ILSE: Your father still wants to go.

ARMAND: I said I'd go with him.

ILSE: How would that look if he goes back and I stay here? My family would never forgive me.

ARMAND: I can go with you both. I'd like to do that.

ILSE: Don't tell Karl about the cancer. Otherwise he'd never agree to go. He's been waiting so long.

[L]

KARL: I could live here no trouble. When I retire they'll pay my pension here. I could live like a king.

MARTA: But if you come to live here I'll miss out on my trip to Australia.

KARL: Don't you worry about that, darling. I'll take care of that. I promised you.

ILSE: [accent] What bullshits you are promising now?

KARL: [accent] What bullshit? Is not bullshit. Mind your business.

OLGA: Swear at him again, Ilse, so we can at least hear English.

ALFRED: Russian is the best language to swear in. You haven't heard swearing till you've heard a Russian in full flight. [Gives us a volley.]

OLGA: Alfred! What's got into you?

ALFRED: I think it's the vodka. Time for another.

    They drink.

[M]

ARMAND: You can come and live with us if you'd like. When we come back from Latvia.

ILSE: Why would I leave then?

ARMAND: Peace and quiet. You wouldn't have to put up with Dad, and we'd love to have you.

ILSE: I've seen him through this far. I'll see him through to the end.

[N]

ILSE: Don't start crying, Marta.

MARTA: But you're leaving.

ILSE: It's time to go home.

MARTA: What if I never see my Karly again?

ILSE: That's how life is.

[O]

KARL: What did my father promise me? Fatherland. Where is it now?

PETER: We were sold out. Latvia was sold out. It started with your parents' generation. You let the Russians in and we accepted the lie and let them stay. We surrendered our land.

ALFRED: We surrendered \ our history.

MARTA: We surrendered \ our culture.

EDVARDS: We surrendered \ our souls.

ANITA: We surrendered \ our language.

OLGA: We surrendered \ our children.

ILSE: We surrendered \ our hope.

KARL: We surrendered \ our lives.

ARMAND: We surrendered \ our identity.

> *The tinkle of the bells. "Latvija".*

ILSE: And yet… and yet… we never surrendered our hearts. Even in the darkest days there was always a little light.

OLGA: It only takes a little light.

ALFRED: Do we have enough strength?

PETER: Enough.

ILSE: I'll drink to that. I could use a little strength.

ALFRED: Get her a glass someone, quickly.

KARL: Here Ilse, you can have mine.

MARTA: And of course you will all come back and see us.

CHORUS: Don't start crying Marta. Not yet.

> *They drink.*

[P]

KARL *on his patio in North Queensland, with a beer.*

KARL: That was my dream. Go back to Latvia, take back my land. But it was never mine. I slept on it, rolled round on the grass, laughing with Marta, not even my name in the tree. Now is not even a dream.

ILSE: Karl, come to bed.

KARL: I can't sleep. I just can't.

ILSE: Neither can I if you're out here talking to yourself.

KARL: I can take care of you, you know.

ILSE: I can still take care of myself.

KARL: I mean later. Stay here. Let me. I know how to.

ILSE: I'll stay for as long as I can.

EDVARDS: There's plenty of time for us.

ILSE: Later, who knows?

KARL: Do you want to be buried in Latvia?

ILSE: How often would you come to visit me? No. I'll sleep here. When I'm finally in this soil, that's true belonging, the last coming home.

> *The ghosts softly start singing "Put, Vejini":*
>
> Put, vejini, dzen laivinu,
> Aizdzen mani Kurzeme;
>
> *The whole cast assemble as ghosts.*

KARL: I won't go back to Latvia again. What for? When Marta dies there's nothing left. My family is here. There's nowhere to go. Right here is where I'll die. Right here is where I'll go on living.

ALL: [*singing*]
> Blow breeze set sail, blow breeze set sail.
> We are leaving our home for a new land.
> Put, vejini, dzen laivinu,
> Aizdzen mani Kurzeme.

THE END

APPENDIX

Substitute scene for existing Scene Twenty-Five if the play is performed without the LEICHHARDT *scenes.*

Latvia. MARTA*'s house. A short time later.*

The bells. The chant of "Latvija".

KARL *comes sprawling into the space. He still has the bottle, now almost empty. He starts to rise slowly, like the man in the prologue. What sounds like a shot.* KARL *falls and lies still.* ARMAND *comes to him.*

ARMAND: Dad?

KARL: Am I dead?

ARMAND: You fell over.

KARL: Was like a thunder clap in my head. Like I was shot.

ARMAND: No.

> *Starts to help him up. Ends up holding him.*

KARL: Too bad.

ARMAND: Don't drink any more.

KARL: My father wasn't shot.

ARMAND: At least now you know.

KARL: Know what? Like I never was here.

ARMAND: Well you're here now.

KARL: Should never've come back. Hey. Maybe I've been asleep all these years.

ARMAND: Just drunk.

KARL: Got drunk with Marta. Fell down asleep. Dreamed of Australia. If I'm awake, I don't like.

ARMAND: [*accent*] What you look?

KARL: You. Maybe my father never was here.
ARMAND: He was. And your father's father.
KARL: Once maybe.
ARMAND: My father is.
KARL: I never held him. My father.
ARMAND: Come on Dad. Let me help you up.

> *They go.*

Latvia—Recent History

In 1795 Latvia came under the control of Russia and remained so—with the exception of a brief incursion by Napoleonic forces in 1812. On 18 November 1918, an independent Latvian republic was declared though armed struggle against both Soviet and German forces was to continue for almost two years. Post World War I, Latvia was a member of the League of Nations, as were the two other Baltic republics. From the 1935 census: 2 million population comprising: Latvians 75%, Russians 10%, Jews 5%, Germans 3%, Poles 2%. In 1939 Germany and the Soviet Union concluded a non-aggression treaty (the Molotov-Ribbentrop Pact) which included the division of Europe into respective spheres of influence. Latvia was included in the Soviet sphere.

In 1940 Latvia, Lithuania and Estonia were occupied by the Soviet Union. Many thousands of Latvians were deported. In 1941 Germany invaded as part of Hitler's thrust into Russia. Many welcomed the Germans as liberators, but under German rule the Latvian Jewish and Gypsy populations were almost completely exterminated, and the arrest and execution of Latvians continued. With the collapse of Nazi Germany in 1945 Latvia was again incorporated into the Soviet Union as a constituent republic. There were 120,000 Latvians in Displaced Person camps in Germany.

In 1979 ethnic Latvians made up only 53.7% of Latvia's population of 2.5 million. In 1989 the indigenous language was declared the state language. Previously Russian was the official language while Latvian was optional. In 1989 Latvia declared republican sovereignty following Mikhail Gorbachev's policies of *glasnost* and *perestroika*. National symbols were rehabilitated: tricolour flags emerged, old coats of arms began to replace the

hammer and sickle; pre-war independence days were once more
instituted as holidays. In 1991 Latvia was granted membership of the
United Nations after diplomatic recognition by the United States on
2 September and four days later by the Soviet Union. The Soviets
agreed to a troop pullout in 1992. The first post-Soviet parliamentary
elections were held in June 1993, with citizenship a major issue.
From the 1994 census: population 2.5 million: 53% Latvian, 33%
Russian, Other 14%. In March 1994 Russia and Latvia agreed to the
final pullout of the Russian troops.

Romuald Misiunas and Rein Taagepera, *The Baltic States, Years of
Dependence, 1940–1990*. Hurst, London, 1983.

Ludwig Leichhardt

Leichhardt was born on October 23, 1813, in Brandenburg, Germany. His interest in natural history was fostered by William Nicholson. In 1841 Nicholson paid for Leichhardt's passage to Australia, providing a letter of introduction to Sir Thomas Mitchell, Surveyor-General of New South Wales, who was interested in employing Leichhardt as naturalist on his next journey. Leichhardt, however, decided to organise his own, private expedition, funded by gifts from pastoralists and businessmen. He set out from Sydney for Moreton Bay on August 13, 1844. The plan was to cover a distance overland of about 4,800 km from Brisbane to Port Essington, north-east of Darwin. The explorer left from Jimbour on October 1 with ten young men, fifteen horses and seventeen bullocks.

He arrived at Port Essington on December 17, 1845, with only seven members surviving the expedition. Their appearance caused a sensation, having been given up for dead. The arduous trek across rugged country was made worse by the inexperience of both leader and party members, and diminishing supplies. Near the Gulf of Carpentaria they had been attacked by Aborigines, who killed John Gilbert with a spear through the neck and severely wounded two others, Roper and Calvert. In July they sighted the Gulf, establishing a line of communication by land between it and the eastern coast of Australia. Abundant water and, in Leichhardt's words *excellent country* meant that large, suitable areas were opened up for settlement. Leichhardt became a national hero.

His second expedition ended on August 1, 1847, having advanced only 500 miles of a journey which aimed to cross Australia from the Darling Downs to Perth. The nine-man party was dogged by terrible terrain and weather conditions, which included torrential rain.

Ludwig Leichhardt. Frontispiece to D. Bunce's 'Australasiatic
Reminiscences'. *(Mitchell Library, State Library of NSW)*

Complaints were made of Leichhardt's behaviour, notably his ill-temper, difficulty in dealing with and selfishness in taking food when in short supply.

Undeterred, Leichhardt set out from the Darling Downs once more in 1848 with a party of six for the same destination. His last letter records the following opinion:

My party has behaved remarkably well. It is without doubt a most difficult task to form a good party. It seems to me that you should be all gentlemen or all working men, for as everyone has to do the same business and as they are all living together, it is extremely difficult to avoid familiarity.

The journey was expected to take at least two and a half years, but late in 1850 there was still no sign of the expedition. On October 30, 1852 a search party, led by a member of Leichhardt's second expedition, Hovenden Hely, unsuccessfully combed a large area of north-west New South Wales looking for the explorer. He concluded that the party had been killed by Aborigines.

It took until 1938 for another version of Leichhardt's first journey to come to light. Gilbert's diary was discovered amongst the Gould collection, recorded by A.H. Chisholm in the book *Strange Journey* (1941).

Patrick White used Leichhardt's journey as one of the bases for his novel *Voss* (1957) which was again the basis for the opera *Voss,* written by Richard Meale and David Malouf and performed by the Australian Opera at the Adelaide Festival in 1986 and at the Sydney Opera House later that year.

Chronicle of Australia; *The Australian Encyclopedia.* Sydney Grolier Society, Sydney, 1983 and copied with the kind permission of Australian Geographic Pty Limited.